DATE DUE

DEC 1 1986		
ILL FAU		
3490898		
4/19/05		

HIGHSMITH 45-220

W9-DDD-857

WAR MOVIES

JAY HYAMS

GALLERY BOOKS
An Imprint of W. H. Smith Publishers Inc.
112 Madison Avenue
New York City 10016

To Harry H. Weiss,
who survived the Great War,
and to Russell B. Clark,
killed in action in Italy,
October 2, 1944

Designed by Eric Marshall

Copyright © 1984 W. H. Smith Publishers Inc.

Published by Gallery Books
A Division of W. H. Smith Publishers Inc.
112 Madison Avenue
New York, New York 10016

A Layla Productions Book

Printed in the U.S.A.

1   2   3   4   5   6   7   8   9   10

Library of Congress Cataloging in Publication Data

Hyams, Jay, 1949–
    War movies.

    Includes index.
    1. War Films—History and criticism.   I. Title.
PN1995.9.W3H9   1984   791.43'09'09358   84-14175
ISBN: 0-8317-9304-X

Page 1: *Lew Ayres (to the right of center)* and
*his schoolmates cheer the end of their classes
and their departure for the "field of honor" in*
All Quiet on the Western Front *(1930).*
Pages 2–3: *Marines wade ashore in* Beach Red *(1967).*
Pages 4–5: *The battle along the highway begins in*
A Bridge Too Far *(1977).*
Page 6: *A German machine gunner and his comrades face
an Allied attack in* The Big Parade *(1925).*
Page 7: *The aftermath of battle in* A Bridge Too Far.
Pages 8–9: *Survivors return from the front in*
Just Another War (Uomini Contro) *(1970).*

Contents

Preface

It is difficult to imagine what our opinion of war would be had there never been any war movies. From the first flickering images of parading soldiers shown in peep-show parlors around the turn of the century to the scenes of blossoming mushroom clouds that end so many contemporary films, war has provided filmmakers with their most compelling subject. Because of their creations, we have seen our history in a way previous generations never saw theirs, and we have come to fear our future. However ignorant of war we may yet be, the images from war movies endure.

This book presents an overview of the history of war movies. The movies covered are those that deal with the major wars of this century. Movies have been made about other wars, of course, but those that deal with the conflicts of the twentieth century are of particular interest because of their close relationship to their subject. Motion pictures and modern war—the movie camera and the machine gun—were born together, offspring of the same technological revolution. The movie camera and the machine gun are both devices made to be aimed at living men, and what each does to the living has changed our world. The machine gun quickly turns living men into corpses; the movie camera just as quickly turns them into immortals. The machine gun denies the living their individuality; the movie camera cherishes it. What the machine gun takes away, the movie camera gives back—or tries to. The history of war movies is the story of people using a powerful new form of communication to make comprehensible an incomprehensible series of events. The tens of millions of people who have died in the wars of the past eighty-odd years do not appear in war movies, and although the movies make use of historical references—the names of men and battles—their version of history is rarely, if ever, accurate. But the movies performed important

functions when they were made and preserve a record of the changing morality of this century.

Born together, motion pictures and modern war have grown up and flourished side by side. Their two histories have become intertwined, and scenes from war movies sometimes come perilously close to being mistaken for scenes from actual history: in the memory of popular culture, they may already be one and the same. And in some ways, scenes from war movies are actual history: they record the ideas and emotions that helped people understand events that were central to their lives. Motion pictures came into being just in time to add a new and perhaps essential dimension to "total" war. Movies are an incomparable form of propaganda; they allow home-front audiences to "see" what their side is fighting for. If the various wars of this century have not always made sense to the people who fought and suffered them, they have made dramatic sense to the noncombatants who experienced them as movies. If the machine gun and the other devices of modern war have left little room for chivalry on twentieth-century battlefields, only rarely has that fact been made apparent to the patrons of movie houses. Perhaps the machine gun would have made warfare more distasteful had the movie camera not been there to make it palatable, to make it into a form of entertainment.

And war makes wonderful entertainment. More movies have been made about war than any other subject, for it is ideally suited to the needs of the filmmaker. At its heart is exciting action, the kind of physical movement essential to the movie camera. It is action with a purpose, of course, and war provides screenwriters with all the ingredients for drama, a conflict of good against evil. The heroes and the villains are there, and their struggle is titanic: they are battling for the fates of nations. The formulas used by filmmakers have changed very little from war to war, decade to decade. The last-minute rescues, heartrending romances, and melodramatic tales of derring-do first used for movies about World War I have been updated for the subsequent wars of this century. On film, war has become the very best example of popular culture, an enthralling mixture of violence and romance.

War movies date more noticeably than the movies of any other genre, and most have more historic interest than artistic merit. The very worst war movies contort history for the sake of entertainment and teach the young that war is exciting; the very best offer at least a hint of the truth of war. It is not accidental that the most famous war movies are antiwar—they may have done nothing to end war, but they have done much to change our opinion of it.

THE GREAT WAR

In 1896, twelve years after Hiram Maxim perfected the machine gun, Thomas Edison perfected his Vitascope, a device for projecting motion pictures. On April 23 of that year, at Koster & Bial's Music Hall in New York City, audiences were treated to the first projected films shown in America. Twelve short movies were presented that night, including some that had been made originally for peep-show machines and some that were pirated copies of European films. Among the latter was *Kaiser Wilhelm Reviewing His Troops*, which offered flickering images of soldiers in fancy uniforms parading past that faraway emperor. The films caused a sensation, and reporters from the city's newspapers were sent to New Jersey to interview Edison at his laboratory. One of these journalists was J. Stuart Blackton, a young English immigrant working as both a reporter and a cartoonist for the New York *World*. Blackton was profoundly impressed by what the great inventor had to say about the future of motion pictures. He quit his job with the *World*, bought a projector from Edison, and in the company of a friend, Albert E. Smith, went into the film business.

By 1897, Blackton and Smith had a camera and had set up a studio on the roof of the Morse Building in downtown Manhattan. They began making movies. Their early efforts were much like the early efforts of other novice filmmakers: they were homemade, composed of what was at hand. Since the studio was located on a roof, rooftop subjects suggested themselves. The first film the two men made was *The Burglar on the Roof*. Blackton took the role of the crook; Smith held the camera. In April 1898, following the American declaration of war on Spain, Blackton and Smith rushed out onto their roof to film *Tearing Down the Spanish Flag*. The film is very concise: hands (Blackton's) reach up and tear a Spanish flag off a flagpole and then run up Old Glory.

Tearing Down the Spanish Flag, made just two years after the first American public exhibition of projected motion pictures, is considered by many film historians to be the first commercial war movie. The very short film was a very great success and prompted Blackton and Smith to make other films about the Spanish-American War. Abandoning the roof for a bathroom, they recreated the Battle of Santiago Bay in a bathtub. Smith aimed the camera at cutouts of battleships maneuvered by Blackton; Mrs. Blackton puffed cigarette smoke at the camera lens for added realism.

Blackton and Smith hauled their camera outdoors to film newsreel shots of US troops, led by Theodore Roosevelt, marching off to the battlefields of Cuba. Like Roosevelt, Blackton was at the beginning of a distinguished career, and the two men were soon to become close friends and neighbors.

Other pioneer filmmakers in other countries had opportunities to film soldiers marching off to war. The growth of the infant film industry was matched by a proliferation of little wars, the first fierce scraps that gave slight hints of the coming debacle. The Boer War, the Boxer Rebellion, and the Russo-Japanese War were each in turn popular subjects for short films. Some intrepid cameramen accompanied the troops and filmed such scenes as soldiers setting up Maxim guns on the veld and cannons being fired at Port Arthur. These films of actual events were shown along with battle scenes reenacted far from the front. American filmmakers recreated incidents from the Boer War on the fields of New Jersey and used local Japanese gardens as the setting for scenes from the Russo-Japanese War.

Mexico is much closer to the United States than either Africa or Manchuria, but American filmmakers neglected the revolution in Mexico until Pancho Villa announced that he wanted to be filmed. The Mutual Film Corporation dispatched Raoul Walsh to cover Villa's exploits. The revolutionary leader was very accommodating to the gringo filmmakers. He agreed to stage his battles during daylight hours whenever convenient, and on at least one occasion he postponed the attack on a city until the cameramen could arrive. Villa was a terrible ham, however, constantly upstaging the camera, and Walsh had difficulty assembling a coherent film: he had abundant shots of the gallant Villa riding at the head of his victorious troops, but little else.

Walsh, who at that time worked as both an actor and director, returned from Mexico in time to participate in a more important venture. He

*The courageous Southern colonel
rams a Confederate flag into the barrel of a
Union cannon in* The Birth of a Nation *(1915).*

was given the role of John Wilkes Booth in D. W. Griffith's *The Birth of a Nation* (1915), the most important film in American history and a landmark war movie.

In the fall of 1913, D. W. Griffith left the Biograph Company, where he had worked since 1908, and joined Reliance-Majestic. He had made more than 450 films during his years at Biograph and had done more than any other filmmaker to establish the structure of narrative film. Griffith gave film its "language." He created or perfected such devices as the flashback, the close-up, the long shot, crosscutting, the moving camera shot, rhythmic editing, and both the fade-in and the fade-out. Although he shunned scripts, he demanded rehearsals (not common in his day) and worked with his performers to develop a restrained but emotive style, making motion picture acting an art. Griffith was a genius at depicting emotion on film, and he knew how to make audiences experience intimately both the most stupendous and the most commonplace events.

Griffith also perfected the thrilling last-minute rescue, was fond of baby animals, and had a fierce sense of morality. The most important and influential man in the history of film, Griffith was a romantic, and he poured his feelings into his films. In a brilliant but subtle way, he used his powers as an artist in a twentieth-century medium to perpetuate the ideals of the nineteenth.

Griffith applied all his skills to the creation of *The Birth of a Nation*, and the result is a film of overwhelming power. It is also a film full of appalling racism. The son of a Confederate veteran, Griffith viewed the Civil War in a thoroughly unreconstructed way, mixing dreamy chivalry with virulent prejudice. He based the film on two inflammatory works by Thomas Dixon, *The Clansman* and *The Leopard's Spots*. The former had already been made into a play, the performances of which frequently ended in riot. The heroes riding to the rescue in the last reel of *The Birth of a Nation* are members of the Ku Klux Klan, and the film led to the rebirth of that organization.

When Griffith set about making *The Birth of a Nation*, the Civil War had been over only fifty years—veterans still turned out for parades, and in fact both Union and Confederate veterans served as advisers on the film. The war was still a controversial subject, and part of the force of Griffith's film is due to its partisan nature. The film recounts, as one of its titles explains, "the agony which the South endured that a nation might be born." The story runs from before the Civil War to Reconstruction and the birth of the Klan.

Only one battle is depicted in the film, but Griffith's handling of it and the other methods of storytelling that he introduced make the film important in the history of war movies.

The film's battle scene is convincingly awesome, a broad tableau of opposing armies, fires raging, shots bouncing wildly, smoke pouring across the field. Griffith's battle was praised for its "realism"—it looked like what most people, including the veterans present, thought a battle looked like.

Perhaps the most important aspect of the film in terms of war movies is the way it weaves together personal stories and historic events: it is history brought to life for the purpose of telling a dramatic story. Griffith could not intercut his film with actual footage (he would do so later in

13

his films about World War I); instead, he modeled his battle scenes after Mathew Brady photographs and inserted throughout the film "historical facsimile" scenes, reconstructions of famous photographs. The film moves from these visual signposts to events in the lives of the members of two families, one Northern, one Southern. General Lee appears on a hill overlooking Petersburg—a famous general at a famous battle—orders an attack, and the attack is led by one of the film's fictional characters. The reasons for the attack are explained: the starving Confederate defenders are trying to reach supply wagons. The viewer understands the reasons for the battle (reasons that are honorable; the heroes are not aggressors) and has sympathy for the participants, even knows some of their appealing life histories. Although frightening, the battlefield is populated by familiar characters. History is being witnessed, and in its midst personal dramas are unfolding.

The most memorable battlefield scenes are of ironic coincidences: two old friends, now on opposite sides in the conflict, meet and die together; the courageous Confederate officer who leads the charge collapses on the Union breastworks and is saved by an old friend, a commander of the defending Union troops. With swift strokes, Griffith makes clear a tragedy soon to become a staple of war movies: brief instances of individual valor are immediately engulfed in the cataclysm of war. These inspiring incidents have another effect, however: they make exciting and understandable what would otherwise be terrifying and bewildering. Seen from above, the battle is chaotic, but when it is seen from the level of the participants, it is revealed as a series of contiguous events. The viewer is presented with a manipulated vision of war in which there is abundant room for morality

Right: The Birth of a Nation. *Sherman's army making its way through the South, described in a title as "a great conqueror marches to the sea."*

since each action is performed separately. Even more important is the fact that the viewer is left with the impression that good people—including the viewer, in his or her imagined participation in the battle—survive. According to Griffith, war is noisy, and some good men die, but the best people, the story's leading characters, live. With all its cannons and banners and opportunities for heroes to be heroic, war is a thrilling spectacle.

The Birth of a Nation includes many scenes soon to reappear in films about World War I: the terrified townspeople fleeing a burning town; the enemy horde entering a town and ransacking the homes of the innocent (a particularly effective scene when the audience has been introduced to the precious but fragile knickknacks in the home of the heroine); the disgusting habits of enemy leaders (an evil mulatto drinks too much and spills his liquor down his shirt). The heroes of the film are pleasingly individualistic and reckless in the face of death; the enemy is coldly machinelike.

One of the film's central themes is that of white women threatened with rape by leering blacks. The device of women faced with "a fate worse than death" was very popular during this period. In westerns, white men surrounded by redskins saved their last bullets to dispatch their womenfolk. The same scene recurs in *The Birth of a Nation* and in films about World War I. The enemy in these films has no apparent political aims and wants only to sexually abuse the pure and innocent women of the nation. The defense of these women was soon to become, on film, an incitement to war.

The barbaric enemy in *The Birth of a Nation* is the black "scalawag" militiamen. Their loathsome characteristics were soon to be attributed to Prussians. Indeed, one of them is played, in blackface, by Erich von Stroheim, shortly to gain fame as the movies' quintessential Prussian.

After enjoying a private screening of the film, Woodrow Wilson declared *The Birth of a Nation* to be "history written in lightning." The vast majority of critics were less pleased with the film, and their outrage eventually caused Wilson to withdraw his praise and Griffith to cut some of the more outrageously racist scenes. The

filmmaker was surprised and hurt by the angry reaction to his epic. He was bewildered by what he considered to be the intolerance around him, and he planned a response.

Some people looked beyond the film's racism and perceived an even more insidious peril: people are greatly impressed by what they see, and those members of the audience unfamiliar with written history might accept as fact the version of events given in the film.

Griffith had demonstrated the ability of film to affect audiences, and because *The Birth of a Nation* was an enormous financial success, other filmmakers paid heed to Griffith's methods. The pioneer filmmaker had shown his peers that history, even current events, could be presented on film, and if the film was exciting enough, full of enough thrilling melodrama, it would be successful. The power of motion pictures to manipulate public opinion had been proven at the exact moment when that power could be utilized.

Like the majority of the epic war movies that have followed it, *The Birth of a Nation* declared itself antiwar. One of its first titles says, "If in this work we have conveyed to the mind the rav- 15

Opposite: The Birth of a Nation. *The Southern colonel collapses on the Union breastworks and is dragged to safety by his friend.*

ages of war, to the end that war may be held in abhorrence, this effort will not have been in vain." Later in the film the title "War's peace" is followed by a scene of dead soldiers.

There was a certain topicality to these statements. Work on the film began in July 1914, one month before war broke out in Europe. By the time the film was nearing completion, war shortages were making themselves felt, and Griffith had trouble locating cloth for his Klan outfits.

Americans were fervently pacifist during the early years of the twentieth century. There were powerful peace organizations in the country, organizations sponsored by wealthy men and their institutions. Americans were also isolationist. The machinations of kings and kaisers were of no concern to democracy-loving Americans.

Even so, the war in Europe was a grand spectacle, and the American film industry did its best to supply its public with something to look at. The old scenes of marching armies were shown, along with newsreels, travelogues, and portraits of the various European leaders. Scenes of Germany's kaiser received as many hurrahs as scenes of Belgium's King Albert, England's King George V, France's Poincaré, and Czar Nicholas of Russia. As one commentator noted, Americans were "neutral with a vengeance."

For the first few years of the war, Americans had the opportunity to view films made by all the warring nations. England presented its case in such films as *The Battling British* and *The Great War in Europe*; German-made films included such titles as *Behind the German Lines* and *The German Side of the War*. The Allied cause received slightly more attention, for not only were Americans more sympathetic to England, but London was at that time the center of the world's film distribution.

In keeping with the policies of President Wilson, neutrality was the national catchword. Among the first American-made war films were *Neutrality* and *Be Neutral*, both released in 1914. The former concerns a German and a Frenchman living in the United States who remain friends despite the events in Europe; the latter involves a heated argument among four men over the subject of neutrality.

The antiwar sentiments of most Americans were well expressed in a Tin Pan Alley hit of 1915: "I Didn't Raise My Boy to Be a Soldier." The tune was dedicated to "every mother, everywhere." American mothers did not want their sons carted off to die on some distant European field, and their apprehensions were utilized by the film industry. The call for peace was frequently directed at the nation's mothers.

Alla Nazimova, a popular stage actress, made her screen debut in *War Brides* (1916), directed by Herbert Brenon. Nazimova plays a courageous woman named Joan, an inhabitant of a small town in an unspecified European country (although nameless, Germany is understood: the country's soldiers wear spiked helmets). War is declared, and Joan's husband and his three brothers are killed in battle. The king (Alexander K. Shannon) declares that all single women in the country must marry and bear children to carry on the war. Pregnant, Joan rallies the other women in a campaign against war. She is imprisoned but escapes, and in the final scene she confronts the king. Declaring, "No more children for war!" she kills herself.

Civilization, or He Who Returned (1916), produced by Thomas Ince (who codirected the film with Raymond B. West and Reginald Barker), was dedicated to "that vast army whose tears have girdled the universe: the Mothers of the Dead." The story takes place in a mythical land named Wredpryd. The women of the country have formed a pacifist organization, the Mothers of Men Society. A young count named Ferdinand (Howard Hickman), inventor of a submarine, is in love with a member of the society (Enid Markey). When the count is sent in his submarine to torpedo a defenseless passenger ship, he refuses, his crew mutinies, and the sub sinks. Christ uses the body of the dead count to return to earth and takes the bellicose King of Wredpryd (Herschel Mayall) on a tour of war's devastation. The king is converted, and peace returns.

A very popular film, *Civilization* was credited with helping reelect Wilson, whose platform was "He kept us out of war." However, by 1915, staying out of the war was no longer the goal of all Americans. A growing number of influential men were pressing for preparedness.

Count Ferdinand, returned from the dead with a message of peace, in Civilization *(1916).*

The ship the count refuses to sink in *Civilization* is named *Propatria*. The reference is to the *Lusitania*, which was sunk in May 1915. The sinking of the *Lusitania* outraged the American public. Americans had already been horrified by newspaper reports of German atrocities in Belgium—the shooting of civilian hostages, the burning of villages, and worse. President Wilson managed to avoid war, but American hatred toward Germany mounted, and public support for neutrality declined. Although their views went against the expressed policies of the government, the exponents of preparedness began to make themselves heard, and the public proved receptive. In the national imagination, the Huns, ruffians of the kaiser, were poised to invade America.

Preparedness for war was very much on the mind of J. Stuart Blackton. The pioneer filmmaker had thrived since *Tearing Down the Spanish Flag*. He was a next-door neighbor of Theodore Roosevelt's at Oyster Bay, Long Island,

and had taken to using the title "Commodore" (he was a member of the Atlantic Yacht Club). Like his neighbor, Blackton was a fierce patriot. The two men were against Wilson's policy of neutrality, and they were determined to "wake up America."

The film Blackton made, *The Battle Cry of Peace* (1915), was dedicated to the mothers of America, but it was anything but a pacifist film. Its subtitle, *A Call to Arms Against War*, gave a clearer notion of its content. Blackton based the film on *Defenseless America*, a book by Hudson Maxim, brother of the man who perfected the machine gun and a leading member of the family-run munitions business. *The Battle Cry of Peace* begins with a lecture given by Maxim at Carnegie Hall. His right hand resting on the barrel of one of his family's machine guns, a map of the United States behind him, Maxim delivers a dire warning about the plight of America. The remainder of the film vividly relates what is in store for the unarmed nation: invasion by a for-

eign power. Although unnamed, the attackers wear distinctly Germanic uniforms. (Their hats do not have spikes, but look like baseball caps worn backward and have large, turned-up earflaps.) The enemy invades New York City, occupies the office buildings, and shows an immediate interest in potent drink and the violation of the local women. Their invasion a success, the ruthless barbarians celebrate their victory. A title reports, "Brutish faces leered drunkenly at each other, glasses were clinked and raised." The film is graphic in its depiction of the impending doom and suggests that the peace movements in the United States were led by enemy agents.

Theodore Roosevelt gushed praise for Blackton's creation: "His film has done more for the Allied cause than twenty battalions of soldiers." Henry Ford, sponsor of the Peace Ship, an expedition sent to Europe in an effort to end the war, was outraged by the film and hastened to alert the public to the fact that Maxim and his munitions-manufacturing family stood to profit from massive armament. Ford's pronouncements went unheeded. *The Battle Cry of Peace*, released shortly after the sinking of the *Lusitania*, was only the first in a series of preparedness films. As the mood of the country changed to militarism, filmmakers rushed to provide suitable fare.

Thomas Dixon, whose works had served as

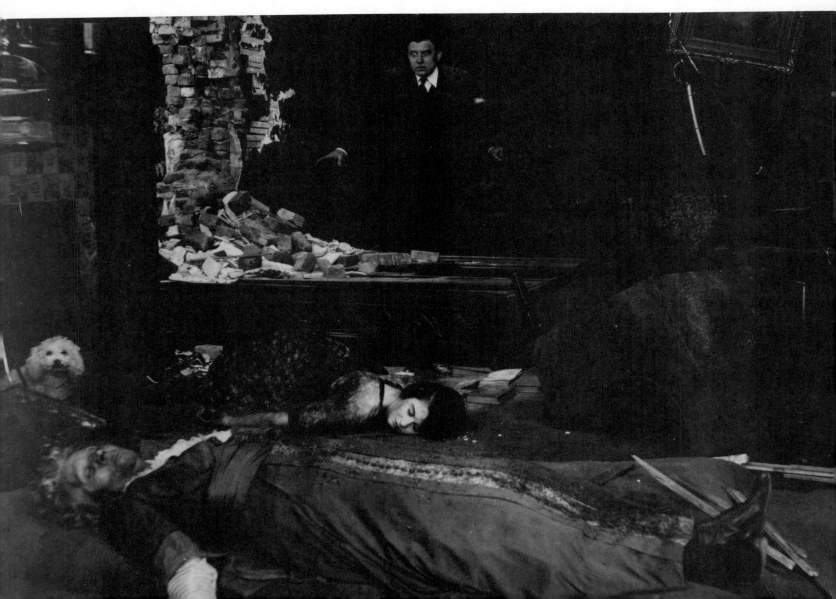

the basis for *The Birth of a Nation*, provided the story line for a prowar film called *The Fall of a Nation* (1916). Once again, defenseless America is attacked by a powerful Hun-like enemy. The film blames pacifist politicians for the nation's weakness.

By 1916, prowar themes were replacing pacifist and isolationist themes in films. The United States was being drawn emotionally into the war. In April of that year, the first American volunteers went to France to fly in the Lafayette Escadrille. Being a pacifist was no longer honorable. Indeed, in films, pacifists were portrayed as either disguised enemy agents or deluded fools.

In-Again, Out-Again (1917) tells the story of a patriotic young man (Douglas Fairbanks) who has a pacifist girl friend. The youth is not deceived by the pacifists and eventually exposes them for what they are: makers of munitions. The cunning enemy agents are packing shrapnel in baby-food cans. *Perkins' Peace Party* (1916) ridicules Henry Ford's Peace Ship. The film depicts a doddering pacifist who in the company of other misguided friends travels to Europe to put an end to the war. They fail miserably and learn their lesson.

It was into this mood of prowar agitation that D. W. Griffith released his monumental film *Intolerance* (1916). The film sought to recount the history of mankind's intolerance—this was Griffith's response to the critics of *The Birth of a Nation*. The film tells four separate stories, one set in Judea at the time of Christ, one set in sixteenth-century France, one set in ancient Babylon, and one set in modern times, and ends with four simultaneous last-minute rescues.

Intolerance was a failure. Audiences had difficulty following the involved plot, but the film had an even greater problem: it assailed the forces of intolerance and prejudice, the forces that lead men to war. Had it appeared a few months earlier, during the period of neutrality films, *Intolerance* might have been a success. Instead, it was banned in some cities, boycotted by religious groups, and largely ignored. (Russia's czarist regime banned the film outright.) Griffith had used his own money on the film and spent the rest of his life paying his debts.

The nation's ardent pacifism had been replaced by equally ardent outrage at Teutonic barbarities, particularly the vile mistreatment of women and children. *The War Bride's Secret* (1916) exposed the truth about German rapine. Thomas Ince, maker of the pacifist *Civilization*, demonstrated his adaptability in *Bullets and Brown Eyes* (1916), a film about Hun horrors (Ince's films were soon to be among the goriest). In these and other films, women were threatened with rape, children bayoneted. Cecil B. De Mille aroused the nation's sense of history in *Joan the Woman* (1916), an inspirational film starring Geraldine Farrar as Joan that goes from a contemporary battlefield in France to a recounting of the life of the martyr. The film was a masterpiece of propaganda. De Mille called it an "age-old call to a modern crusade."

On April 6, 1917, the United States declared war on Germany. Pacifist films were immediately banned. *War Brides* was withdrawn with the explanation that its philosophy might be "easily misunderstood by unthinking people." The nation's peace movements aligned themselves with the government's promise that this was to be the "war to end all wars"; Henry Ford turned his powers toward the production of tanks, airplanes, and ambulances. The popular tune changed to "It's Time for Every Boy to Be a Soldier."

The country became anti-German. Vienna-born actor Erich von Stroheim found himself suddenly without work, a situation that would not last long, however, for he was quickly given plenty of opportunities to portray that most sinister of villains: the Prussian.

Von Stroheim was the ideal actor for the role, and he performed it in numerous films. He perfected the character and even identified himself with it. Von Stroheim claimed to be a member of a Prussian noble family, a graduate of Heidelberg, and a cavalry officer. With his shaven head and monocle, his European politeness cut with cruel arrogance, he presented the epitome of the "cultured swine" Hun, the aristocratic officer who, while sipping the best champagne and listening to Wagner, orders women and children to be tortured.

Von Stroheim was actually the son of a Jew-   19

The shocking fate that awaits "defenseless America" as presented in The Battle Cry of Peace *(1915).*

ish hatter and had no rightful claim to the "von," which he had simply inserted in his name. He had immigrated to the United States in 1909, created a new identity for himself, and made a career as both a director and an actor. As a director, he made some of the greatest films of the silent era; as an actor, he became, in a phrase thought up by a studio publicity department, "The Man You Love to Hate."

The country also became vehemently pro-Ally. A producer named Robert Goldstein made the error of releasing *The Spirit of '76* (1917), a film about the American Revolution in which, as history would have it, the British are the enemies of the Americans. Goldstein was sentenced to ten years in prison under the Espionage Act (he was released after serving only one year, by which time the wartime hysteria had abated).

The US government took films very seriously. Shortly after war was declared, the government created a Division of Films as part of the Committee on Public Information. Its job was to sell the war to Americans, and it not only made its own films but involved itself in the commercial film industry. Independent filmmakers were given access to government services, including a real army of extras. Films became an essential "weapon" in the government's arsenal. Moviegoers paid a special admission tax and were bombarded by films promoting recruitment and Liberty Bonds, but more importantly, films provided the government with direct access to the thoughts of its citizens. There were no more antiwar films; the films shown glorified the war and stressed the virtues of courage and self-sacrifice. The actors and actresses who appeared in the films took part in Liberty Bond drives and publicly donated money to the Red Cross.

America's filmmakers rushed to create films about the war. The films they made are remarkably alike and betray the distance of the moviemakers from the actual war. The themes of these movies are few and are repeated over and over: the invasion of Belgium; the sinking of the *Lusitania;* and the wickedness of the kaiser—that syphilitic madman, "the Potsdam Attila"—and his subhuman "kaisermen." The German soldiers in these films are porcine slobs—to open a beer bottle, they smash its neck across the edge

Erich von Stroheim in a characteristic pose.

of a table; to drink, they tip the bottle toward their mustachioed mouths, half the liquid flowing down their chests toward their protruding bellies.

Curly-haired Mary Pickford, "America's Sweetheart," confronts all these perils in *The Little American* (1917), directed by Cecil B. De Mille. Pickford plays an American girl named Angela Moore who has a German boyfriend (Jack Holt) and a birthday on July 4. When war erupts in Europe, her boyfriend goes back to Germany to fight for his country, and Angela, too, soon departs for Europe, summoned to France by an ailing aunt. The innocent girl books passage on a ship called the *Veritania*; in mid-ocean, the ship is torpedoed by a German submarine. Angela survives and makes it to her aunt's château in time to witness the German invasion and the subsequent Hun atrocities. One of the most dramatic moments in the film takes place in the cellar of the château, where Angela comes upon a dazed and battered young girl clutching a rosary. The girl has been raped by the Germans. When Angela confronts the Prussian colonel (Walter Long) with this outrage, he sneers and replies, "My men must have relaxation." Angela takes sides (her boyfriend eventually switches), declaring, "I was neutral until I saw your men attack innocent women and murder old men. Then I stopped being neutral, and I became human." She acts as a spy for the French, is caught by the Germans, and is saved from a firing squad at the very last moment.

Like "Little Mary," Americans had moved from neutrality to involvement. The conversion of Americans from pacifists to soldiers of democracy was a common theme in films. Even the enemy (witness Holt in *The Little American*) could realize the error of his ways. In *The Unbeliever* (1918), a wealthy young American full of upper-class snobbism learns the truth about people ("Class pride is junk!" he exclaims) by witnessing the heroism of his fellow soldiers. Erich von Stroheim plays the despicable Prussian officer, and in one scene he puts an elderly woman and a child before a firing squad. Von Stroheim is ultimately killed by a German soldier who can take no more of his outrages.

Distribution of *The Little American* was held

up briefly in Chicago, where a German-American censor was offended by the film's anti-German sentiments. Local magistrates acted quickly, and the film was shown.

The presence of German immigrants in this country became a cause for alarm: they were all potential spies and saboteurs. *The Hun Within* (1918) deals with a young German-American tempted to commit sabotage. *The Prussian Cur* (1918), directed by Raoul Walsh, was advertised as "The Master Drama of the War, featuring Captain Horst van der Goltz, for 10 years Secret Agent of the Kaiser, exposing the intricate workings of the whole dastardly system of crimes German agents have committed in America." The film suggests a solution to the problem of criminal Germans in America: lynching, by a hooded gang that resembles the Ku Klux Klan. The film was withdrawn.

Identifying the enemy was rarely a problem, but newspaper publisher William Randolph Hearst got a quick response from the government when he included the Japanese as enemies in a serial he produced called *Patria*. The Japanese were on the Allied side; the villains in the film were changed to Mexicans.

The Germans were the enemy, and the atrocities attributed to them grew in outrageousness. Few people balked when newspapers reported that the Germans had set up special factories behind their lines and were boiling down the corpses of their dead soldiers to distill glycerine for use in munitions. It was reported that in Belgium the Germans had skinned babies (and kittens) and nailed their flesh to church doors.

James W. Gerard, American ambassador to Germany from 1913 to 1917, claimed to have proof of the German barbarities. *My Four Years in Germany* (1918), directed by William Nigh, was based on Gerard's memoirs and was advertised as a compilation of newsreel films taken in German prison camps (the film was actually shot in New Jersey). *My Four Years in Germany* created a sensation and was immensely popular. The Germans could be blamed for anything—like the Indians in westerns, they had no way to complain. *The German Curse in Russia* (1918) "proved" that German propaganda lies had led to the revolution there.

The perpetrator of these outrages against humanity, the enemy of all civilization, was Germany's kaiser. Produced by Carl Laemmle, *The Kaiser, the Beast of Berlin* (1918) was written and directed by Rupert Julian, who also took the title role. The film begins in a peaceful Belgian town named Louvain, home to a blacksmith named Marcus. The Germans invade the town, but the film does not linger there. Rather, it goes on, without a plot, to cover the requisite events. The *Lusitania* is sunk, and the commander of the guilty submarine is decorated—and then goes insane. Important figures appear, including Von Hindenburg, General Pershing, and Admiral von Tirpitz (played by Lon Chaney). "Newsreel" film explicitly shows the German atrocities. The film finally returns to Louvain, where the kaiser has been taken as prisoner by the victorious Allies. Marcus becomes his jailer.

The Kaiser, the Beast of Berlin was quite popular and led to imitations, including the comic *The Geezer of Berlin* (1918). In 1940, the title was adjusted for another war: *Beasts of Berlin (Goosestep)*, directed by Sherman Scott.

The popular archvillain Gustav von Seyffertitz assayed the role of an evil Prussian in *Till I Come Back to You* (1918), a film about the German mistreatment of Belgian children. In response to the powerful anti-German feelings in the country, Von Seyffertitz changed his name to C. Butler Clonebaught; not every actor wanted to be identified with the unpopular roles—Rupert Julian was hissed in public.

While Germans were lambasted as militaristic louts, America's allies were praised for their courage and virtue. Films about the Allies frequently concerned women, as in *For France* (1917) and *The Maid of Belgium* (1917). In countless films, innocent women were threatened with rape at the hands of the Boche. They would invariably be rescued at the last instant, and as just retribution, the kaiser would be made to kiss or salute the American flag. The most honorable and defenseless women were nurses. Edith Cavell, the English nurse executed by the Germans in 1915, was immortalized in such films as *Lest We Forget* (1918) and *The Woman the Germans Shot* (1918). (The memory of her martyrdom was revived in 1939, during another period of anti-German feelings, in *Nurse Edith Cavell*, directed by Herbert Wilcox.)

American history and pride in American military might were used to inspire patriotism and enlistment. Such films as *The Spirit of '17* (1917) and *Over There* (1917) were little more than animated recruitment posters. Draft dodgers were scorned in films like *The Slacker* (1917), in which a man is convinced to enlist after being reminded of great American heroes of the past, including Nathan Hale and Abraham Lincoln. There was also a *Mrs. Slacker* (1918), about a wife who inspires her husband to enlist.

Spy films also were popular, and in *The Spy* (1917), *Berlin via America* (1918), *The Kaiser's Shadow* (1918), and many others, the sneaky Hun agents were uncovered and routed; those citizens who could not serve in uniform and had to stay home could always hope to foil enemy agents. Even children managed to do their bit, inspiring enlistment and bearing up bravely under duress.

Although war films comprised only part of the film industry's production, they were very popular. They informed people (not always accurately) of events overseas and helped cheer them through wartime deprivations. They gave the relatives and friends of fighting men an idea, however slanted, of what the war was like. Even more, the films provided moviegoers with an outlet for their tensions, an opportunity to hoot at the kaiser and rejoice in victory.

The films were also thrilling. Viewers were fascinated by scenes of warfare's new weapons—airplanes and tanks, machine guns and submarines. It was noted that Americans showed an increasing taste for gore, for the most gruesome scenes of battlefield carnage. War was coming into its own as a form of entertainment on film.

Most of the comedy films of the war were more cruel than funny. In *The Kaiser's New Dentist* (1918), a Mutt and Jeff cartoon, the German leader is forced to submit to true torture. There was one outstanding exception to these films: Charlie Chaplin's *Shoulder Arms* (1918), a parody of trench warfare in which the man with the famous little mustache undergoes the rigors of

war. Chaplin fights back with humor, infiltrating the German lines disguised as a tree and donning a gas mask to throw a stinking cheese into the German trenches. In a dream, the brave soldier captures the kaiser and victoriously takes him to London.

In the spring of 1917, D. W. Griffith went to London for the British premiere of *Intolerance*. There, he was asked by the British government to make a film about the war, a film to help convince America to join the Allies. Griffith's film, *Hearts of the World* (1918), was released a few months before the armistice. Although it did not serve its original purpose, the film remains one of the best of World War I.

The War Office Committee of the British Ministry of Information told the famous American director that he could make the film any way he wished. The committee helped finance the film and gave Griffith access to actual combat footage. Even more important—and more exciting to fans in America—was the fact that Griffith visited the front, the only American director to do

Lillian Gish being whipped by one of the "kaiser's ruffians" in Hearts of the World *(1918).*

so. A steel helmet substituted for his usual felt hat, he was taken on guided tours of the trenches—publicity agents claimed he had been up to within fifty yards of the German positions. Griffith chatted with the soldiers and posed for photographers. He and his crew shot film in villages near the front and then returned to America to finish the film.

The scenario for *Hearts of the World* is credited to M. Gaston de Tolignac; the translator is given as Captain Victor Marier. Both names were pseudonyms for Griffith. The subtitle of the film is *The Story of a Village:* the village is unnamed.

The film begins with newsreel shots of Griffith walking through the trenches. He is next seen doffing his hat and shaking hands with Lloyd George at 10 Downing Street. Its credentials thus assured, the story begins, declaring itself "an old-fashioned play with a new-fashioned theme." The action is set in a small French village. The year is 1912, and life in the peaceful village is pleasant, full of humorous incidents, warm family ties, and tender love. A boy (Robert Harron) is in love with the girl next door (Lillian Gish). The girl and boy plan to wed. The only hint of the trouble to come is a man named Von Strohm, described in a title as a "tourist, sometime servant of the mailed fist." (Von Strohm is played by George Siegmann; Griffith had asked Von Stroheim's permission to use this abbreviated form of his name. Von Stroheim also appears in the film—as a Prussian officer, of course—as does Noel Coward, in his screen debut.) Von Strohm strolls through the town, "much interested in village architecture and foundations." The film abruptly cuts to German militarists planning "the dastardly blow against France and civilization." Back in the village, the town crier, banging a drum, announces war.

The film cuts to one of Griffith's "historical facsimiles," a reconstruction of the English houses of Parliament, where Sir Edward Grey asks the Commons for their support of France and Belgium; the next scene is a reconstruction of the French Chamber of Deputies. This is followed by a scene of Herbert Henry Asquith, David Lloyd George, Grey, and Winston Churchill sitting in a room awaiting Germany's response to England's ultimatum. A clock ticks on the mantel. The hours pass. It is war.

Back in the village again, the sons of France, including the boy, march off to war dressed in Zouave-like uniforms with kepis. There are flowers stuck in the barrels of their rifles. The soldiers from the village are put in trenches outside it, while the enemy hordes mass. On the day that was to have been their wedding day, the boy and the girl are far apart: he and his comrades are fighting a losing battle against the Huns; she is in the village, where enemy shells blast the houses as the townspeople flee or hide. Her "simple soul broken by terror" and clutching her wedding gown in her hands, the girl wanders the battlefield in search of the boy.

The boy survives the battle and returns to the front. Gone are his baggy pants and kepi—he wears a steel helmet and the uniform of a poilu. The girl returns to the village and undergoes the cruelty of the Prussian invaders. She is made to work in the fields, and when she fails to lift a basket of potatoes onto a wagon, she is mercilessly whipped. The German officers pass their time in "The Dungeons of Lust," where they drink too much and enjoy lewd dancers. Von Strohm is attracted to the girl. He begins to make barbaric advances. As he is attacking the girl, the boy enters the village. He rescues the girl from Von Strohm, and the two lovers take refuge in a room. The Germans begin breaking down the door; the boy prepares to kill the girl should the worst occur. They are saved by the last-minute arrival of French soldiers joined by victorious American doughboys.

Griffith was quite successful in his use of combat footage: scenes of tanks, poison gas, and horse-drawn artillery are skillfully intercut with the staged battle scenes. And in his created battles, Griffith showed that he had found room for valor and irony even on the flat, muddy plain of World War I. A brave soldier runs toward a pillbox, throws himself on the ground beneath it, and tosses in a hand grenade; a wounded soldier is pulled from a shell hole, and in the next instant another shell explodes in the hole; a line of prisoners is interrogated, and a captor

offers them cigarettes. The scenes could be taken from a vast number of films of World War I—and World War II. The new-fashioned war displayed old-fashioned themes.

In a scene near the front lines in *Hearts of the World*, French soldiers are seen near their dugout, which they have named on a sign over the entry: Hotel Richelieu. American soldiers in World War I were fond of naming their dugouts after film companies: Keystone Kottage or Vitagraph Village. The soldiers at the front showed a preference for comedies; the citizens at home enjoyed films about hand-to-hand struggles in no-man's-land. Thanks to the film companies, the war took place on both sides of the ocean.

The "war" at home ended as abruptly as the war overseas. Immediately after the armistice of November 11, 1918, no one wanted to see war movies. There was no market for the war films then in production, a situation producers were not soon to forget. Cinema owners put up signs to draw the public to new films: "This is not a war film."

World War I changed the American film industry immeasurably. With its foreign competition eliminated, Hollywood had flourished and become the center of the world's film production. Films had proven their power and were viewed with a new seriousness. Filmmakers had developed new skills during the war years, producers had established a mammoth industry—and in the midst of it all the war movie had been given its essential design.

When D. W. Griffith, returned from the front-line trenches, had been asked his opinion of the real war, he had answered honestly, "Viewed as a drama, the war is in some ways disappointing." Griffith and a host of other filmmakers had managed to put into modern war the drama they thought it lacked. Although Mr. Maxim's rapid-fire gun left no place for nineteenth-century idealism and chivalry on the battlefields of the modern world, the pioneer filmmakers, following their own dreams and opinions of war, had found room for them on film. They had proved that war was the perfect subject for films—and World War I had not ended all wars.

WHAT
PRICE
GLORY?

D. W. Griffith was the only American director to visit the trenches during World War I, but he was not the only director to witness the war. The French director Abel Gance had already made a name for himself as an important film-maker when he was drafted into the French Army during the last months of the war. Poor health had kept him out of the army, but by 1918 France was in desperate need of soldiers, and Gance was sent to the front.

He never forgot what he saw there. Discharged, he had reenlisted—he wanted to make a film about the war. He obtained permission to film at the front so that he could incorporate actual scenes of combat in his movie.

Released shortly after the armistice, *J'accuse* (1919) presents Gance's vision of the war, his rage at the purposeless waste he had witnessed. The story of the film concerns two friends. The wife of one is raped by Germans; the husband suspects his friend, Jean Diaz. The two men are sent to the front, where the husband is killed. Diaz, a poet and a visionary, is driven mad by the terrible sights he has seen in the trenches. He summons his neighbors—those who have not fought, including the war profiteers—and tells them of a dead soldier who rose up and called on the other war dead: "My friends, my friends. . . . Let's go see if the country is worthy of us and if our deaths have served some purpose." Diaz's vision comes true. The dead do arise, and they pay the living a horrific visit.

In 1919, Gance was angry at what he perceived as the terrible stupidity of the war; he would later have another reason to be angry, for the peace the young men had died to establish was itself short-lived. In Germany in 1919, Adolf Hitler became the seventh member of the committee of the German Workers' party; he was soon to find the means of venting his own rage over the outcome of World War I.

The end of the war left anger in the United States, too. Although few war movies were shown after the armistice, there was a brief but caustic spurt of revenge movies, films in which the kaiser and his homeland are made to atone for their deeds. *Why Germany Must Pay (The Great Victory)* (1918) reminded audiences of such German atrocities as the murder of Nurse Cavell and went on to propose methods for dealing with the dangerous German people. Before putting forth its theories for establishing a lasting peace, *The Heart of Humanity* (1919), directed by Allen Holubar, recapitulates the story of Germany's bestiality in Belgium. Erich von Stroheim appears as a Prussian lieutenant named Von Eberhard, who, eyes bulging, attempts to rape a Red Cross nurse (Dorothy Phillips). He chases her around a room and tears at her clothes, while a child cries from a crib and the town outside is engulfed in flames. She is saved by the last-minute arrival of her soldier-husband (William Stowell).

Getting revenge is the theme of *Behind the Door* (1919), directed by Irvin Willat and produced by Thomas Ince. The film gives a sense of how bloodcurdling Ince's films had become since *Civilization*.

A German-American taxidermist named Oscar Krug (Hobart Bosworth), living in Maine and constantly pestered by his neighbors because of his Teutonic heritage, enlists in the navy. His wife (Jane Novak) manages to get aboard the same ship, which is torpedoed in mid-ocean by a German submarine. Mr. and Mrs. Krug are the only survivors. After spending several days adrift in a small boat, they are spotted by another German submarine. The sub surfaces, and the Germans rescue the wife but leave the husband to die. He survives, living only for revenge, and eventually succeeds in sinking the German submarine and taking prisoner its captain (Wallace Beery). Krug wines and dines the German and extracts from him the story of his wife's fate (Germans in submarines, like Germans in châteaux, need "relaxation": she was raped by the crew and then killed). The enraged Krug takes the German "behind the door," opens a razor, and prepares to exact his revenge. When he reappears, he reports, "I swore I would skin him alive, but he died on me—damn him!"

Abel Gance's *J'accuse* was released in the United States in 1921 as *I Accuse*. This was not the same as the 1919 French film; it had been heavily edited. The accusations hurled in the original at the Germans, war profiteers, and, fi-

nally, war itself, were cut down to just the Germans. The American version was also given a happy, victorious ending.

The brief period of revenge films was followed by a pause in the production of war movies. During this respite, there were a few films about veterans returning home, including some about wounded veterans trying to fit back into society. Hoot Gibson plays a shell-shocked veteran in *Shootin' for Love* (1923). He overcomes his fear of gunplay in time to rescue his girl friend from outlaws. *Humoresque* (1920), directed by Frank Borzage, is about a concert violinist who returns from service in the army wounded in both arms. He, too, is cured of his wounds by the love of a woman.

The British government asked playwright Arthur Wing Pinero to write a play that would in

some way ease the agonies of war-maimed soldiers. The play he wrote, *The Enchanted Cottage*, was made into an American movie in 1924, directed by John S. Robertson. A shell-shocked and disfigured soldier (Richard Barthelmess) comes home to find himself rejected by his family and former sweetheart. He seeks an abode far from his relatives and ends up in an isolated cottage, where he meets an unattractive (she has protruding teeth and a very large nose) girl (May McAvoy). The two are affected by the cottage: it has been used by generations of honeymooners, and in the atmosphere of love the veteran and the girl fall in love and are transformed. They appear beautiful to each other.

The most important war movie to appear during this lull was *The Four Horsemen of the Apocalypse* (1921), directed by Rex Ingram, the 29

Above left: Behind the Door *(1919). The German submarine submerges, leaving Hobart Bosworth to die.*

Above right: *Rudolph Valentino* (left) *in a scene from* The Four Horsemen of the Apocalypse *(1921), the film that made him a star.*

film that launched Rudolph Valentino on his short but spectacular career as a screen idol. The Germans in the film are as evil as ever, and the battle scenes are full of convincing destruction, but it is the poignant love story of Valentino and Alice Terry that made the film a tremendous success and set the style for the war movies to come: the application of romance and adventure to vaguely antiwar themes.

The veterans of World War I were the first war veterans to have the motion picture as a medium for recounting their combat experiences. They could *show* audiences how awful the war in the trenches had been; they could make audiences *see* the terrible true nature of war. But the battles were over, and the war continued only as memories and nightmares unevenly distributed among the surviving participants. There was nothing left to point at: to

show the war, it would have to be recreated, and to do so required making sense of the memories, putting them into coherent form as a story, adjusting agony to accommodate plot.

Films reflect the period in which they are made more than the subject with which they deal, and the American veterans of World War I returned to a nation that was going on a spree—the Roaring Twenties, the Jazz Age, a period of economic prosperity and joyous immorality. Beneath the glossy surface of the Jazz Age languished the "lost generation," those who saw, according to F. Scott Fitzgerald, "All gods dead, all wars fought, all faiths in man shaken." How would the veterans remember the war? In terms of 1917 innocence, or 1920s savvy? How could they, in 1920, convey their feelings of rage and loss without resorting to the stories then popular, stories of brash young men and sassy women?

The experience of the war remained within

The Big Parade (1925). As the doughboys march to the front, Renée Adorée (lower right) searches through the ranks for her lover.

those who had fought it, but the war itself was rapidly passing out of their possession: it was becoming a national property, and as such it was viewed by the living—by those who had not fought and by those who had survived the fighting—as a great victory overseas, America's salvation of Europe. The war had been won, and all the dead were heroes: the veterans did not object to this interpretation, and in the prevailing attitude of the times they could both scorn the medals they had won as emblems of tragedy and embrace the theme of war as great adventure.

World War I has remained a popular film topic, divided into two distinct categories: the "antiwar" film about the ground war and the chivalric dream of the air war. Both types were established during the twenties. The ground war came first.

Laurence Stallings returned from World War I with only one leg; he had lost his right leg to wounds suffered during the Battle of Belleau Wood. The ex-marine became a critic for the New York *World* and began writing about his wartime experiences. His novel, *Plumes*, was published in 1924. That same year, in collaboration with playwright Maxwell Anderson, Stallings wrote a play about marines called *What Price Glory?* The play's appealingly rowdy characters and abundant profanity delighted the public, and it was a big hit on Broadway. King Vidor, who had recently begun working as a director for the newly formed Metro-Goldwyn-Mayer, thought that attitudes had changed and the public again was ready for a war movie. He was right. Vidor used a story by Stallings as the basis for *The Big Parade* (1925), the first in a series of war movies and one of the biggest money-makers of the silent era, second only to *The Birth of a Nation*.

The Big Parade begins with a parade. The flags and music have a hypnotic effect on the spectators. Drawn away from their work by the stirring music, ordinary citizens are transformed by the romantic dream and enlist. The story concerns three "typical" American boys: Jim Apperson (John Gilbert), the profligate son of a wealthy mill owner; Slim (Karl Dane), a steelworker; and Bull O'Hara (Tom O'Brien), a bartender. All three enlist in the army and have become good friends

by the time they are sent overseas as part of the "big parade" of American soldiers. As a title states, "The Yanks came to France in the spring—millions of 'em. Heads up. And tails over the dashboard!" In France, Apperson meets a farmer's daughter named Melisande (Renée Adorée), and the two fall in love. When Apperson's unit is ordered to the front, Melisande is distraught, and as the rows of men march off, she runs through the ranks, searching for her lover. She finds him, and they embrace. They are separated, Apperson is put on a truck, and as it pulls away, he tosses Melisande some keepsakes, including a boot, which she hugs to her chest.

The three friends take part in a terrible battle; only one survives. The battlefield scenes are famous for their harrowing atmosphere. Vidor made great use of rhythmic movement, and the scenes of men and trucks moving toward the front follow a compelling tempo. Soldiers making their way through woods are mowed down by machine guns. There is a rhythm and symmetry to the spectacle—it is as though the entire battle were an irresistible force, pulling the participants toward death. The enormous battle is experienced by each soldier as a personal event. Vidor said he wanted to show the experiences of an ordinary man, a man with no particular opinions about the conflict, who is thrust into war. By making the battle personal, it becomes even more frightening. The loneliness and fear of the individual soldiers are painfully clear; the instances of courage appear futile.

When Slim is killed, Apperson, enraged, leaps into a German trench and grapples with an enemy soldier. The two struggle, Apperson gets the upper hand and poises to kill the man, but seeing that the German is already wounded, he pulls back and offers his enemy a cigarette. The German dies—Apperson finishes the cigarette. Another soldier, crossing a field with artillery shells exploding around him, throws up his arms and cries, "They cheered us when we went away, and they'll cheer us when we return. But who the hell cares after this?"

It is Apperson who survives—he is the better-looking one of the trio, the one involved with the French girl. The experience of the war has

31

knocked the wastrel out of him. Like the hero of *The Unbeliever*, he has learned life's true values. Like Stallings, he has lost a leg, and when he returns home he finds that no one there can understand him. He goes back to France and the waiting Melisande.

British critics assailed *The Big Parade* for its implication that Americans had won the war single-handedly—using fisticuffs. American audiences loved the film, for without denying the horrors of the war, it reinforced the national sense of pride in the heroism of American soldiers. The swearing done by the heroes (to be lip-read, of course) was titillating, and the love story was touching. By making war a personal experience, *The Big Parade* avoided war's more dire aspects. There were no political or philosophical statements to be made. The war was a molder of character, a means of displaying the true personalities of protagonists. The moments of battlefield horrors were only part of the story, background to the adventure of war with its romantic possibilities. As an advertisement for the film announced, "The life stories, the little group of people one comes to know and love, amid the clash of huge, unknown forces. Epical in background; individual in romance." The "huge, unknown forces"—the forces that tore off men's legs—were to remain unknown; World War I had been successfully fit into the form of a story about love and adventure in foreign lands.

The enormous success of *The Big Parade* did not go unnoticed by American filmmakers, and the remaining years of the twenties were full of movies about wartime adventure and romance. A great many of these films follow the same pat-

tern: two pals are sent to France (or Nicaragua, or any other scene of action), where they meet a girl; they argue over possession of the girl, exhibit disdain for officers, and fight both each other and the enemy. The prototypes for these buddies were Captain Flagg and Sergeant Quirt, the "hard-fisted" professional marines of *What Price Glory?* (1926).

In the stage version of *What Price Glory?*, the roles of Flagg and Quirt were taken by Louis Wolheim and William Boyd; in the screen version, directed by Raoul Walsh, the roles were given to Victor McLaglen and Edmund Lowe. The stage play had antiwar themes, but these were discarded in the film, which gave audiences the kind of comic excitement then popular: bawdy humor, playful fisticuffs, close-ups of bosoms and buttocks, and plenty of profanity (again for lip-readers). The battle scenes are powerful—including one famous scene in which a row of infantrymen standing in a trench is buried by the explosion of a mine, leaving only the points of their bayonets sticking up through the earth—but it was the ongoing squabble between Flagg and Quirt that delighted viewers. The two "brothers in arms" exchange dirty looks when at a distance and enormous fists when within range. The film begins with the pals bickering in China, they continue their dispute in the Philippines, and arrive in France still knocking each other around. Although they are brave soldiers and respond without hesitation to their country's call, it is their personal feud that is of primary importance to them: the war is an inconvenience, an interruption in their brawl. Even the feminine charms of Dolores Del Rio as a French girl named Charmaine are less appealing to the rough pair than their friendly enmity. Quirt eventually wins Charmaine, but when he sees his buddy "moving on," he calls out, "Hey, Flagg, wait for baby!"

Too popular to be separated, Flagg and Quirt appeared in three sequels to *What Price Glory?*, all directed by Raoul Walsh. The first of these, *The Cock-Eyed World* (1929), was written by Stallings and Anderson. McLaglen and Lowe carry on their exchange of comic insults, argue over Lili Damita, and battle insurgents in Central America (probably meant to be followers of

Nicaraguan revolutionary Augusto Sandino). *Women of All Nations* (1931) again united Flagg and Quirt; their careers as buddies came to an end in *Under Pressure* (1935), in which the two pals, now called Jumbo and Shocker, are involved in digging a tunnel under New York City's East River. The war was not necessary to Flagg and Quirt: like digging a tunnel, it was merely an excuse for action. (John Ford directed a remake of *What Price Glory?* in 1952, in which James Cagney and Dan Dailey play Flagg and Quirt.)

McLaglen and Lowe were not the only buddies in uniform delighting audiences. In *Tell It to the Marines* (1926), directed by George Hill, a tough veteran sergeant named O'Hara (Lon Chaney) gives a humorous hard time to Private "Skeet" Burns (William Haines). The two go from the marines' San Diego training camp to a battleship in the Pacific to a battle with "bandits" in the Philippines. (Haines has a love affair with Eleanor Boardman.) The film was made with the cooperation of the Marine Corps and is remarkable because scenes of the annual battle practice of the US Pacific Fleet were used as a

Opposite: *Aircraft support an Allied advance in* Wings *(1927).*

Above: *Edmund Lowe* (third from left), *Dolores Del Rio, Victor McLaglen, and other cast members of* What Price Glory? *(1926).*

background to some of the action, the first time that any fleet maneuvers had been filmed for use in a movie.

Robert Graves and Jack Holt were teamed in a series of adventure films that got the two buddies involved with modern technology and current events. In *Submarine* (1928), directed by Frank Capra, Holt is a deep-sea diver and Graves is a navy petty officer. The two friends fall out over a dance-hall girl known as Snuggles (Dorothy Revier). When Graves's submarine is rammed and sinks to the bottom, only Holt can save the crew, but his jealousy over his pal's relationship to the girl makes him hesitate—while the men in the sub, slowly suffocating, writhe in agony. The movie was quite topical: two submarines had recently been rammed and sunk.

In their next film, *Flight* (1929), also directed by Frank Capra, Holt and Graves fly around in airplanes and argue over the affections of a girl (Lila Lee), while fighting bandits in Central America. Once again, jealousy over the girl makes one of the pals think twice before saving his friend. Like *Submarine* and *The Cock-Eyed World*, *Flight* was quite topical: the action takes place in Nicaragua, and the "bandits" handily dispatched by the heroes are guerrillas fighting with Augusto Sandino.

Wallace Beery and Raymond Hatton formed yet another team. They were first united in a comedy version of *The Big Parade*, the title of which recalls an earlier Beery film, *Behind the Door: Behind the Front* (1926), directed by Edward Sutherland. The two pals, Riff (Beery) and Shorty (Hatton), take part in the fighting in France and get themselves in a lot of trouble. They are thrown in the brig for pricking an officer's derriere with a bayonet, and they fall for the same girl, who happens to be their captain's sister (as inseparable as any pals, they inform the captain that he is soon to be their brother-in-law). During a big battle, Riff and Shorty find themselves behind the German lines. They put on German officers' uniforms, and while stumbling around, Riff experiences a typical battlefield coincidence: he meets his New York butcher, a German who has come to fight for his fatherland. The butcher presents Riff with an unpaid bill for eight dollars. Money finally in hand, the butcher walks away and is blown up.

Beery and Hatton left the army in their next film together, also directed by Edward Sutherland, called *We're in the Navy Now* (1926). The two would-be sailors get involved with another girl and have comic difficulties with a hammock. The last of this series, *Now We're in the Air* (1927), directed by Frank Strayer, finds the pals competing for the affections of a comely girl named Grisette.

Nineteen twenty-seven was the right year to be in the air. Charles Lindbergh's solo flight across the Atlantic that year thrilled the nation, but the airplane received an even greater boost in *Wings*.

The Big Parade had established World War I on the ground, but there was another story to tell. Among the returning veterans were men who had served in airplanes. John Monk Saunders had not seen action overseas, but he had served in the aviation section of the Army Signal Corps, and the young writer was full of exciting tales about airmen. Another young man, William Wellman, had gone to France and flown with the Lafayette Flying Corps, an outfit similar to the Lafayette Escadrille. When the United States had entered the war, he had transferred to the Army Air Corps. By 1927, Wellman was working as a film director. *Wings* (1927), directed by Wellman and based on a story by Saunders, was the first, and perhaps the best, movie about the air war of World War I.

The plot of *Wings* concerns two friends (Charles "Buddy" Rogers and Richard Arlen) who join the Army Air Corps. There are romantic complications involving their girl friends, one of whom (Clara Bow) shows up in France as a nurse. Shot down behind enemy lines, Arlen steals a German plane and flies it back toward the Allied lines; he is shot down mistakenly by his friend and dies in his arms.

Wings is famous for its scenes of aerial combat, not its plot. Wellman had the full assistance of the US War Department—the most government help ever given a filmmaker—and a group of talented stunt pilots, including Dick Grace, who had served in the Naval Air Service during

34

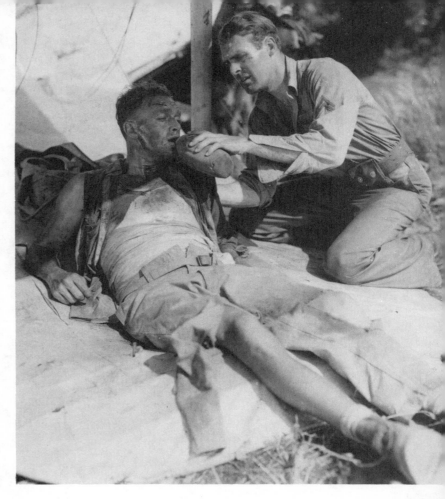

Right: *A scene on the ground in* Flight *(1929).*

the war. The aerial warfare in *Wings* set the style for all future aviation films: planes swoop out of the sky to strafe trains and troops on bridges; burning planes spin to the earth and crash; planes loop the loop and dive and soar at terrific speed.

These thrilling action sequences had a powerful effect on audiences in 1927, for few people had had the opportunity of flying in a plane. The film opened a whole new world, peopled by daring young pilots with their own chivalric code. High over the heads of the grappling doughboys and Boche, knights of the air exchanged machine-gun blasts and heroic courtesies. The foe in the air was not the hated Hun: the enemies in *Wings* are the members of the Flying Circus of Captain Kellerman (modeled after Baron von Richthofen, "the Red Baron," and his Flying Circus). They are menacing but not inhuman, and the dogfights are contests, feats of skill, not senseless slaughter.

Wings won the first Academy Award for best

picture of the year (the awards were initiated in 1927) and led to a flock of imitators, many of which were based on stories by Saunders, were directed by Wellman, and contained footage from *Wings*.

The Legion of the Condemned (1928), directed by Wellman and based on a story by Saunders, stars Gary Cooper. Cooper had had a small scene in *Wings* as an experienced pilot who chats with the two stars ("Luck or no luck, when your time comes, you're gonna get it," he says) and then, after taking a bite of a chocolate bar, goes off to perform "a flock of eights before chow," only to be killed in a crash. In *The Legion of the Condemned*, Gary Cooper is one of a group of young men who join the Flying Squadron of the French Foreign Legion because they "have tried everything in life but death." Most of them are seeking to escape some unfortunate incident in their past. One has gambled away his money at Monte Carlo (when he attempts to shoot himself, the poor fellow is stopped by his mistress, who tells him, "Don't try to blow out what you haven't got"); another has killed a girl in a car crash;

some are there to forget failed love affairs. All of these pilots are described as "the rarin', tearin' galoots who aim to die in their tall, brown boots."

The assignments given the pilots are truly suicidal: they fly spies behind the enemy lines, and they do so during daylight hours. The Germans, led by a Prussian with a monocle, have little trouble rounding up and shooting the pilots and their spy passengers. Cooper is given Fay Wray as his spy to bear, and he eventually saves her from a firing squad.

Cooper plays a British airman in *Lilac Time* (1928), directed by George Fitzmaurice. The story of the film was adapted from a Broadway play by Jane Cowl and Jane Murfin—the play had been about ground warfare and was altered to accommodate the popularity of the air war. Captain Philip Blythe (Cooper) is a member of a squadron of the Royal Air Force billeted in France near a farmhouse that is home to a pretty young French girl named Jeannine (Colleen Moore). Captain Blythe and Jeannine fall in love. When the fearsome German "Red Ace" shoots down Blythe, he manages to crash-land near the farmhouse. Jeannine signals for an ambulance but is not allowed inside it to be with her lover. As the ambulance moves off, she grabs desperately onto its tailgate.

Romance was the primary ingredient of the air-war films that immediately followed *Wings*. The war demanded only the simplest of plots and served as the opportunity for romantic encounters. Any handsome American actor could be put behind the controls of a biplane, and when not roaming the skies in search of the Red Baron, he would have plenty of time on the ground during which to meet enticing "foreign" women. In *Captain Swagger* (1928), the matinee idol Rod la Rocque plays an American aviator serving in the French Air Force who meets and becomes romantically involved with Sue Carol, a popular screen flapper. The soil of Europe was not so very foreign after all. In *A Dog of the Regiment* (1927), directed by Ross Lederman, an American flier (Tom Gallery) shot down behind the German lines runs into a German nurse (Dorothy Gulliver). The two fall in love despite the

belligerencies of their respective homelands and receive support from the star of the film, the nurse's dog: Rin Tin Tin. (The canine hero belonged behind the German lines: he had been found in a German trench during the war by an American infantry officer, who then had taken him home and made him into a movie star.)

The most important successor to *Wings* was *Hell's Angels* (1930), produced and directed by Howard Hughes. An avid promoter of aviation, Hughes had begun work on his epic film in 1927 and had just finished a silent version, starring Norwegian actress Greta Nissen, when sound arrived. Hughes canceled the film and at great expense reshot much of it with sound and replaced Nissen, whose heavy accent was unsuitable for her role, with Jean Harlow. The final film is in transition from silent to sound. As planes take off into darkness, a title states, "Everybody gets it on the night patrol"; as Harlow turns to Ben Lyon, one of two brothers vying for her attention, she asks, "Would you be shocked if I got into something more comfortable?"

The plot of *Hell's Angels* concerns two broth-

Above: *Tom Gallery ponders his fate with the aid of Rin Tin Tin in* A Dog of the Regiment *(1927).*

ers (Ben Lyon and James Hall), their dispute over Harlow, their combat with Baron von Richthofen's deadly aces, and their own battle (one kills the other to prevent him from leaking important information to the enemy). As with *Wings,* it is not the plot of *Hell's Angels* that is important: it is the action sequences. Hughes filled the air with planes. Their motors roaring and machine guns hammering away, flocks of biplanes participate in spectacular dogfights. One of the film's most exciting sequences is a night bombing raid on London by a zeppelin. The giant, dark craft ominously moves in and out of clouds as it approaches the city. When the zeppelin is attacked by British planes, the Germans throw material overboard in an effort to lighten the airship. Finally, declaring, "For kaiser and fatherland!" loyal crewmen jump to their deaths, sacrificing themselves for the rest of the crew.

Hughes's investment paid off. *Hell's Angels* was a great success, and its dramatic flying sequences were used, like scenes from *Wings,* in many other films. (These scenes had proven expensive in many ways—it was reported that three stunt fliers had died during production of the film.)

One of the films to benefit from *Hell's Angels* footage is *Sky Devils* (1932), a Howard Hughes production directed by Edward Sutherland. The film is a comedy (Robert Benchley contributed to the dialogue) and involves a pair of quarreling friends (Spencer Tracy and George Cooper). The story begins with the two draft-dodging buddies working as lifeguards at Coney Island in 1917. Since neither of the two can swim, they do poorly at their job, and after a series of misadventures they end up in France as fliers who can't fly. However, few of the Americans can fly. As one reports after crashing a plane, "I bring down one more of our planes, and I'll be a German ace." Tracy separates from Cooper and teams up with an actor well-suited to the role, William Boyd, the man who had played Sergeant Quirt in the stage play of *What Price Glory?* Forever anxious to escape the rigors of army life, Tracy eventually gets himself, Boyd, and the girl they are arguing over (Ann Dvorak) in a plane headed for Switzerland. Spotting some cows in a field, they decide they have arrived and land the plane.

The sound of yodeling convinces them that they are indeed in Switzerland, but the music is coming from a record being played in the German officers' headquarters.

The adventurous aspects of the war on the ground, as portrayed in *The Big Parade* and *What Price Glory?*, were short-lived—within a few years the trenches were to become a symbol of doom. But the war in the air as established in *Wings* and *Hell's Angels* has never lost its aura of romantic spectacle. Even when, in 1930, the theme of war's futility made its way into movies about the air war, the planes maintained their fascination.

The submarine, another piece of modern technology made famous by the war, was less popular with filmmakers than the airplane. There was no Stallings or Saunders to come forward with a dramatic story, and in nearly all of the few films about submarines, the story is the same: the sub sinks. Added to this fatalistic view of undersea warfare is the fact that it is difficult to include women—and romance—in tales about men at sea.

The title of John Ford's first important sound film, *Men Without Women* (1930), reflects one of the drawbacks to naval stories. Although there are a few scenes with women in the beginning of the film, most of the story concerns fourteen men in a submarine. The submarine sinks, and one of the crewmen sacrifices himself to save the others. (Among the submariners is John Wayne.)

Another submarine sinks in *Hell Below* (1933), directed by Jack Conway, a movie about American submarines in the Adriatic Sea during World War I (the film was photographed in the clear waters around Pearl Harbor and had the cooperation of the US Navy). Unlike Ford's film, *Hell Below* manages to find room for plenty of romance (between Madge Evans and Robert Montgomery) and humor—the sub's cook, known as Ptomaine, is played by Jimmy Durante. Walter Huston is the commander, and when the sub sinks, divers attempt to save it.

Hell Below, with its exciting scenes of undersea melodrama and its heroic, self-sacrificing sailors, was propaganda for the navy. Similar films were being made in Germany. *Mor-*

genrot (Dawn) (1933), directed by Gustav Ucicky, is about a German submarine that is rammed by a British destroyer and sinks: two of the crewmen kill themselves to save the remaining men. The film displays remarkably few traces of anti-Allies propaganda, but it promotes duty, self-sacrifice, and national pride. As one of the crewmen declares, "We Germans may not know much about living, but we know how to die." The film was released the day after Adolf Hitler became Reich chancellor.

John Ford solved the problem of getting women in a navy picture in *Submarine Patrol* (1938), a film about the sub chasers of World War I, the frail, wooden boats that were used to protect American troopships. The hero of the film (Richard Greene) is aboard one of the ships; he falls in love with the daughter (Nancy Kelly) of the captain of the ship being escorted. The girl has come along for the voyage.

In 1930, the image of the western front of World War I was changed forever by a group of films led by *All Quiet on the Western Front*. These films were hailed as powerful antiwar statements, and their popularity led to a brief cycle of pacifist films, a cycle that came to an end with the films promoting preparedness for the next war. Some of these films, particularly *All Quiet on the Western Front*, have remained popular, and their visions of trench warfare have become the dominant images of World War I. The popularity of these films did nothing to prevent World War II, and that war locked them securely in the past: they are no longer antiwar, merely anti-World War I.

Erich Maria Remarque served as a German soldier on the western front during World War I. He drew on his memories of the war for his first novel, *All Quiet on the Western Front*, which was published in 1929 and became an immediate international best-seller. The movie version of the book, produced by Carl Laemmle (who had produced *The Kaiser, the Beast of Berlin*) and directed by Lewis Milestone (a Russian-born director who had served in the US Signal Corps

during the war), appeared in 1930.

The film begins during the early months of the war. As soldiers in spiked helmets march off to battle with flowers stuck in the barrels of their rifles, a schoolteacher calls on his students to enlist. They are "the iron men of Germany," he tells them, and "the field of honor" calls to them. Full of visions of the glory to be theirs (and eager to get away from their classes), the boys, including Paul (Lew Ayres) and his friends, enlist. Sent to the front, they soon learn the truth about war: it is not a matter of heroism, only survival. Led by a veteran sergeant named Katczinsky (Louis Wolheim, Captain Flagg in the stage version of *What Price Glory?*) and a corporal (Slim Summerville), they try to stay alive. The French attack; they retreat. They attack, and the French retreat. The fighting in the trenches is shockingly brutal, men killing one another with bayonets and shovels. One by one, the friends are killed or maimed. The war itself is a mystery to them. "How do they start a war?" one asks, and the others try to answer. "Somebody must have wanted it," says one. "It must be doing somebody some good." "Every full-grown emperor needs one war to make him famous." One boy thinks war is a kind of fever: no one wants it, but everyone catches it. They also worry about what will happen to them after the war: "What have we got to go back to?"

The war goes on. The only thing that changes is their helmet (the spiked helmet is replaced by the bucket-shaped helmet). During a bombardment in a cemetery, the corpses are tossed to the surface. Paul takes refuge in a shell hole, and a poilu (Raymond Griffith) jumps in after him. Paul stabs the man and then finds that he cannot leave the trench, because of enemy fire. During the night, he listens to the Frenchman die and begs forgiveness of the man he has killed, promising him that after the war he'll write to the man's wife and parents. The Frenchman does not reply: he is dead.

Sent home after recuperating from a wound, Paul finds that he cannot stay there. No one understands what he has experienced. He glances at his butterfly collection and visits his old professor, whom he finds delivering another prowar harangue to another room full of eager young men. The professor asks Paul to speak to the class, but Paul has little to say. As he tells the professor, "When it comes to dying for your country, it's better not to die at all."

He is killed when he returns to the front. Reaching from his trench toward a butterfly, he is shot by a French sniper. The last scene of the film is of soldiers marching off into the sky over fields of crosses, each soldier turning to look back at the audience.

Although the roles were played by Americans, *All Quiet on the Western Front* is about Germans, and a great deal of its power lay in that one fact: it "revealed" the enemy. The film also promoted the popular sentiment that the German people had been against the kaiser's war—when you got to know them, German soldiers were boys very much like American boys (indeed, the actors are so obviously American that the viewer is challenged to remember they are supposed to be German). Perhaps the most important aspect of the film is that the enemy of the Germans is French. Paul and his comrades are not shooting at American doughboys. The war and its suffering remained foreign, and the film's antiwar themes were not applied to America's involvement in the war. Americans were free to view the war as a European affair that Americans had had to end.

All Quiet on the Western Front won the Academy Award as best picture, and Milestone won as best director; the producer, Carl Laemmle, was considered for a Nobel Peace Prize. The film was not well received in Germany. The Nazi propagandist Joseph Goebbels condemned it when it appeared there, and Nazis stormed the theater where it was being premiered and released white rats into the audience; they returned the next night with snakes. Hitler then banned the film in Germany, and Mussolini banned it in Italy. Because of its depiction of French soldiers, the film was also banned in France (the ban lasted until 1962). The book also was banned in Germany and was thrown on pyres beginning in 1932. Remarque left Germany in 1931 and went to Switzerland, but he did not stop writing.

Lew Ayres, the central character of the film, went on to other acting roles and gained national acclaim in the role of young Dr. Kildare in a series of films. His popularity ended in 1941,

when he declared himself a conscientious objector. (Rather than fight, he served as a volunteer medic and showed courage under fire.)

The German director G. W. Pabst spent World War I in a French camp for enemy aliens. Although he did not experience the fighting firsthand, he was an ardent pacifist and wanted to make a film about the senseless waste of war, a film that would be a plea for European unity. Pabst based *Westfront 1918* (1930) on a novel by Ernst Johannsen, *Four Men of the Infantry*. Like *All Quiet on the Western Front*, *Westfront 1918* is about German soldiers on the western front who experience the war as a relentless destroyer of hope and purpose. The story follows four soldiers, friends who are trapped in a squalid wasteland. Their existence alternates between periods of boredom and sudden moments of chaotic slaughter. The men stare blankly over the top of their trench at a nightmare landscape in which mangled corpses stick up from the flat mud (the film was quite graphic; people fainted at its Berlin premiere). The war is nothing but death, and all human values become meaningless in the overwhelming despair. Karl (Gustav Diessl), the central character, goes home on leave to find his wife in bed with the son of the local butcher. He returns to the front and, like his friends, is finally wounded. He is taken to a bombed-out church and laid on a cot next to a wounded French soldier. The Frenchman takes Karl's hand and whispers that he is a friend, not an enemy. But Karl is already dead. The film ends with a question: "End?"

Westfront 1918 was banned in Germany in 1933.

In both *All Quiet on the Western Front* and *Westfront 1918*, the war is not the background to individual acts of valor. Rather, it is the foreground, and it leaves no room for heroic actions. The atmosphere is one of death and hopelessness; the only human response is sorrow. Both films were based on works by Germans, for whom the war had the aspect of defeat: Paul and Karl die for no reason. The suffering and disillusionment of the Depression made their way into American-made films about World War I, but since the outcome of the war for Americans had been victory, the themes of the films about it are different: the dead have made heroic sacrifices, and the war recedes into the background, making room for a dignified response. The futility of the war, however powerfully expressed, serves to add poignance to the heroes' actions.

R. C. Sherriff, who had served as an infantry captain in the British Army during the war, achieved his first great success as a playwright with *Journey's End*. The film version of the play, made in the United States, was directed by James Whale, a Briton who had spent most of World War I in a German prisoner-of-war camp. Almost all of the action in *Journey's End* (1930) takes place inside a dugout at the St. Quentin, France, headquarters for a group of British officers. The plot concerns the various officers and the ways in which they contend with the boredom and anxiety of the war—and with one another. The central character of the film is Major Stanhope (played by Colin Clive, who had had the lead in the play). Stanhope, who has been in the trenches for more than three years, is being destroyed by his awful responsibilities, sending young men to their deaths. He gets by on gulps of whiskey.

The scenes of trench fighting in *Journey's End* are fearsome, and the film was acclaimed as an important antiwar statement, but the film is not antiwar in the sense of *All Quiet on the Western Front*. It is about officers, men who suffer the emotional and physical strain of the war but continue doing their parts. They are courageous because they do not give in to their fears—the war is bad because it destroys men's spirits.

The character of Stanhope emerged as a popular symbol, and various Stanhopes appear, under different names, in other films of the early thirties. They are always recognizable by the nearby bottle of whiskey.

Other British officers are faced with the utter waste of war in *Tell England* (1930), directed and cowritten by Anthony Asquith. Based on a novel by Ernest Raymond, the film relates the events of the disastrous Gallipoli campaign as experienced by two young officers, whose initial patriotic zeal is slowly replaced by bitter disillusionment. The film is powerful precisely because it deals with an actual battle, a battle that was a terrible defeat. It is not an antiwar statement, however, for although the war is terrible, it is not stronger than the courage of the men involved.

The view of war as a horrific, man-devouring waste spread to movies about aerial combat: the war in the air was as harrowing as the war on the ground. John Monk Saunders, author of *Wings*, supplied the stories for a number of films in which the air war is no longer the scene of gallantry: the fliers, constantly facing death, are afraid; their commanders are destroyed by their responsibilities.

The Dawn Patrol (1930), directed by Howard Hawks, was based on "The Flight Commander," a story by Saunders about the 59th Squadron of Britain's Royal Flying Corps in 1915. The Allied fliers are being slaughtered by the Germans, and they blame their squadron commander (Neil Hamilton) for the appalling death rate. When the commander is promoted, the task of leadership falls to his most outspoken critic (Richard Barthelmess). He soon learns the truth about command, and, his nerves shattered by the anguishing responsibilities, he takes to the bottle. When he sends the younger brother of his best friend to his death, he takes off on a suicidal mission and is killed. His friend (Douglas Fairbanks, Jr.) assumes the terrible post of flight commander.

Another pair of friends faces the strain of

Left: *Colin Clive (left) as the whiskey-drinking Stanhope in* Journey's End *(1930).*

aerial warfare in *The Eagle and the Hawk* (1931), directed by Stuart Walker and based on a story by Saunders. Fredric March and Cary Grant train together in England and are sent to France, where they fly in the same plane: March is the pilot, Grant is the observer. March becomes a famous ace, but the killing has its effect on him, and after a dinner given in his honor at which he is awarded a medal for his exploits, he commits suicide. Grant takes the body up in a plane and crashes it, sacrificing himself to preserve his friend's honor.

The effect of war on character is even more vividly presented in *Ace of Aces* (1931), directed by J. Walter Ruben and based on a story, "Bird of Prey," by Saunders. Richard Dix stars as Rex Thorne, a sensitive young sculptor who enlists when his wife (Elizabeth Allan) accuses him of cowardice. The war has a brutalizing effect on the artist, who is transformed into a bloodthirsty killer; after shooting down forty German planes, he becomes the "ace of aces." His wife becomes a Red Cross nurse and runs into her changed husband in a Paris bistro. She does not like what she sees: the war has ruined him.

A novel by Saunders, *Single Lady*, served as the basis for *The Last Flight* (1931), directed by William Dieterle. The story concerns four fliers who go on a binge across Europe immedi-

ately after the armistice. Each is in some way wounded: one has a burned hand; one suffers from a tic in an eye; one has become a violent bully; and one cannot keep himself awake. The end of the war has left them wounded and without a purpose. They are joined by a girl traveling with a pair of pet turtles. Nothing matters to the little group: they are lost in despair.

The title of *Beyond Victory* (1931), directed by

Right: *Cary Grant* (left) *and Fredric March in* The Eagle and the Hawk *(1931).*

Left: *Lionel Barrymore* (left) *and Phillips Holmes* in The Man I Killed (Broken Lullaby) *(1932).*

man's girl friend, Elsa, is consumed by grief, but she is deeply affected by Paul's sincerity and his interest in her dead lover. Paul is very much like the man he killed, and he fits into the dead man's family. The father, his hatred gone, hands Paul his dead son's violin, and while Elsa, her grief abated, accompanies on the piano, Paul plays a lullaby.

Far from the grim trenches, the despair of antiwar themes could be translated into sentimentality, a proper setting for romance. Ernest Hemingway's novel *A Farewell to Arms* was made into a stage play by Laurence Stallings in 1930; in 1932, it was made into a movie, directed by Frank Borzage. The story concerns a poignant love affair between an English nurse (Helen Hayes) and an American in the Italian ambulance service (Gary Cooper): the war is far in the background. Two endings were made for the film, one, true to the book, in which the nurse dies giving birth to his child, and one in which she survives. The happy ending was used in the first American release of the film; Hemingway complained.

The first work by William Faulkner to make it to the screen was his story "Turnabout," used as the basis for *Today We Live* (1933), directed by Howard Hawks. Gary Cooper plays an American aviator who comes between an Englishwoman (Joan Crawford) and her boyfriend (Robert Young). The Englishman serves on a torpedo boat in the company of the girl's brother (Franchot Tone). When it is clear that the girl really loves the American, the two Englishmen sacrifice themselves in a suicidal mission.

Self-sacrifice is also the theme of *The White Sister*, a novel by F. Marion Crawford that has been made into a film three times: in 1915, 1923, and 1933. The heartrending tale is always the same—a nun is torn between devotion to her vows and her love for a former boyfriend—only the war changes to suit the period. In the 1933 version, directed by Victor Fleming, the woman (Helen Hayes), believing that her Italian aviator lover, Giovanni (Clark Gable), has been killed, enters the convent of the White Sisters. Giovanni is not dead. Captured by the Austrians, he escapes and comes to her, but she refuses to break her vows.

John Robertson, is from the phrase, "Beyond victory lies the dream of man's desire." The film begins with five American soldiers ordered to hold off the Germans while the remainder of their unit pulls back. Only two of the men survive, and they end up in a German hospital, where they are befriended by a nurse. Looking at the medals on one of the soldiers, the girl asks, "What did you get them for?" "For killing a lot of guys," answers the war-weary doughboy.

The films of World War I are full of fearful scenes of advancing soldiers being mowed down by machine guns. Individuals, men with names and families, are slaughtered in droves. "Killing a lot of guys" might earn a soldier medals, but it did not give meaning to the carnage: beyond victory lay cynicism.

Many of the films of World War I also include scenes of individuals confronted with the killing of one enemy soldier. Jim Apperson leaping on the wounded German in the trench in *The Big Parade* is like Paul in the shell hole with the dying Frenchman in *All Quiet on the Western Front*. Killing one man is not heroic, and the memory of having done so survives all victories.

The Man I Killed (Broken Lullaby) (1932), directed by Ernst Lubitsch, is about a French soldier named Paul (Phillips Holmes) who kills a German soldier and, plagued by guilt, goes to Germany after the war to visit the family of the man he killed. The man's father (Lionel Barrymore) is consumed by hatred for the French, but when he learns that Paul has come to put flowers on his dead son's grave, he relents; the dead

44

Opposite: *Spencer Tracy and Gladys George* (right) in They Gave Him a Gun *(1937).*

The fate of ex-soldiers in the postwar world
became a popular subject during the Depression: men who had served their country in war
were without work. William Wellman, famous for
his aviation films, directed *Heroes for Sale*
(1933), a film about a veteran (Richard Barthelmess) who, unable to find employment, takes to
drugs. Dick Grace, the stunt pilot who had
worked with Wellman on *Wings*, wrote the story
for *The Lost Squadron* (1932), directed by George
Archainbaud. The members of the "lost squadron" are unemployed former aviators forced to
take dangerous work as stunt pilots in Holly-

wood. (The reports of pilots killed in the making of such films as *Hell's Angels* made this film topical.) The pilots find work on a movie being directed by a certain Von Furst (Erich von Stroheim). Von Furst wants to make a dramatic war film and doesn't care about the risks involved. Displeased with the way a scene is going, the tyrannical Teuton yells, "This is supposed to be war, death, destruction—not a Sunday-school picnic!"

They Gave Him a Gun (1937), directed by W. S. Van Dyke, presents a grim view of war's effect on character. A circus barker named Fred (Spencer Tracy) and a small-town bookkeeper named Jimmy (Franchot Tone) become friends in the army and serve together in France, where they both fall in love with a nurse named Rose (Gladys George). Believing Fred dead, Rose marries Jimmy. But the war has had its effect on him—he has become a killer, and when the war is over he becomes a gangster. (Rose thinks he is an insurance adjuster and enjoys their wealth.) Fred turns up when the circus comes to town, and Jimmy is ultimately killed. "He always seemed like such a mild little guy," comments a policeman.

"He was," replies Fred. "Until—until they gave him a gun."

Another man trained to kill "brings the habit back with him" in *The Road Back* (1937), directed by James Whale. The screenplay for the film was written by R. C. Sherriff and Charles Kenyon from the novel *The Way Back*, written by Erich Maria Remarque as a sequel to *All Quiet on the Western Front*. The film is about young Germans who return home after serving in the army only to find that there is no road back to peace. They cannot fit into society, they are not understood at home, and they cannot readjust to school. Instead, they become involved in the political turmoil around them. One of them is shot down in a public square while participating in a hunger riot; another finds that his girl friend is having an affair with a war profiteer and kills the man. He is tried for murder, and in his defense, one of his friends tells the jury, "You taught him to kill men who never did him any harm. Now you wonder why he killed the man who ruined his life." The future looks bleak: in one scene, the friends

come upon a mustachioed dwarf drilling schoolboys (who wear Nazi-like uniforms) for the next war.

The cast of *The Road Back* includes Andy Devine and Slim Summerville (who plays a role similar to his role in *All Quiet on the Western Front*). The two provide much unneeded comedy. The German consul in Los Angeles saw nothing funny about the film and warned the actors and technicians involved in the production that if the film contained anything anti-German, it would be banned, along with all their other films.

F. Scott Fitzgerald and Edward E. Paramore wrote the screenplay for *Three Comrades* (1938), another film based on a novel by Remarque. Directed by Frank Borzage, the film deals with three members of Germany's "lost generation" (Robert Taylor, Robert Young, and Franchot Tone) who return from military service to poverty and political chaos. The three comrades meet a girl (Margaret Sullavan) who is dying of tuberculosis and sacrifice everything in vain attempts to cure her. The little group tries to make a living running a repair shop, but there is no hope: their personal tragedies are overshadowed by a greater national tragedy. One of the three (Robert Young) is killed in a riot. His assailants are not identified—Fitzgerald had named them in his original screenplay, but the Hays Office had censored all references to Nazis.

In 1934, Laurence Stallings assembled a documentary history of the war using Signal Corps footage and, it was claimed, films taken from the secret archives of the various nations involved in the conflict. With a running commentary by Stallings, the film relates the major events of the period, beginning with a scene of Germany's Bismarck in 1901 and ending with the current situation. The film was given an ominous title: *The First World War*. It was no longer the Great War or the German War. It was only the first; everyone knew another was coming.

Antiwar films slowly disappeared during the mid-thirties. John Ford's *The Lost Patrol* (1934), the story of a group of British cavalrymen lost in the Mesopotamian desert, was among the last. Officerless and without orders, the men are led by their sergeant (Victor McLaglen). They take refuge at an oasis, where they are surrounded by Arabs. One by one, they die, some courageously, some in abject fear. Boris Karloff appears as a religious fanatic on his way to insanity.

In *The Road to Glory* (1936), Howard Hawks repeated the theme of *The Dawn Patrol:* the transmission of the responsibilities of command. The screenplay for the film was written by William Faulkner in collaboration with Joel Sayre based on a French film, *Les Croix de Bois.* The film begins with Captain Paul Laroche (Warner Baxter) speaking to a group of replacements. He reminds the new recruits of the glory of the regiment they are in, the 39th, which was founded by Napoleon. The famous regiment is suffering terrible losses, and Laroche, who keeps himself full of brandy, is blamed. He is particularly disliked by Lieutenant Denet (Fredric March), who is appalled by the captain's methods. When one of the men is caught, wounded, in the barbed wire in front of their trenches, several of the man's friends try to save him and are killed. The captain coldly shoots the wounded man, ending his misery and preventing further rescue attempts. The two officers also argue over a nurse named Monique (June Lang). When she asks the lieutenant why men go to war, he answers, "Do not ask me that. Men always have died in wars and probably always will. For what reason we do not know."

The captain's father, Papa Laroche (Lionel Barrymore), a veteran of the Franco-Prussian War, joins the regiment, toting the bugle he blew at Sedan. He and his son die gloriously, and Lieutenant Denet assumes command of the regiment. Denet has learned the truth about Laroche—he was a compassionate man in a terrible situation. The film ends with Denet delivering the speech about the famous regiment to another group of recruits.

The Road to Glory was hailed as an important antiwar film, but reviewers were quick to inform people that the film had nothing to do with a current novel by Humphrey Cobb called *Paths of Glory;* that story of World War I would have to wait.

Papa Laroche was not the sole Franco-Prussian War veteran to turn up in a film about World War I. In *Surrender* (1931), directed by William

Erich von Stroheim in Grand Illusion *(1937).*

K. Howard, a German count who was a general during the earlier war argues with his son, a soldier of World War I, about the differences between the two wars. The count's castle is being used to house French prisoners of war, among them Warner Baxter. The commandant of the prison, Captain Elbing, has been disfigured by a wound and wears a handkerchief over half his face. The film is a romance: given the task of wiring the castle for electricity, Baxter meets the fiancée (Leila Hyams) of the count's son. They fall in love, and she saves his life when he tries to escape. When the armistice is declared, Elbing commits suicide, and the count laments that the world he knew and cherished has been destroyed—all the distinctions of class and rank are gone.

Surrender is similar to another film, set in another German castle being used to house French prisoners: *Grand Illusion (La Grande Illusion)* (1937), directed by Jean Renoir. Son of the painter Pierre Auguste Renoir, Jean Renoir served as an officer in the French Army during World War I and had vivid memories of the war. When the threat of another European conflict arose, he made *Grand Illusion* to remind the peoples of Europe of their common interests and their shared humanity. The title of the film does not refer to any one illusion: indeed, the film is composed of many illusions, each subtly exposed. Although many critics consider it the greatest antiwar film ever made, there are no scenes of warfare in *Grand Illusion.* The war is examined from behind, from the causes of con-

flict: the lines that separate countries; the societal customs and economic barriers that separate people; the beliefs, the prejudices, even the songs and games that people adopt to establish separate identities. All are imaginary, created by men. By displaying these illusions in a gentle, noncritical way, the film shows the viewer the commonality of humankind.

Grand Illusion begins with three French officers—an aristocrat named De Boeldieu (Pierre Fresnay), a former mechanic named Marechal (Jean Gabin), and a Jewish banker named Rosenthal (Marcel Dalio)—taking off on a reconnaissance flight. They are shot down by a German ace named Von Rauffenstein (Erich von Stroheim) and are treated to a formal breakfast in the German officers' mess. Von Rauffenstein is immediately drawn to De Boeldieu; the two members of the military aristocracy share common acquaintances and social rank. According to Von Rauffenstein, the two other Frenchmen have their rank as a "gift" of the French Revolution—they are not the same as he and De Boeldieu. Dressed in their heavy coats—the entire film takes place in winter—the three French officers are taken to a prisoner-of-war camp, where they become involved in escape attempts. They are transferred to another prison, and because of their continued efforts to escape, they are finally taken to the escape-proof castle-prison of Wintersborn, the commandant of which is Von Rauffenstein. Delighted to see his friend again, Von Rauffenstein takes the Frenchmen on a tour of the impregnable castle, stopping to show off his Maxim guns (Marechal allows that he prefers the restaurant of the same name). Von Rauffenstein presents an imposing presence. He has been wounded, and his jaw is supported by a brace. To his dear friend De Boeldieu, he explains, "My backbone fractured in two places, mended with silver plates. Silver strut in my chin, also a silver kneecap . . . I owe all this wealth to the misfortunes of war." The Prussian aristocrat has nothing to look forward to: "The end of this war will be the end of the Von Rauffensteins and the De Boeldieus."

Marechal and Rosenthal plan an escape; as is his duty, De Boeldieu helps them, acting as a decoy. Following his own code of honor, Von Rauffenstein shoots De Boeldieu and grieves when the Frenchman dies. Marechal and Rosenthal make their way toward Switzerland, stopping at the home of a German woman whose husband and three brothers have all been killed in battles proclaimed great German victories. The two men finally reach the Swiss border, an invisible line in the snow. A German patrol spots them, but the soldiers stop firing when they realize their targets are in Switzerland.

National boundaries are meaningless, and men who care for each other kill each other because of illusory principles. The various nationalities in Grand Illusion—German, French, English, and Russian—all speak their native languages, but they all share the same interests and desires. The common humanity of the men overpowers their assigned roles. They are divided only by illusions.

Perhaps the greatest illusion was that a film could prevent a war. Grand Illusion was awarded a special prize at the Venice Film Exposition of 1937. It was then banned by the Fascists. Goebbels banned the film in Germany, and when the Nazis entered Vienna in 1938, one of their first acts was to stop all performances of the film. When the Nazis occupied Paris in 1940, they confiscated and either destroyed or reedited all the prints of the film they could find. The original film was believed lost, destroyed in a bombing, until an intact version was found in Munich in 1957. Renoir restored the film, and when it was shown at the Brussels Film Festival in 1958, it was selected as one of the best films of all time.

Jean Renoir was not the only French director troubled by the threat of another European war. Abel Gance remade J'accuse in 1938. In this new version, the protagonist, Jean Diaz (Victor Francen), is a scientist, the only survivor of a patrol sent out on the eve of the armistice. Diaz promises his dead comrades that there will never be another war, and he spends the next twenty years preaching peace and working on a device to put an end to war. His invention—bullet-proof garments—is usurped by warmongers preparing for a new war. Diaz goes crazy and calls on the dead of World War I to arise in protest of the coming war. They do. (To take the roles of the

dead soldiers, Gance enlisted the help of the French association of war-wounded men, and their mutilated bodies present a frightening spectacle.) Gance dedicated the film "To the war dead of tomorrow, who will doubtless look at it skeptically, without recognizing themselves in its image."

The German government banned *J'accuse*, as did the French government, deeming the film counterproductive.

An edited version of the film, entitled *That They May Live* (a title taken from Ezekiel 37:1-10), was shown in New York City in November 1939, accompanied by an old Donald Duck cartoon. Reviewers of Gance's first *J'accuse* (1919) had expressed the opinion that had the film been shown in 1913, it might have prevented the war. The folly of that notion was proved by the 1938 version. The New York audiences were deeply moved by the mystical, nightmarish film, but the war it had been made to stop was already three months old.

THE
WORLD
WAR

The world war did not come without warning. Italy invaded Ethiopia in 1935; civil war erupted in Spain in 1936; Japan invaded China in 1937; and Nazi Germany remilitarized the Rhineland in 1936, annexed Austria and Czechoslovakia's Sudetenland in 1938, and signed a nonaggression pact with the Soviet Union in 1939. War was coming—Britain and France knew it, and, far across the Atlantic, so did the United States. It is ironic that the first motion pictures decrying Nazism and the ominous events in Europe came not from the countries facing imminent danger but from America. Even more remarkable is the fact that these films were made without government approval.

The end of World War I had left Hollywood the center of the world's film production. By 1930, American filmmakers enjoyed a worldwide market for their product, and the product they created was "entertainment"—the movies were made to sell to the largest possible audience, both in the United States and abroad. Nearing the apogee of their power, the major studios knocked out readily marketable commodities, including romances, musicals, comedies, westerns, thrillers, horror stories, and gangster films. All were shiny, exciting films, carefully preened and meticulously clear of any political or philosophical shadows. If a film had a "message," it was buried beneath the glossy entertainment, where it would disturb no one. And the messages were usually delivered late; Hollywood followed events at a safe distance, waiting for public opinion to solidify before taking a stance, however vague, in film.

There were sound business reasons for being chary of propaganda in films; Europe was an important market for the studios. If offended by American "propaganda," Europeans might ban Hollywood's films. Furthermore, American audiences were quick to reject anything that smacked of propaganda. The experience of World War I had turned Americans against all films with political statements. Many Americans were convinced that the US entry into World War I had been a mistake, that Americans had been tricked by cunning British and French propagandists. Munitions manufacturers, men who stood to profit from war, were blamed. A Senate investigation into the role played by US businessmen in the American entry into the war, headed by Senator Gerald P. Nye, led to the Neutrality Act passed by Congress in 1935. Americans wanted nothing to do with foreign wars: the events in Europe were suitable subjects for newspapers or newsreels, but not movies. Americans wanted escape, not tirades.

By the mid-1930s, those distant events in Europe were having an effect on American filmmakers. Although the rest of the United States remained adamantly isolationist, Hollywood, with its many Jewish and British constituents, aligned itself against Hitler. The Nazi takeover of the German film industry led to the emigration of scores of actors, writers, and directors to the United States. Very much aware of the power of film, the Nazis began banning American-made movies, frequently for reasons the Hollywood producers had not foreseen. Sometimes the Nazis banned all the films of a certain actor because the actor was Jewish (Johnny Weissmuller) or otherwise non-Aryan (Charlie Chan); sometimes the ban seemed to be the result of whim.

It was the civil war in Spain that first drew the attention of American filmmakers. *The Last Train from Madrid* (1937), directed by James Hogan, was the first Hollywood film about the Spanish Civil War, but it is hardly controversial. The story of a group of disparate people trying to get aboard the last train from besieged Madrid, the film resembles *Grand Hotel* (1932) and makes no references to the controversy in Spain, no political statements. The turmoil of the civil war provides nothing more than an exciting background to the personal stories of the various characters.

Somewhat more controversial was *Blockade* (1938), directed by William Dieterle, who had emigrated from Germany to Hollywood in 1930, and written by John Howard Lawson, who, like Ernest Hemingway, John Dos Passos, and e. e. cummings, had served as a volunteer ambulance driver in Europe during World War I. *Blockade* is also set in the Spanish Civil War, and as in *The Last Train from Madrid*, the opposing sides are never named and there is no mention of Mussolini or Hitler. Even so, the sympathies of the film are with the Loyalists. The film stars

Preceding pages: Guadalcanal Diary *(1943).*

Opposite bottom: *Well-indoctrinated American children salute the arrival of Dr. Kassel (Paul Lukas) in* Confessions of a Nazi Spy *(1939).*

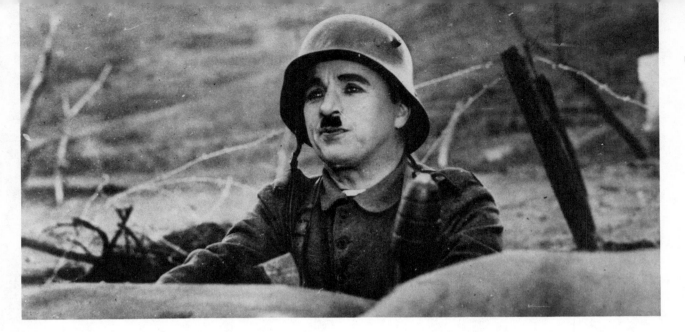

Henry Fonda and Madeleine Carroll and ends with a passionate plea from Fonda, as an embattled farmer: "Where is the conscience of the world that it allows the killing and maiming of civilians to go on?"

Although its politics were bland, *Blockade* was banned in many countries and was picketed in several American cities. Catholic organizations were particularly outraged by the film, for the Spanish Loyalists were considered atheistic Communists. Lawson went on to write screenplays for other films, and in 1948, when ideologies had changed, he was blacklisted as one of the Hollywood Ten.

Warner Brothers, a studio known for its fast-paced, exciting action films, many of which dealt with social problems or with "headline dramas," produced the first explicitly anti-Nazi American film. Released before the outbreak of war in Europe, *Confessions of a Nazi Spy* (1939) was based on contemporary headlines: FBI investigations recently had led to the arrest of Nazi spies operating in the United States. The screenplay for the film was based on a book by Leon G. Turrou, *The Nazi Conspiracy in America.* Turrou, a former G-man who had exposed Nazis in the German-American Bund, acted as technical adviser for the film. The star is Edward G. Robinson, already the preeminent figure for any gangland story.

Warner Brothers had plenty of foreign actors for *Confessions of a Nazi Spy.* The film was directed by Anatole Litvak, a Russian-born director who had fled Germany when the Nazis came to power, and its cast included several foreign-born actors: Francis Lederer, George Sanders, and Paul Lukas.

Confessions of a Nazi Spy declares itself a story "stranger than fiction," but it is really a preparedness film presented in the format of a standard crime drama. An unseen narrator recounts the FBI's investigation of Nazi operatives in America, revealing German consulates as fronts for spies and German Bund meetings as centers of Nazi propaganda at which American citizens of German extraction are terrorized into complicity with the ruthless Nazis. Those who speak out against the Nazi propagandists are dragged out of the meetings and savagely beaten; those who refuse to comply with the orders of the Nazi spies are told that their relatives in Germany will suffer or that they themselves will be sent back to Germany, where the Gestapo will take care of them. The Nazis even set up camps at which children are indoctrinated. The information the Nazi operatives want— American plans for the mobilization of the East Coast, blueprints for battleships, codes, the numbers of troops in the Northeast—makes it clear that they are planning an invasion of America. There is also discussion of the Panama Canal. The orders come from Goebbels (played by Martin Kosleck, an impersonation he was to repeat in several films); they are dispersed from a German ship in New York harbor. The FBI, led by Robinson, manages to expose the spy ring when one of the spies, disgruntled with the wages the Nazis pay, agrees to talk.

While the film was being made, the actors and producers received death threats. When it was released, the German chargé d'affaires, Hans Thomsen, threatened reprisals, and the movie was banned in Germany and in those neutral countries that feared offending Hitler's

Charlie Chaplin in The Great Dictator *(1940).*

Reich. The film aroused ire in other places, too: theater managers received word from the Irish Republican Army that they would be harmed if they continued to show "British propaganda films."

It was a propaganda film, but it was also an exciting crime drama based on contemporary headlines. Nazi spies made perfect gangsters, and throughout the forties, the Nazis in American films were made to resemble gangsters. Nazism was a crime, and Hitler's henchmen were hoodlums. In the absence of more information about Nazis, the formula worked.

Many Americans, including members of the government, did not see things that simply. Warner Brothers had broken out of the familiar terrain of American movies, had encroached into an area outside the accepted domain of films. The ramifications of this action were soon to make themselves felt.

The most important American film of 1939 was *Gone with the Wind*. On the brink of world war, Americans looked back with nostalgia at the Civil War; they had done the same with *The Birth of a Nation* prior to World War I. And, as they had in 1915, Americans in 1939 prized their isolation from the pernicious continent of Europe, with its marching armies, chanting mobs, and barking rulers dressed in gold braid. When the long-awaited war finally began, it hardly began at all. In September 1939, the German Army invaded Poland—and then the war seemed to end. American filmmakers, remembering how they had been caught with unsalable war movies when World War I had ended suddenly, were reluctant about investing in war-related subjects.

Charles Chaplin had begun work on *The Great Dictator* in 1939. "The story of a period between two world wars," it appeared in 1940 and was not well received by critics, who thought Chaplin had overstepped his bounds—the fact that "the little tramp" resembled Hitler was only mildly amusing, and there was nothing funny about concentration camps. Chaplin himself later admitted that had he known the actual horrors of the German concentration camps, he would not have made the film.

Chaplin plays two parts in the film: Adenoid Hynkel, the dictator of Tomania; and a Jewish barber. The story begins in 1918, with Germans on the western front firing Big Bertha at distant Notre Dame; yanking the lanyard is the little barber. The monstrous projectiles don't travel very far, however, and before long Chaplin is having comic difficulties heaving grenades at the approaching enemy. He then takes off in a plane carrying important dispatches. The plane crashes, and the barber suffers amnesia, only to awaken in a world ruled by "the double cross." While the barber shaves customers in the ghetto, his look-alike, Hynkel, discusses the coming invasion of Osterlich with his ministers, Herring (Billy Gilbert) and Garbitsch (Henry Daniell). They also discuss matters of race. "After killing off the Jews, we'll wipe out the brunettes," exclaims Hynkel. When Garbitsch assures him that he will someday rule the world, Hynkel dances with a balloonlike globe. He is visited by his imposing ally, Benzino Napaloni (Jack Oakie), dictator of Bacteria. Osterlich is invaded, but following a case of mistaken identity, it is the little barber and not Hynkel who addresses the troops. It was this six-minute speech, an impassioned plea from Chaplin for reason and brotherly love, that disturbed critics. "The way of life can be free and beautiful," he says, "but we have lost the way. Greed has poisoned men's souls—has barricaded the world with hate—has goose-stepped us into misery and bloodshed. . . . Let us unite and fight for a new world . . . let us fight to free the world. . . . In the name of democracy, let us all unite!" Some people claimed to perceive Communist overtones in the speech.

By 1940, Hitler had done more than invade Austria, but the films released in the United States dealt with events before the war (because of the time involved in their production, films must necessarily follow behind events). *The Mortal Storm* (1940), directed by Frank Borzage, is about a German university professor (Frank Morgan) who enjoys a peaceful life, surrounded by his students and his family, until Hitler comes to power. The professor is Jewish; his wife (Irene Rich) is Aryan. When he refuses to teach Nazi ideology, the professor is put in a concentration camp. His family falls apart, divided by Nazism. The professor's stepsons (Robert Stack and William T. Orr) become Nazis; his daughter (Margaret Sullavan) ends her engagement to a Nazi zealot (Robert Young) and falls in love with one of the professor's students (James Stewart). When the two lovers learn that the professor has died of a "heart attack" in the concentration camp, they decide to flee Germany. They head for Austria, but she is shot as they reach the friendly border and dies in his arms. He is alone but free in Austria.

The film was a little late. By 1940, Austria no longer offered freedom from Nazis; indeed, *The Mortal Storm* was released in June 1940, the month in which Hitler's army paraded into Paris.

A Metro-Goldwyn-Mayer production, *The Mortal Storm* led to the banning in Germany of all that studio's films. The movie refers to Hitler and Germany by name, recreates scenes of Nazi book burnings, and portrays Gestapo officials as cruel. MGM made another very similar film in 1940, *Escape*, directed by Mervyn LeRoy.

Escape is about a German actress who has lived in the United States for many years and returns to Germany in an effort to sell her house there. (The actress was played by Alla Nazimova, who had made her screen debut in 1916's *War Brides* and had retired from films in 1925; she made her return to the screen in *Escape*.) She makes the mistake of trying to get American dollars for her house, and, an outspoken woman, she falls afoul of the Nazis and ends up in a concentration camp, condemned to death. Her American son (Robert Taylor) sets about rescuing her. He receives help from an American-born countess (Norma Shearer) and a Nazi doctor (Philip Dorn) sympathetic to his mother. The leading Nazi, a general who wears a monocle and delights both in cruelty and Wagner, is played by Conrad Veidt. (A German, Veidt had fled the Nazis with his Jewish wife in 1929; on a visit to Germany in 1930, he had been nabbed by Nazi officials who then claimed he was "sick" and couldn't travel. Rescued by the studio he was working for, Veidt came to Hollywood and had a brief career playing evil Nazis—he died in 1943.) His chloroformed mother disguised as a corpse, the son spirits her out of the concentration camp and gets her on a plane for America.

The struggle against the Nazis remained a family affair in *Four Sons* (1940), directed by Archie Mayo. John Ford had directed a silent version of *Four Sons* in 1928. Ford's film was the story of a Bavarian mother whose sons leave her to fight in World War I—one on the American side. The screenplay for the 1940 film, written by John Howard Lawson, relocates the mother and her sons to Czechoslovakia. One of the sons goes to America; one of them becomes a Nazi and is killed by his brother, a loyal Czech. The patriot is killed by the Nazis in revenge. The fourth son enlists in the German Army and is killed during the invasion of Poland. There is nothing left for the mother to do but join her one remaining son in America.

In *The Man I Married* (1940), directed by Irving Pichel, yet another family is wrecked by Nazis. A German-American (Francis Lederer) and his American wife (Joan Bennett) visit Hitler's Germany. She is appalled by what she sees; he is taken in by Nazi propaganda.

Alfred Hitchcock left England for the United States in 1939. One of his last films in England was *The Lady Vanishes* (1938), a melodramatic comedy about the disappearance of an elderly governess aboard a train traveling through Austria. The lady (Dame May Whitty) is a British agent, and she is kidnapped by a nasty bunch of Germanic operatives. The English people on the

train, convinced that nothing untoward can happen to them because they are English subjects, are eventually drawn into grave danger. There is a pacifist aboard the train who, in the tradition of pacifists in films made just before wars, is a fool. "After all, they wouldn't shoot unarmed people," he announces, moments before he is shot.

With the outbreak of the war, the British government asked Hitchcock to remain in America and make films to urge America's entry into the conflict. He did so, creating one of the most popular anti-Nazi films of the period: *Foreign Correspondent* (1940).

Dedicated "to the forthright ones who early

Opposite left: *Margaret Sullavan* (center) in The Mortal Storm. **Opposite right:** *Robert Taylor* (left) in Escape. *Both films were made in 1940 by MGM. Note the identical upholstery.*

saw the clouds of war while many of us at home were seeing rainbows," *Foreign Correspondent* is a suspenseful and sometimes humorous thriller. The movie begins with a newspaper editor frustrated by the reports his foreign correspondents are sending him from Europe. "There's a crime hatching on that bedeviled continent," he says, and he decides to send a crime reporter to root out the story. The man he selects, Johnny Jones (Joel McCrea), is a particularly good choice because he has a "fresh, unused mind."

In Europe, the naive crime reporter encounters a crime. Van Meer (Albert Basserman), a Dutch diplomat and member of the Universal Peace party, is kidnapped by German agents because he knows a secret clause to a treaty. The agents make it appear that Van Meer has been assassinated, but Jones knows better, and during the last days before the war, he pursues Van Meer and his captors from London to Holland (where, in one of the film's most famous scenes, he locates Van Meer in a windmill) and back to England. He also falls in love with a woman (Laraine Day) whose father (Herbert Marshall) happens to be the archconspirator.

The Universal Peace party is revealed to be a cover-up for spies and traitors. His crime solved (and the war declared), Jones and his girl friend board a plane for New York. The plane is shot down, and the film ends with the couple back in London, where Jones delivers a radio broadcast to America. As he begins to speak, German planes roar overhead and bombs fall. While sirens wail and the lights behind him flicker, Jones declares, "The lights have gone out everywhere except in America. Hello, America! Hang onto your lights. They're the only ones left on in the world!"

Foreign Correspondent was a masterpiece of propaganda. Even Joseph Goebbels expressed his admiration for the film. Of course, by the end of 1940, American films were banned in most of Europe. Goebbels probably obtained his copy of the film through Switzerland.

Another couple fleeing war-torn Europe is forced to return in *Arise, My Love* (1940), a comedy-drama directed by Mitchell Leisen. The film begins with ace pilot Tom Martin (Ray Milland) in a prison in Spain, joking with a priest while awaiting execution. He is sprung by a mysterious woman claiming to be his wife. Augusta Nash, called Gusto by her friends (Claudette Colbert), is actually a newspaper reporter. Martin is in Spain because "a couple of big guys are kicking around a lot of little guys," and he wants to help the underdogs; she is there in search of exciting news. Exchanging glib remarks, the two escape in a stolen plane and go on to fall in love while witnessing most of the important events of the period. They arrive in Paris shortly before the Nazis and are in the woods of Compiègne for the French surrender ("Old trees practicing curtsies in the wind because they still think Louis XIV is king," remarks Martin). The two lovers decide they've had enough of the war and book passage for America on the *Athenian*. (Mary Pickford made a similar error in *The Little American* when she got aboard the *Veritania*.) The ship is sunk, but the two lovers are rescued, and they return to Europe, where she continues her reporting and he joins the RAF.

The title of the film, taken from the Song of Solomon 2:13, was understood to be an appeal to the United States. However, such exhortations did not have an immediate effect on Americans.

Teutonic Knights in Alexander Nevsky (1938).

It was the Germans who mastered propaganda. Well before Hollywood undertook its first, halting attempts to influence public opinion in the United States, the Germans, led by Joseph Goebbels, had perfected one of their most fearsome weapons. Nazi propaganda weakened the French resolve to fight in 1940 and inculcated in many German soldiers and civilians the determination to die rather than surrender in 1945. From the indoctrination of the young to the propagation of the biggest lies, Nazi propaganda changed the world Germans lived in.

When the Nazis came to power in 1933, Goebbels was made director of the Ministry for Public Enlightenment and Propaganda. He had complete control over the radio, newspapers, theater, and films. Jews and liberals were purged from the film industry; films were censored or banned. Goebbels did not put Nazi propaganda into all German films; the majority were made for escapist entertainment. However, the films made to promote the Nazi party were heavily larded with propaganda. Among the first, in 1933, were two films about Nazi martyrs killed by the Communists: *S. A. Mann Brandt*, directed by Franz Seitz, and *Hans Westmar*, directed by Franz Wenzler. Leni Riefenstahl created a landmark in the exploitation of mass psychology in *Triumph of the Will* (1935), ostensibly a documentary of the 1934 Nazi party rally held in Nuremberg. As Riefenstahl later admitted, "The preparations for the rally were made in concert with the preparations for the camera work." It is not a documentary, but contrived and skillful propaganda: the star of the film is Adolf Hitler, who gave the film its title.

The Nazis used films to spread the lies essential to national socialism. Following the German invasion of Poland, the Nazis made films explaining the reasons for the attack. In *Heimkehr (Homecoming)* (1941), directed by Gustav Ucicky, ethnic Germans living in Poland are cruelly mistreated by the Poles. The Poles whitewash the homes of the Germans and forbid them to speak German. In one scene, a German child cries as the Poles ransack his school, throwing the furniture out into the street and then setting it afire. The suffering Germans are rescued by the arrival of the German Army.

The most vicious films made by the Nazis—the most evil films ever made—were those promoting anti-Semitism. *Jud Süss* (1940), directed by Veit Harlan, relates the fictional story of a Jew during the Middle Ages. A disgusting degenerate, the Jew rapes an innocent young girl before he is finally executed. *The Eternal Jew* (1940), directed by Franz Hippler, uses scenes of Polish Jews in the ghettos to establish the "racial inferiority" of Jews. The "documentary" proves that Jews are unclean and uncivilized, hence unfit for survival in the Aryan world.

Although the Nazis found American audiences unreceptive to their propaganda, the powerful image of Germany exported by the Nazis helped maintain American neutrality. In 1936, Charles Lindbergh visited Germany and was impressed by the Luftwaffe, Germany's air force. He returned to America and gave radio broadcasts in which he claimed the Germans were invincible. He also said, "The greatest advocates of bringing us into war are the British, the Jews, and President Roosevelt."

The Soviet Union was very much aware of the power of motion pictures. (Lenin had been so impressed by D. W. Griffith's *Intolerance* that he had offered the American director the leadership of the Soviet film industry.) Soviet leaders were also aware of the danger looming across their western borders. Sergei Eisenstein's *Alexander Nevsky* appeared in 1938 as a warning to all potential invaders of Russia. With a stirring musical score by Sergei Prokofiev, the movie recounts the defeat of the Teutonic Knights at the "Battle of the Ice," the decisive encounter in 1242 on frozen Lake Peipus. Led by Alexander Nevsky, the heroic Russians rout the German invaders (who, with their closed helmets and interlocked shields, resemble tanks). Nevsky condemns the few remaining knights to be sold "for soap" and sets free the German foot soldiers, telling them, "Go home and tell all in foreign lands that Russia lives. Let them come to us as guests without fear. But if anyone comes to us with the sword, he shall perish by the sword. On this the Russian land stands and will stand."

Alexander Nevsky was suppressed in 1939 following the Nazi-Soviet nonaggression pact.

When the Germans invaded Russia in 1941, the film was brought out again with great fanfare.

Viewed from the threshold of another world war, World War I lost most of its despair and became again the scene of heroism. *The Dawn Patrol* was remade in 1938, directed by Edmund Goulding. Although the film uses aerial footage from the 1930 original, it does not share that film's sense of doom. Starring Errol Flynn and David Niven, the 1938 *Dawn Patrol (The Flight Commander)* displays prowar sentiments, if only in the contagiously heroic characters of its stars.

The Fighting 69th (1940), directed by William Keighley, reminded Americans of the glorious exploits of New York's famous "Irish" regiment (the 165th Infantry, part of the Rainbow Division). Many of the characters portrayed in the film are historical, including the regiment's celebrated chaplain, Father Francis Patrick Duffy (Pat O'Brien), and its poet laureate, Joyce Kilmer (Jeffrey Lynn). James Cagney plays a street-wise Brooklyn boy, a cynical noncomformist whose cowardice endangers the regiment. (Cagney and O'Brien had already been matched as priest and unregenerate in 1938's *Angels with Dirty Faces*.) As Kilmer recites his poems and Father Duffy makes his parish rounds through the muddy trenches, Cagney becomes the first man to "let the regiment down." He is court-martialed and

condemned to be shot, but with his faith restored, he instead dies heroically, saving his compatriots by throwing himself on a hand grenade. The film ends with Father Duffy standing beside the Duffy memorial in Times Square delivering an inspiring speech, which ends, "Amid turmoil . . . let the tired eyes of a troubled world rise up—to see America!"

The Fighting 69th tells a fictional tale of a smart-alecky punk who dies a hero. *Sergeant York* (1941), directed by Howard Hawks, recounts the true story of a deeply religious man who abandoned his pacifism and became, in the words of General John J. Pershing, "the greatest civilian soldier of all time." On October 8, 1918, Alvin C. York single-handedly killed 25 Germans and captured 132. For more than twenty years, Hollywood filmmakers tried to obtain permission to film York's heroic deeds, but he had refused. He finally relented, pleased by the choice of Gary Cooper to portray him.

The screenplay for *Sergeant York*, written by John Huston and Howard Koch, presents York as a perfect symbol for the nation. The lanky Tennessee backwoodsman does not want to fight. He abhors the idea of killing, but after long meditation, comparing the teachings of the Bible with a book of American history, he decides that it is sometimes necessary to kill to protect peace and freedom. As a soldier, York uses his turkey-

Opposite: *Pat O'Brien* (left) *trying to comfort an overloaded James Cagney in* The Fighting 69th *(1940).* Right: *Gary Cooper as* Sergeant York *(1941).*

shooting expertise (making clucking sounds to attract the birds) to kill Germans. Unlike the soldiers in *All Quiet on the Western Front*, the civilian soldier York found meaning in the war, and his dramatic exploits present a different view of the conflict: American soldiers were more than a match for Germans.

By 1941, there were plenty of civilian soldiers to take inspiration from York: the United States had instituted its first peacetime conscription in 1940. In a series of so-called service comedies, the "selectees" included comedy stars, who usually wound up in uniform as the result of some silly misunderstanding. Bob Hope, accompanied by his valet (Eddie Bracken), goes through basic training in *Caught in the Draft* (1941), directed by David Butler. Bud Abbott and Lou Costello became stars in their second film together, *Buck Privates* (1941), directed by Arthur Lubin. The film begins with the two clowns hawking neckties on the street; they are chased by a policeman and seek refuge in what they think is the line for a movie—it turns out to be a line for a draft board, and they enlist; so does the policeman (he becomes their sergeant). Among the other recruits is Lee Bowman, a millionaire's son who manages to overcome that handicap and prove himself a worthy soldier. The Andrews Sisters are there, too, singing about that "Boogie Woogie Bugle Boy." Abbott and Costello again encounter the Andrews Sisters in a wartime setting, this time afloat, in *In the Navy* (1941), also directed by Lubin.

The popularity of fliers begun with *Wings* was continued in a cycle of films about pilots undergoing training. These films promoted preparedness (the United States was not yet at war) and usually dealt with the theme of military service as a "melting pot" in which men of differing social rank become equals in uniform.

I Wanted Wings (1941), directed by Mitchell Leisen, concerns a wealthy polo-playing playboy (Ray Milland), a college football hero (Wayne Morris), and an auto mechanic (William Holden) who go through aviation school together. All three are confronted by the rigors of training and the charms of Veronica Lake.

Robert Preston plays a football hero, Buddy Ebsen plays a hillbilly, and Edmund O'Brien is

Above: *Dick Powell* (left), *Lou Costello, and Bud Abbott in* In the Navy *(1941).*

the cowardly son of the commanding officer (Robert Barrat) in *Parachute Battalion* (1941), directed by Leslie Goodwins. O'Brien overcomes his fear of jumping and even saves the lives of a few instructors when not battling with Preston for Nancy Kelly.

Errol Flynn plays a flight surgeon trying to solve the problems of blackouts, chronic fatigue, and high-altitude sickness among fliers in *Dive Bomber* (1941), directed by Michael Curtiz.

The seriousness of war was brought home to cocky aces in films that involved Americans in the plight of Britain. In *International Squadron* (1941), directed by Lothar Mendes, Ronald Reagan flies bombers to England and learns the truth about heroism. (This was actor Helmut Dantine's first film in America. Vienna-born, he had fled Austria after spending three months in a Nazi internment camp.)

Tyrone Power is an American pilot delivering a bomber to England in *A Yank in the RAF* (1941), directed by Henry King. While in London, the jaunty American airman discovers a former girl friend (Betty Grable) dancing in a nightclub. He decides to stay around, and signs up with the RAF. When not dancing at the Regency House, Grable works as a volunteer nurse; Power is less dedicated until he sees one of his buddies killed. He then takes part in the evacuation of Dunkirk. The Britons in the film display their famous stiff upper lips. When Power asks a British flier, "How is it at Dunkirk?" the unflappable Briton replies, "Very cloudy." The British government had a hand in the production of the film, and the ending was changed at the request of the British. The original script called for Power to die in the Blitz; it was changed to allow him to live.

The heroic character of the British people was used in many films to try to promote American aid to the embattled British Isles. *Man Hunt* (1941), based on a novel called *Rogue Male*, by Geoffrey Household, tells the story of a British big-game hunter who decides to stalk the world's most dangerous quarry: Adolf Hitler. The sportsman (Walter Pidgeon) positions himself in the woods overlooking a terrace at Berchtesgaden. When Hitler appears on the terrace, the hunter gets the Fuehrer in his sights and pulls the trigger. The gun is empty, for this was only a "sporting stalk." After a moment's reflection, the hunter slips a cartridge into his rifle and again takes aim, but he is surprised by guards before he can fire. A Gestapo official (George Sanders) tortures Pidgeon in an effort to force him to sign a confession that he was working for the British government. When Pidgeon stubbornly refuses, the Germans throw him off a cliff. He survives the fall and returns to England, followed by Sanders and some ruthless Gestapo agents. In his final confrontation with Sanders, Pidgeon demonstrates great resourcefulness, fashioning a makeshift bow and arrow and using the weapon to dispatch the Nazi. The film ends with the hunter and his rifle being parachuted into Germany.

Man Hunt was directed by Fritz Lang, another émigré director from Hitler's Germany. In 1933, Goebbels had offered Lang the directorship of the Nazi film industry—Hitler had loved Lang's *Metropolis*. Lang had immediately fled Germany; he arrived in the United States in 1935.

Hitler was not the first European megalomaniac the British had stubbornly and victoriously resisted. *That Hamilton Woman (Lady Hamilton)* (1941), directed by Alexander Korda, presents the story of the love affair between Britain's naval hero Lord Nelson (Laurence Olivier) and Lady Hamilton (Vivien Leigh). The screenplay for the film is attributed to R. C. Sherriff and Walter Reisch, but Winston Churchill is credited with writing some of the speeches, particularly one in which Nelson (speaking of Napoleon but referring, of course, to Hitler) declares, "You cannot make peace with dictators. You have to destroy them!" The film was potent pro-British propaganda and was popular not only in the United States, but in the Soviet Union. Stalin said it was his favorite film; so did Churchill, who tried the patience of those around him by having the film screened at every opportunity.

Not everyone was pleased with *That Hamilton Woman,* and Korda found himself summoned to appear before a Senate subcommittee. The hearings, chaired by Senators D. Worth Clark and Gerald P. Nye, had begun in September 1941. Citing seventeen films, including *Confessions of a Nazi Spy, The Great Dictator, The Mortal Storm, Escape, Four Sons, Sergeant York,* and *Man Hunt,* the senators were investigating charges of "war propaganda in motion pictures." Clark and Nye wanted to know why Hollywood films presented only one side of events in Europe. The Senate itself was involved in debates over American foreign policy: how was it that Hollywood had already decided the course for the rest of the country? Why were filmmakers trying to create war hysteria?

Senator Nye accused the motion picture industry of fostering pro-British sentiments, and he implied that this prowar attitude was the result of foreigners—particularly Jews—working in the film business. (Nye was quoted in *Variety* as saying, "If anti-Semitism exists in America, the Jews have themselves to blame.") The senators charged the filmmakers with using their thea-

ters to spread propaganda, propaganda that was not necessarily in the best interests of the country.

The filmmakers, with Wendell Willkie as their counsel, replied that they were doing what they had always done: following popular opinion and making entertainment out of factual events. After all, both *Escape* and *The Mortal Storm* were based on best-selling books. Speaking for Warner Brothers, Harry M. Warner stated, "*Confessions of a Nazi Spy* is a factual portrayal of a Nazi spy ring that actually operated in New York City. If that is propaganda, we plead guilty."

The hearings never reached a verdict, and Korda never had to appear before Senator Nye. He had been summoned to appear on December 12: five days earlier the Japanese had rendered the hearings moot.

The Japanese made a fatal error when they attacked the United States, and they compounded the error by making it a surprise attack. Their heinous act defined their character for Hollywood scriptwriters and put revenge in the hearts of the most die-hard isolationists. The United States declared war on Japan on December 8, 1941. Three days later, Germany and Italy declared war on the United States, and Congress reciprocated.

It was a world war, a "total" war: the entire nation was thrown into the war effort, and the government was quick to enlist the services of the film industry. The producers, distributors, and exhibitors of America's films had already

organized a committee, the Motion Picture Committee Co-operating for National Defense (founded around the time of Dunkirk), to distribute government films. Within a week of the attack on Pearl Harbor, this organization was renamed the War Activities Committee of the Motion Picture Industry (WAC), and it eventually worked with the Office of War Information (OWI). The film industry agreed to distribute (and in some cases create), free of charge, the government's films, of which there were more than 140 by the end of the war.

Many of these films were poorly made and tedious; some were excellent. There were training and orientation films for soldiers, and films to boost morale, inspire enlistment, and promote conservation (such as *Frying Pan to Firing Line*, a film about saving cooking fats). There were films explaining the necessity of gasoline rationing and increased income taxes (in *The New Spirit*, a Walt Disney cartoon, Donald Duck pays his taxes). Many films were made about Red Cross and War Bonds drives. There were films to recruit factory workers (such as *Women in Defense*, written by Eleanor Roosevelt and narrated by Katharine Hepburn) and films to show workers how the weapons they made were used (Orson Welles narrated *Tanks*, the story of an M-3 tank from its manufacture in Detroit to its delivery for combat). There were also war information films and combat films made by the various armed services, and many of Hollywood's best directors served in uniform and directed these government documentaries. John Ford served in the navy and was responsible for such films as *The Battle of Midway*; William Wyler enlisted in the Army Air Force and directed *The Memphis Belle* while stationed with a bomber squadron in England; John Huston joined the Signal Corps and made what is perhaps the best documentary of the war, *The Battle of San Pietro*. Frank Capra directed the "Why We Fight" films, a series of seven films made to explain to American soldiers the background of the war up to America's entry; only three of the films were shown in the United States.

Both Congress and the film industry were against the domestic distribution of government propaganda films. Rather, the government provided the filmmakers with six categories to serve as guides for Hollywood's contribution to the war. These included the issues of the war; the nature of the enemy; the nature of America's allies; the production front; the home front; and the fighting forces. The filmmakers had no trouble inserting these themes in their films.

Hollywood lost nearly one quarter of its male employees during the war, including forty-nine leading actors, among them David Niven, Clark Gable, James Stewart, Robert Montgomery, Henry Fonda, Tyrone Power, Mickey Rooney, Victor Mature, Gene Autry, and Douglas Fairbanks, Jr. More than three thousand actors gave free appearances through the United Service Organizations (USO), and many of them—Joe E. Brown, Bob Hope, Jack Benny, Al Jolson, Ray Bolger, Gary Cooper, Bing Crosby, Fred Astaire, Ann Sheridan, Paulette Goddard, and others—followed "the foxhole circuit" to military bases throughout the world, entertaining troops. As they had done during World War I, popular screen personalities traveled the country promoting War Bonds; Carole Lombard was killed in a plane crash while returning from a bond drive. Hollywood itself welcomed men in uniform. At the famous Hollywood Canteen, servicemen could dance with actresses and eat off plates washed by such notables as Humphrey Bogart.

The war had further effects on Hollywood: blank ammunition and hair for wigs became scarce, travel restrictions hampered location shooting, materials for the construction of sets became difficult to obtain, even the celluloid film had to be rationed. Hollywood did not suffer because of these deprivations; indeed, the war brought the film industry its most profitable years, leading up to 1946, the most profitable year in the industry's history until 1980. Whether to see the most recent newsreel or to forget the war in a comedy or musical, Americans flocked to movie theaters. The war brought employment and prosperity to the nation: Americans had money, wartime restrictions made the movies one of the few sources of entertainment available, and, thanks to a government tax on movie tickets, going to see a movie became an act of patriotism.

For both soldiers and civilians, films played an important role during the war. Movie theaters stayed open all night for the benefit of factory workers on late shifts; in London, movie theaters remained open even during the worst period of the Blitz. At "beachhead bijous" throughout the war zones, soldiers crowded to see the latest films, and films were projected on hospital ceilings so that wounded men could watch.

The majority of the films Hollywood made during the war years were not about combat—war movies are expensive to make, servicemen wanted to see neither war movies nor westerns, and although American citizens wanted war movies, they could not abide them as a steady diet.

The war movies that were made have dated more quickly than the films of any other genre. The fervid patriotism and fantastic heroics of these films make them embarrassing today. However, while these films may not present an accurate account of the conflict, they capture the mood of the period. The world at war portrayed in these films has the aspect of a wonderful, romantic adventure. The sense of purpose, the spirit of being united in a just cause—absolute right against absolute wrong—makes them exhilarating. The war put pressure on the morals and ideals of the nation, and filmmakers recorded them in their clearest form. The war was the best of times for the filmmakers, and as a result of their efforts, the war is remembered as having been the best of times for Americans.

The expense of making war movies was offset by government assistance. The government recognized motion pictures as its best source of public relations, an ideal means of boosting morale and encouraging enlistment, and offered filmmakers enormous cooperation in the making of films about the armed services. This cooperation included all the extras the filmmakers needed (in perfect uniforms with proper weapons); the use of tanks, planes, and ships; access to actual battle footage; and expert technical advice. The government required only that it have approval of the script, and the filmmakers had no reason to complain about such a formality. The situation was ideal: the filmmakers sincerely wanted to help the war effort; the government wanted them to do so and offered assistance; and the American public was eager to see films about the war if only because the films offered them an opportunity to experience something of the enormous conflict of which they and their families were part.

In 1942, however, the government could offer little assistance to American filmmakers—the nation's soldiers were desperately needed for duties more pressing than facing cameras. Although it took great effort to organize the rest of the nation's industries for the war, Hollywood was prepared. World War II, a conflict of good versus evil, fit effortlessly into formulas Hollywood had been using for years, and the heroic struggle could be carried out by ordinary Americans as well as by soldiers.

One of the first movies released after the attack on Pearl Harbor was *A Yank on the Burma Road* (1942), directed by George B. Seitz. The story concerns a New York taxi driver (Barry Nelson) who takes a job in the Far East driving a supply truck and ends up leading a convoy of medical supplies through Burma to China, witnessing Japanese barbarities along the way. *Joe Smith, American* (1942), directed by Richard Thorpe, pits an ordinary American against ruthless Nazis. Based on a story by Paul Gallico, the film stars Robert Young as Joe Smith, a mechanic in an aircraft factory and a regular sort of guy who likes movies and bowling. Because he has knowledge of a new bomb sight, Joe is kidnapped by Nazis, who blindfold him and take him to a house on the outskirts of town, where they mercilessly torture him for information. Surviving the agony by losing himself in memories of his happy family life, he escapes and succeeds in leading FBI agents to the house and the Nazis.

Joe Smith, American delivers a clear message to America's factory workers: no matter how dull or unimportant their work might have seemed, they were heroes.

Even the most unlikely citizens could become heroes. *Two Yanks in Trinidad* (1942), directed by Gregory Ratoff, is a comedy about two New York racketeers (Pat O'Brien and Brian Donlevy) who find patriotism. The two hoods squabble, and to escape his former pal's wrath,

O'Brien enlists; Donlevy enlists, too. In Trinidad, O'Brien becomes involved with a café performer (Janet Blair). The café happens to be a refueling station for Nazi submarines, and when the news of the Japanese attack on Pearl Harbor reaches the two Yanks, they forget their differences and know just what to do to the Nazi depot.

Humphrey Bogart stars as the suave Gloves Donahue in *All Through the Night* (1942), directed by Vincent Sherman. Bogart and his cronies stumble on Nazi spies who plan to blow up a battleship in New York harbor. The Nazi spygangsters include Conrad Veidt and Peter Lorre (who, in 1933, had fled Hitler's Germany). In a more serious film, *Across the Pacific* (1942), directed by John Huston, Bogart, as a US Army Intelligence officer, tracks Japanese agents and ends up in Panama on December 6, 1941, just in time to foil a Japanese plot there.

Training films were popular throughout the war. Such films showed potential enlistees what they could expect and made the drudgery seem almost appealing. Production of *To the Shores of Tripoli* (1942) began before the war broke out. Directed by H. Bruce Humberstone, with a prologue by Lowell Thomas, the film was set firmly in the mold of 1941's *Parachute Battalion*. A cocky young man (John Payne), son of a veteran of World War I, arrives at the Marine Corps base at San Diego and goes into training under the same sergeant (Randolph Scott) who trained his father. Like the country of which he is a symbol, the young man has to calm down before he can receive the mantle being passed to him—the glory and traditions of the marines. There is a nurse (Maureen O'Hara) for Payne to pursue, and in the tradition of training films, he manages to prove himself by saving the lives of other cadets and instructors, but most of the film concerns the training of marines.

The core of *Captains of the Clouds* (1942), directed by Michael Curtiz, is a documentarylike account of the training of Royal Canadian Air Force pilots. Wrapped around this is the story of three unruly bush pilots (James Cagney, Dennis Morgan, and Alan Hale) who fly supplies to settlers in northern Canada. Following one such mission, the three men overhear a radio broadcast of Churchill's "We Shall Never Surrender"

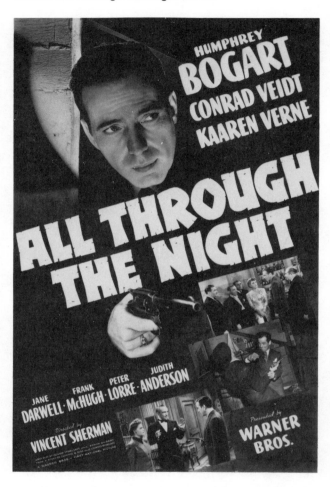

speech (delivered in June 1940, after Dunkirk). More for adventure than patriotism, the three go to Ottawa and enlist. Even the recalcitrant Cagney comes through in the end. The three pilots are given the assignment of flying unarmed bombers to England, and when they are attacked by Messerschmitts, Cagney crashes his plane into a German plane to save his friends. (Phillips Holmes, the sensitive French soldier of *The Man I Killed*, was killed in a collision aboard a Royal Canadian Air Force plane in 1942.)

Eagle Squadron (1942), directed by Arthur Lubin, continued the story of Yanks in the RAF. Based on a story by C. S. Forester, the film begins with a prologue by war correspondent Quentin Reynolds (whose voice, like that of Lowell Thomas, provided the aura of factuality). Chuck Brewer (Robert Stack), one of the Ameri-

66

cans serving with the RAF, doesn't like the British at first—he mistakes their stoic acceptance of the deaths of friends for callousness. He is fond of one Briton, however, Anne Partridge (Diana Barrymore, daughter of John Barrymore, in her screen debut). Chuck proposes to Anne, but she turns him down, preferring to wait for the end of the war before committing herself. The film follows the daily lives of the fliers, shows how they receive and carry out their orders, what happens to them if they are shot down over the Channel, and ends with the planning and execution of a commando raid in France. The objective of the raid is to steal a special new German plane, the Leopard. Chuck takes part in the raid and succeeds in nabbing one of the planes, which he flies back toward England, pursued by three German fighters. Chuck shoots down the Germans while reproposing marriage to Anne, who happens to be in the operations room listening to his radio transmissions. Even contemporary audiences found the movie beyond silly.

The contrived heroics of these animated recruitment posters are excusable: there was a war on. And the films did affect audiences and in-

spire enlistment. A popular film about marines would lead to increased enlistment in the Marine Corps. After seeing a dramatic movie about the navy, farmboys from Nebraska or Oklahoma who had never seen the sea volunteered for the navy.

Access to the enemy was denied most American forces during the first months of the war, but American fliers with the RAF could shoot at Messerschmitts, and, even more gratifying to the American public, fliers with General Claire Chennault's American Volunteer Group could shoot at Jap Zeros. Chennault had gone to China to organize air defenses for Chiang Kai-shek and

"The people's war" of Mrs. Miniver (1942).
As German bombs fall on their village,
Mrs. Miniver (Greer Garson) seeks shelter with
her children (Claire Sanders and Christopher
Severn) and her maid (Brenda Forbes).

had formed his squadron of volunteers in 1941. Known as the Flying Tigers because of their winged tiger insignia (designed by Walt Disney Studios), the American airmen became national heroes, and their P-40 Warhawks with tiger shark's teeth painted beneath the propeller entered popular folklore.

Flying Tigers (1942), directed by David Miller, begins with a quotation from Chiang Kai-shek in which he calls the Flying Tigers "symbols of invincible strength" and says, "The Chinese people will preserve forever the memories of their glorious achievements." The first scenes of the film are of hungry children receiving food from the United China Relief. There is then the sound of approaching Japanese planes, which begin dropping bombs on the civilians. As nurses with glowing faces watch, the planes of the Flying Tigers roar into the sky for revenge. In one of the first encounters, an American pilot sends a burst of machine-gun fire through the cockpit of a Japanese plane. The enemy pilot puts his hands to his face, blood spurting between his fingers. American audiences could righteously applaud.

The price of revenge is high. One of the American pilots is killed, and the commander of the squadron (John Wayne) wraps the dead man's belongings in a scarf and places the small package in a drawer full of similar packages. The Americans are vastly outnumbered; Wayne is therefore willing to accept any volunteers, even John Carroll, who joins because he needs the money. An egotistical braggart, Carroll argues with the other fliers and competes with Wayne for a nurse (Anna Lee). In the end, he redeems himself with a fatal act of heroism.

The inhabitants of the British Isles were having no difficulty making contact with the enemy; even the most ordinary family was drawn into the war. *Mrs. Miniver* (1942), directed by William Wyler, tells the story of one such family, the Minivers, for whom the war becomes a very personal matter. Mr. Miniver (Walter Pidgeon) goes in his boat to Dunkirk to help in the evacuation; Mrs. Miniver (Greer Garson), a popular woman who has a rose named after her, captures a downed German flier (Helmut Dantine); their son (Richard Ney) joins the RAF, and his young wife (Ter-

esa Wright) is killed in an air raid; their home is partially destroyed by German bombs, as is the rest of their village.

The film's final scenes take place in the roofless, bombed-out church, where the local vicar delivers a passionate speech about the effect of war on ordinary people: "The homes of many of us have been destroyed, and the lives of old and young have been taken. There's scarcely a household that hasn't been struck to the heart. . . . Why, in all conscience, should these be the ones to suffer? . . . Are these our soldiers? Are these our fighters? Why should they be sacrificed? I shall tell you why! Because this is not only a war of soldiers in uniform—it is a war of the people, and it must be fought not only on the battlefield but in the cities and in the villages, in the factories and on the farms, in the home and in the heart of every man, woman, and child who loves freedom! . . . This is the people's war! It is our war! We are the fighters! Fight it, then! Fight it with all that is in us. And may God defend the right." As he finishes, British planes fly over the church on their way to Germany, and the chorus sings, "Onward, Christian Soldiers."

Although English critics felt the Minivers resembled no English family they had ever known, American audiences tearfully embraced the film, which reinforced American notions of what the British were like: cheerfully courageous and polite even under extreme duress. The movie won seven Academy Awards, including best picture, best director, and best actress, and did much to strengthen American support for Britain. Garson and Pidgeon repeated their roles as Mr. and Mrs. Miniver in a sequel to the film, *The Miniver Story* (1950), directed by H. C. Potter, in which the family is reunited after the war. Mrs. Miniver is dying of an unnamed dread disease and has only six months to live. She does not worry her family with this news and bravely solves all their problems within her allotted span.

Americans were further rallied to the British cause in *This Above All* (1942), directed by Anatole Litvak. The screenplay for the film, based on a novel by Eric Knight, was written by R. C. Sherriff. The story concerns an English soldier who, on leave following the debacle of Dunkirk, be-

gins to question the reasons for the war. The soldier (played by Tyrone Power, who had already seen action at Dunkirk in *A Yank in the RAF*) doesn't like the British caste system and believes there is no reason for fighting in an "aristocrats' war." He overstays his leave, becoming a deserter, but during a blackout he meets and falls in love with a woman (Joan Fontaine) who is a member of the upper class. She convinces him that the war has an important purpose that goes beyond class differences, and he returns to the army.

The British film industry, which experienced a period of listlessness during the 1930s, was wrenched from its doldrums by the war. Whereas American filmmakers responded to the war by fashioning it into standard forms of entertainment, British filmmakers developed a documentary approach to the conflict, a combination of realism and restraint. Instead of melodramatic heroism, there is the understated performance of duty; instead of individual heroes changing events, there are groups of men calmly working together to do the best they can. By placing emphasis on the characters of the men involved, by basing the stories on actual people or events, and by presenting the servicemen as no greater than they really were, the filmmakers created a different form of propaganda. British audiences could take pride in the actions of their soldiers, 69

Below: *Niall MacGinnis, as one of the stranded Nazis, scratches a reminder into the wall of a Canadian trading post in* 49th Parallel *(1941).*

even when it was a matter of valor in defeat. The films did not try to wreak righteous vengeance upon the enemy; rather, they sought to reinforce the British public's sense of who they were and what they were doing. These films are notable for their ability to inspire confidence in victory through the portrayal of grim determination.

One of the first films to display the influence of the documentary on fictional drama was *49th Parallel (The Invaders)* (1941), produced and directed by Michael Powell with a screenplay by Emeric Pressburger. The title of the film refers to the boundary between the United States and Canada; the story is set in 1940, when Canada was at war with Germany, but the United States was neutral. The movie begins with a German submarine sinking a Canadian freighter in the St. Lawrence. "The curtain rises on Canada," gloats the submarine's commander. The sub takes refuge in Hudson Bay, and a detail of six men is put ashore to collect food and fuel, the commander telling the men that they are "the first German soldiers to set foot on Canadian soil—the first of many thousands. Today, Europe—tomorrow, the world!" No sooner are the men ashore than the sub is sunk by Canadian

planes, stranding the Germans in Canada.

The remainder of the film follows their flight across Canada toward the US border. Along the way, the Germans encounter various representatives of democratic civilization, each encounter illuminating the character of the Nazis. At a Hudson's Bay Company trading post, the Germans run into a French-Canadian fur trapper (Laurence Olivier), whose isolationist view of the war quickly turns to patriotism when he witnesses Nazi brutality. The Nazis are also coldly antireligion: when the wounded trapper asks for his rosary, it is refused him. He promises the parting Germans, "When we win the war, we send you some missionaries." Coming upon a religious community composed of German refugees, the Nazis use their strident propaganda in an effort to enlist the people in the Nazi crusade. They fail, of course, for Nazism represents precisely that which the members of the commune had fled Europe to escape: intolerance. True Nazis, the fleeing Germans even take the time to burn a book by Thomas Mann, the property of a Canadian-Scottish artist (Leslie Howard) whose initial timidity becomes courage when he is confronted by the murderous Germans. One by one, the Nazis are killed or apprehended, until only one (Eric Portman) remains, and he has the misfortune of encountering a disgruntled Canadian soldier (Raymond Massey) who, while making full use of his democratic right to grouse, is eager to get his big hands on a Nazi.

Although the Nazis are presented as thoroughly demonic, some Americans, always sympathetic toward the underdog, found themselves drawn to their plight: outlaws on the lam attract a modicum of commiseration. Powell and Pressburger, who collaborated on several films between 1942 and 1956, reversed the situation in One of Our Aircraft Is Missing (1941).

Dedicated to the people of Holland and made with the cooperation of the exiled government of the Netherlands, One of Our Aircraft Is Missing begins with a British Wellington bomber on a raid over Stuttgart. Returning to England, the plane is hit, and the fliers are forced to bail out over Nazi-occupied Holland. With the aid of the courageous Dutch people (including Peter Ustinov as a parson), the fliers make it safely back to England. The last scene shows them taking off in another bomber, their target Berlin.

One of Our Aircraft Is Missing combines the documentarylike approach popular among British filmmakers with a fictional story. Desperate Journey (1942), directed by Raoul Walsh, shows how a similar theme was handled by an American filmmaker. When their Liberator bomber is shot down on a raid over Germany, five RAF pilots—Errol Flynn, Ronald Reagan, Alan Hale, Arthur Kennedy, and Ronald Sinclair—bail out and find themselves deep in the heart of Germany. Undaunted, the five airmen set off toward Holland, and along the way they blow up various portions of Germany, get their hands on important military secrets, meet a German girl (Nancy Coleman) sympathetic to their cause, and, using fisticuffs, prove themselves superior to the German armies sent by a Gestapo major (Raymond Massey) to capture them. Commandeering a car and chased by Germans on motorcycles, they ultimately get aboard a captured British bomber and fly it back across the Channel, Flynn declaring, "Now for the Pacific and a crack at those Japs!"

Behind One of Our Aircraft Is Missing is the heritage of British documentary filmmakers; behind Desperate Journey are Mack Sennett and Superman.

Perhaps the best example of the documentary style of British war movies is In Which We Serve (1942). Produced, written, codirected (with David Lean), and scored by Noel Coward—who is also its star—the film tells the story of one British destroyer, the HMS Torrin, from its construction to its sinking off the coast of Crete.

"Fast and powerful," the ship is cheered at its launching by the men who made it; their affection is shared by the men who serve on it, led by their captain (Coward). The ship is next seen in battle near Crete in May 1941. German dive-bombers attack the ship, and one succeeds in hitting it before being shot down. The captain comments, with great reserve, "Well done. We got him, but I'm afraid he got us, too." As the ship rolls over in the ocean, the survivors hold onto a rubber raft, and in a series of flashbacks, the lives of the various crewmen and the previous history of the ship are revealed. The men are 71

rescued by another ship and, in one of the film's most moving scenes, the captain bids farewell to each of them as they go off to serve on other ships. For, as the narrator reminds the audience, "There will always be other ships, for we are an island race. . . . There will always be other ships and men to sail in them. It is these men, in peace or war, to whom we owe so much. Above all victories, beyond all loss, in spite of changing values in a changing world, they give, to us their countrymen, eternal and indomitable pride. God bless our ships and all who sail in them."

One of the most powerful aspects of the film is its presentation of the enemy. Except for a brief glimpse at the beginning of the film, the Germans do not appear, but as the unarmed, wounded sailors cling to their raft, a German plane repeatedly strafes them, displaying very clearly the character of the enemy.

In Which We Serve is also important because it was the screen debut of Richard Attenborough, destined to create notable war movies of his own.

Not all of Britain's war movies were of the caliber of *In Which We Serve*. *Ships with Wings* (1941), directed by Sergei Nolbandov, uses a feeble melodrama—a disgraced pilot (John Clements) who saves the day by suicidally crashing his plane into a dam, thereby flooding a Nazi base—to glorify the Fleet Air Arm of the Royal Navy. The star of the film is the aircraft carrier *Ark Royal*; however, by the time the film was released, the *Ark Royal* had been sunk by an Italian submarine.

Spitfire (The First of the Few) (1942) recounts the story of R. J. Mitchell, the man who invented the plane that was so instrumental in the defense of Britain. Directed by Leslie Howard, who also plays the role of Mitchell, the film deals with the period before the war and the valiant efforts of Mitchell to see his invention recognized. This was Howard's last film as an actor (he coproduced two others after it): he was killed in 1943, when the passenger plane he was aboard was shot down by German fighters (the Germans believed Winston Churchill was among the passengers).

Eight months after the Japanese attack on Pearl Harbor, American marines waded ashore at Guadalcanal in America's first big amphibious assault. The news of the battle coincided with the release of Hollywood's first major motion picture about American soldiers in combat, *Wake Island* (1942), directed by John Farrow. The story of the Japanese invasion of Wake Island, which took place in December 1941, following the attack on Pearl Harbor, the film is fundamentally true to its subject: all the Americans are

Opposite: *Outnumbered but firmly united in their cause, the American defenders prepare to open fire in* Wake Island *(1942).*

Opposite: *Noel Coward* (lower right) *and the other survivors of the* Torrin *cling to their raft in* In Which We Serve *(1942).*

killed. There is room for heroism in defeat, however, and with its doomed but stubbornly courageous American soldiers holding out to the last against enemy hordes, *Wake Island* established the classic type of Hollywood war movie. The screenplay, by W. R. Burnett and Frank Butler, has its roots in both American history and American film: as the Japanese landing craft approach, an American officer instructs his men, "Don't fire until you see the whites of their eyes"; William Bendix (as Smacksie Randall) and Robert Preston (as Joe Doyle) play a pair of tough but undisciplined marines who delight in bickering—audiences had no trouble recognizing them as Flagg and Quirt. The commander of the small force (Brian Donlevy) never considers surrendering to the Japanese, and when they call on him to do so his response is, "Tell them to come and get us." The Japanese do, but each of the marines puts up a terrific battle before being killed. At the film's conclusion, with all the marines dead, a narrator states, "This is not the end."

It was a grim ending, but in the summer of 1942, Allied victory was a long way off; one of the important turning points came in the autumn, and once again an American assault co-incided with the release of a topical film. On November 8, 1942, American troops landed on the coast of North Africa; before the end of the month, audiences were delighting in *Casablanca*, directed by Michael Curtiz.

One of the most popular films ever made, *Casablanca* is the best example of Hollywood's ability to wrap political propaganda in entertainment. From its opening sequence of a Resistance member shot dead beneath a poster of Marshal Pétain, leader of the Vichy government, to its closing scenes in which a bottle of Vichy water is tossed in the trash before Rick Blaine (Humphrey Bogart) and his new ally, Captain Renault (Claude Rains), walk off together into the fog, *Casablanca* is about commitment to the Allied cause. At the center of the film is a love story, and the genius of *Casablanca* is that it uses the love story to emphasize the self-sacrifice necessary for victory.

The setting is the Moroccan city of Casablanca, a magical place full of refugees from Nazi-occupied Europe. While waiting for exit visas that will enable them to take the next step on their journey to freedom, the mixture of nationalities is free to enjoy the unique atmo-

sphere of the city, and everybody goes to Rick's Café Americain, certainly the most romantic establishment yet created on film. Although he claims his nationality is "drunkard," Rick is an American, and from running guns to Ethiopia in 1935 to fighting for the Loyalists in Spain in 1936, he has been involved in the war. Something has made him bitter and cynical and weakened his commitment to the Allied cause, and that something arrives in his café. Ilsa (Ingrid Bergman) was once Rick's lover. They were together when the Germans entered Paris ("The Germans wore gray. You wore blue," he recalls), and she left him then, with no explanation. She now arrives with her husband, Resistance leader Victor Laszlo (Paul Henreid), and wants Rick to help them get to America. Rick eventually does, realizing that he can no longer remain uninvolved. Once again, he loses the woman he loves, but it is a sacrifice made toward a higher goal. As he himself says, "I'm not much good at being noble, but it doesn't take much to see that the problems

of three little people don't amount to a hill of beans in this crazy world."

Casablanca is famous for its memorable dialogue (most of it written by Howard Koch); its music; and its cast, including Bogart in one of his greatest performances, the intensely feminine Bergman, Claude Rains as a corrupt but sincere prefect of police, Conrad Veidt as a Gestapo officer, Sydney Greenstreet as a rival café owner, Peter Lorre as a shifty operator, and Dooley Wilson as Sam, Rick's ever-loyal, piano-playing friend. The film is perhaps most remarkable for the way it romanticizes the Allied cause, imbedding it inextricably in a Hollywood dream of love. Seen today, the film is striking for its tone of assured victory; the war seems already won—all that was necessary was the will to fight it.

When Churchill and Roosevelt held a conference in Casablanca soon after the film's release, the city's fame was secure. Morocco itself was teeming with Americans in 1942. Along with the

74

American soldiers were Bob Hope and Bing Crosby helping everyone escape the war in *The Road to Morocco*, directed by David Butler. It was a good year to celebrate Americans, and Gary Cooper as Lou Gehrig in *The Pride of the Yankees* and James Cagney as George M. Cohan in *Yankee Doodle Dandy* helped fortify national pride. *Yankee Doodle Dandy*, an unabashedly patriotic musical, was directed by Michael Curtiz, and he followed it with *This Is the Army*, another flag-waving musical. *This Is the Army* is composed of two Irving Berlin stage shows, 1917's *Yip Yip Yaphank* and 1942's *This Is the Army*. The two are joined in the screen version by George Murphy, cast as the director of both. The many musical numbers include Kate Smith singing "God Bless America" and Berlin himself singing "Oh, How I Hate to Get Up in the Morning." All of the actors involved, among them Joan Leslie, George Tobias, Alan Hale, and Ronald Reagan, donated their services, and the profits from the film were given to the Army Emergency Relief.

National pride was further boosted in such films as *We've Never Been Licked* (1943), directed by John Rawlins, the title of which refers to the record of America's military forces. Most of the film is about Texas Agricultural & Mechanical University, an institution that claimed to have graduated more army officers than West Point. The smart-alecky son (Richard Quine) of an officer rebels against the school's traditions before embracing them and going to war.

Everyone was rallied to the cause. Basil Rathbone as Sherlock Holmes and Nigel Bruce as Dr. Watson uncovered Nazi plots in *Sherlock Holmes and the Voice of Terror* (1942), directed by John Rawlins, and *Sherlock Holmes and the Secret Weapon* (1942), directed by Roy William Neill. Invisibility was used against the Nazis in *Invisible Agent* (1942), directed by Edwin L. Marin, in which a very special spy (Jon Hall) is parachuted into Berlin to disrupt the Nazis. And, although Rin Tin Tin died in 1932, the tradition of canine valor was continued by Lassie and her son, Laddie. In *Son of Lassie* (1945), directed by S. Sylvan Simon, Laddie and his RAF master are shot down over Norway and have to make it back home. In *Courage of Lassie* (1946), directed by Fred Wilcox and starring Elizabeth Taylor and Frank Morgan, the brave collie wanders from home, serves in the army as a killer dog, suffers shell shock, and finally finds her way home.

Opposite: *Claude Rains* (second from left), *Paul Henreid, Humphrey Bogart, and Ingrid Bergman in* Casablanca *(1942).*

75

The majority of the combat films made by Americans during World War II are set in the Pacific. In fact, until the last year of the war, there were few films about American infantrymen in Europe. One reason for this is that the time necessary for the production of films forces them to follow behind events, and until 1943, there were no American soldiers in Europe. There is also the fact that the war in the Pacific was, for Americans, more emotionally charged than the war in Europe. The Japanese had seen to that when they attacked Pearl Harbor.

Throughout the war, the original ideas for almost all of Hollywood's war movies came from the filmmakers themselves, and they followed public opinion. The war in the Pacific provided them with ample subjects: the undeniable heroism of the Americans was matched by the undeniable cruelty of the Japanese. Furthermore, the war in the Pacific was a racial conflict, a fact overlooked by neither American filmmakers nor the American government. For its "yellow" Japs, Hollywood had to make do with Chinese and Filipinos; the government had interned most of the West Coast's American citizens of Japanese ancestry in "relocation centers," depriving Hollywood of an army of extras and thousands of Americans of their civil liberties.

The story of doomed Americans making a last stand against the Japanese, initiated in *Wake Island*, was continued in *Bataan* (1943), directed by Tay Garnett. *Bataan* tells the story of thirteen American soldiers assigned to delay the Japanese advance; as in *Wake Island*, all of the Americans are killed. The film strikingly depicts Japanese cruelty, including the slaughter of civilians, and it makes the deaths of the Americans more tragic by giving each of the soldiers a distinct character. The result, of course, is the standard American platoon, composed of ethnic stereotypes representing a cross-section of American society. *Bataan* is remarkable because along with the inevitable Irishman (Thomas Mitchell), Pole, and California "jitterbug" (Desi Arnaz), there is a black (Kenneth Spencer). Added to the ethnic identities are personal stories, including that of a murderer (Lloyd Nolan) who redeems himself, and a graduate of West Point (Lee Bowman) who proves himself. One by one, they are all killed by the Japanese (one dies of malaria), and one by one they are buried. In the end, the last surviving soldiers face wave after wave of charging Japanese. Whether with a machine gun or with bare hands, each American kills a crowd of Japs before being killed. The last man alive is the leader of the group (Robert Taylor). He buries his dead comrades, digs his own grave, and sets up his machine gun over it.

That is where he dies, firing away at the approaching enemy.

The fact that it was Robert Taylor, one of the period's leading male stars, who was being killed by the Japanese made the film even more powerful for American audiences. Veronica Lake, whose "peekaboo" hairstyle became a fad (when women working in factories began having accidents because of the long hair, the government asked Lake to have her hair trimmed for the duration), meets a similar fate in *So Proudly We Hail* (1943), directed by Mark Sandrich.

The screenplay for the film, written by Allan Scott and Sandrich, was based on the experiences of army nurses in the Philippines during the Japanese invasion. A mixture of tear-jerking romance and flag-waving patriotism, the film tells the story of a group of American nurses—including Claudette Colbert, Paulette Goddard, and Veronica Lake—and their experiences during the fighting before the fall of Bataan and Corregidor. In the face of the murderous Japanese, who machine-gun their hospital, the nurses take part in a holding action, giving the other Americans time to retreat. Lake plays a woman who has vowed eternal vengeance against the Japanese after seeing her fiancé killed at Pearl Harbor. She gets her opportunity when a Japanese patrol arrives to capture the nurses. Putting a hand grenade in her blouse, she goes out to meet the enemy, and her explosive death allows the other nurses to escape.

The final scene of *Cry Havoc* (1943), another film about nurses on Bataan, is even less pleasant. Directed by Richard Thorpe, the film is based on a play by Allan R. Kenward. As with many films based on plays, most of the action of the film is restricted to one location, in this case a dugout on Bataan in which a group of army nurses and volunteers cares for wounded soldiers (including Robert Mitchum in a bit part) and tries to survive the desperate fear and constant danger. The thirteen women, like the thirteen soldiers in *Bataan*, represent a mixture of American types, with a southern belle, a former telephone operator, and a burlesque queen working alongside the career army nurses (led by Margaret Sullavan). The women discuss their former lives and help one another endure the stress; they go from being a crowd of disparate people to being a group of dedicated, courageous nurses. In the end, they are forced to surrender to the Japanese, and they leave their dugout with their hands raised, their fate in the hands of the enemy.

Salute to the Marines (1943), directed by S. Sylvan Simon, recounts another tale of American heroism against the Japanese in the Philippines. The film begins at the Marine Corps training camp in San Diego, where a general delivers a speech to the troops about a certain Sergeant Major William Bailey, who gave his life in the defense of the Philippines and was awarded the Medal of Honor for his heroism. Wallace Beery stars as Bailey, a career marine who, after thirty years in the service, ends up in the Philippines training recruits. His wife (Fay Bainter) and his daughter (Marilyn Maxwell) convince him to retire (his wife attempts, unsuccessfully, to get him to stop chewing tobacco). The victim of Japanese propaganda, his wife has become a pacifist. Bailey, who calls the Japanese "mustard-colored monkeys," knows better. His time comes after December 7, when he and a group of Filipinos fight a heroic holding action at a bridge. He dies, and so does his wife.

Howard Hawks directed *Air Force* (1943), a movie that covers most of the important events in the Pacific war up to the Battle of the Coral Sea. Dudley Nichols used actual Army Air Force files for the preparation of the screenplay, which follows the story of one B-17 Flying Fortress, the *Mary-Ann,* and its crew. The film begins with the *Mary-Ann* taking off from San Francisco on December 6, 1941, on a training mission to Pearl Harbor. The next morning, as the plane approaches its destination, the radio picks up the shouts of Japanese fighter pilots. From the disaster at Pearl Harbor, the *Mary-Ann* flies to doomed Wake Island, from there to battle-torn Manila, and then on to take part in the Battle of the Coral Sea. Damaged and out of fuel, the *Mary-Ann* is finally crash-landed in Australia. The film ends with the crew taking off in their plane with a new target: Tokyo.

The center of the film is inside the *Mary-Ann:* the crew, a group of nine men who, sharing in both defeats and victories, become a team of professionals, dedicated to their mission. The men are presented as equals; even the film's stars—John Garfield, Gig Young, Arthur Kennedy, Harry Carey—share the lead. The brutality of the conflict is clear ("Fried Jap going down," announces George Tobias as a gunner), and the film has plenty of heroics, but its overall theme is commitment to the group and the cause.

The unavoidable gap between the conception of an idea for a film and the film's release is well illustrated by *The Story of Dr. Wassell* (1944), produced and directed by Cecil B. De Mille. In April 1942, during one of his fireside chats, President Roosevelt mentioned the heroic actions of a navy doctor who had rescued wounded men during the Japanese invasion of Java and had managed to get them all safely to Australia. De Mille was among the many Americans listening to the radio broadcast, and he decided to make the incident into a film. Gary Cooper was chosen for the role of Dr. Corydon M. Wassell, the Arkansas country doctor who became a medical missionary in China and joined the navy when war was declared; novelist James Hilton, working from interviews with the real Dr. Wassell, created a story, which was made into a screenplay by Alan Le May and Charles Bennett. The resulting film, which included a love story (with Laraine Day) and scenes of dancing girls (Java, after all, is in the exotic Far East), was released around the time of the D-day invasion of Europe.

The most important wartime Hollywood movie about the war in the Pacific was *Guadalcanal Diary* (1943), directed by Lewis Seiler. The film is about the battle and the lessons the marines learned while adding a new verse to their hymn; it is also about the changes wrought on Americans by the experience of the war. Learning to fight the Japs successfully ("They aren't supermen, just tricky," comments one marine) in-

volved changing attitudes about fighting and killing.

Based on a best-selling book by war correspondent Richard Tregaskis, the movie presents a day-by-day account of the battle, beginning with the marines aboard their transport ships and ending with them marching past a road sign pointing to Tokyo. In between, they meet and, after hard fighting, defeat the Japanese defenders of the island. Although their landing is unopposed, the marines soon encounter fierce resistance, with Japanese snipers "hiding up in the trees, like apes." The marines are armed with more than their weapons, however—they have seen movies. One American soldier attracts Japanese soldiers by making turkey sounds. "Are you Sergeant York or Gary Cooper?" asks a buddy. "Scratch one squint-eye," ex-

claims the other, plugging the enemy soldier.

Among the marines—who are described as high school athletes, grocers, clerks, and taxi drivers—are the Brooklyn cabbie William Bendix, connecting the film to *Wake Island*, and the tough sergeant Lloyd Nolan, connecting the film to *Bataan*. All of the marines treasure thoughts of home: the film makes clear their joy in receiving mail, in listening to a radio broadcast of the World Series, and in singing traditional songs (on the eve of a big battle, they sing, "Home on the Range"). The battles are presented as a series of individual encounters, for the most part scenes of marines running forward shooting at the fleeing Japs, and the men who are shot die by seeming to fall asleep suddenly, but there is a hardness to the film. Richard Jaeckel made his film debut in *Guadalcanal Diary*, and with his

79

Opposite: *Gig Young* (left), *Arthur Kennedy, and James Brown in Air Force (1943).*

smooth, beardless chin, he was about the right age (the average age of the marines at Guadalcanal was nineteen). He learns his lessons well. When he sees one of his buddies killed by a Japanese soldier pretending to be dead, Jaeckel uses the same ruse to trick a Japanese soldier, yelling at the man he is killing, "That's one you taught me, Tojo!"

The Marine Corps recognized the importance of the film and helped in its production. Their investment paid off: they set up recruiting stations near theaters showing the film and received more than twelve thousand new recruits.

Richard Tregaskis, who had landed with the marines at Guadalcanal, lived through World War II (he was wounded during the Italian campaign). He was tall—six feet seven inches—and his fellow correspondents warned him that if he were captured by the Japanese they would use him as an observation post. In 1963, he published an account of another war, *Vietnam Diary*.

There is far more jingoism and bloodletting in *Gung Ho!* (1943), directed by Ray Enright, a step-by-step account of the marine assault on Makin Island. The technical adviser for the film was Evans F. Carlson, the man who had led the actual raid, and seven of the marines who had taken part in the raid were given roles in the film. It was Carlson, who had served as an observer with the Chinese Army in 1937, who popularized the phrase *gung ho*, a Chinese Army motto meaning "work together." Carlson made it the password of his marine raiders. Randolph Scott, as Colonel Thorwald, plays the role of Carlson in the film.

Although of particular importance to Americans, the Pacific was not the only theater of war. The war in the deserts of North Africa involved a different cast of characters, an international mixture of which the leading participants were the British under Montgomery and the German Afrika Korps under Rommel. Fighting alongside the Germans were Italians; the Allied forces included Australians, Americans, Free French, and various other nationalities.

The first Hollywood film about the fighting in North Africa was *The Immortal Sergeant* (1943), directed by John Stahl and based on a novel by John Brophy. The story of a British patrol

in the Libyan desert, the film stars Thomas Mitchell and Henry Fonda. Mitchell plays the sergeant of the title, a wise and resourceful veteran of World War I; Fonda is his corporal, a timid man afraid of the responsibility of command. When the sergeant, wounded, kills himself to unburden the imperiled patrol, the corporal must take command, and—inspired by the example set by the sergeant (whose disembodied voice offers encouragement)—the corporal succeeds in getting the remaining men back to safety.

"A sergeant's the same in every army in the world," laments a British soldier in *Sahara* (1943), directed by Zoltan Korda. The sergeant in question is indeed a tough character: Sergeant Joe Gunn (Humphrey Bogart), commander of a redoubtable M-3 tank named *Lulubelle* (the sergeant named it after a horse, not a woman). *Sahara* begins in the deserts of Libya following the fall of Tobruk; as the sergeant and his crew coax the temperamental *Lulubelle* back toward the safety of Allied lines, they come across assorted stragglers. Although vexed by the insults they direct toward his beloved air-cooled tank, the sergeant offers these Allied troops a lift, and before long *Lulubelle*'s passengers include four British soldiers, one South African, a Free French soldier (who comes along because he enjoys the sergeant's cigarettes), and a proud Sudanese corporal with an Italian prisoner (who claims to have an uncle in Pittsburgh). A Messerschmitt appears and strafes the tank a few times before the sergeant shoots it down, adding a German prisoner (who speaks English but doesn't let on) to the already crowded *Lulubelle*.

The passengers hanging on to the lurching steel box and the sergeant squinting through the hatch, sand blowing in his face, the little group, composed of members of most of the warring nations, makes its way to a well. They are pursued by Germans, but rather than leave the well to the enemy, they decide to stay and fight, thus buying time for the rest of the retreating Allies. When not shooting at the five hundred Germans who soon surround the water hole, the defenders talk and discover they are all really very much alike. The two Axis allies do not get along well, however, and the German ends up killing the

80

Opposite: *Henry Fonda* (left), *Melville Cooper, Allyn Joslyn, and Morton Lowry in* The Immortal Sergeant *(1943).*

men who died defending the well, the sergeant says that they would have enjoyed the news: "They stopped them at El Alamein."

Critics, particularly British critics, complained about *Sahara*, pointing out that there were no American tanks fighting alongside the British during the period dealt with in the film, but such cavils did nothing to deflate the film's popularity. An exciting action story, it stimulated patriotism and allowed audiences to delight in the wonderful array of international characters allied against the Germans. The character of the Germans was also made clear in such scenes as that in which the German flier refuses to be touched by a member of an "inferior race"—the Sudanese corporal.

Italian. It is the Germans who are different. As one of the British soldiers says, "We're much stronger than they are. Those men out there have never known the dignity of freedom." Most of the defenders are killed, but the well is held, and the parched Germans ultimately surrender. The film ends with the sergeant and *Lulubelle* back at the Allied lines, where news arrives of the victory at El Alamein. Reciting the names of the

By the time *Five Graves to Cairo* was released, in May 1943, the fighting in North Africa was nearly at an end. Directed by Billy Wilder with a screenplay by Charles Brackett based on a play by Lajos Bira, *Five Graves to Cairo* offers an entertaining, if farfetched, explanation of the British victory at El Alamein. Like *Sahara*, the film begins in 1942, just after the fall of Tobruk. A British soldier (Franchot Tone), the only survivor of a tank destroyed by the enemy, is rescued by a Turkish innkeeper (Akim Tamiroff). At the inn, the British soldier assumes the identity of a clubfooted servant recently killed in an air raid. The dead man turns out to have been a spy in league with the Germans, and with the help of a French girl (Anne Baxter), the British soldier obtains secret information that explains the ability of the German tanks to race around in the desert without supplies. In 1936 (with wicked foresight), the Germans had buried supplies of fuel, water, and ammunition at five places in the desert; the key to their locations is on a map, which the soldier gets to the British Army.

The film includes some memorable characterizations. The French girl hesitates before helping the soldier because her brother was killed at Dunkirk, and she accuses the British of having deserted France. The opportunity to filch the map occurs when the German General Staff uses the inn as its headquarters. Among the officers is Rommel, played by that paragon of Prussian officers, Erich von Stroheim. In one scene, the girl makes the mistake of addressing the field marshal at an early hour; he curtly explains to her that he has an aversion to being around females in the morning. There is also an Italian general (Fortunio Bonanova), who has trouble getting along with his Teutonic allies.

"How can a nation that belches understand a nation that sings?" he asks. Although the Italians were enemies of the United States, Hollywood scriptwriters had trouble casting them as villains.

It was the Germans who were the enemy, but even had they known the facts, the world's filmmakers could not have created accurate films about the barbarities committed by the Nazis. In the half century since the war, no one yet has succeeded, for the Nazis bequeathed to the twentieth century a horror beyond the scope of narrative film. Along with countless lives, the Nazis took away the parameters of humanness: the traits of Nazis are believable only when attributed to aliens from distant galaxies, and their actions mock those who try to describe them, devaluing any medium of expression.

And even had the filmmakers been able to express the truth, few would have believed them. Many Americans were skeptical of reports of Nazi brutality. The World War I rantings about Belgian babies had made them think that such atrocity stories were nothing but propaganda.

The films made during the war about the Nazis reflect popular opinion and the film-inspired conviction that the Nazis were gangsters. The well-publicized eugenic theories of Nazi Germany provided hints of manipulated sexuality. In *Women in Bondage* (1943), directed by Steve Sekely, Nancy Kelly is condemned to enforced sterilization when she speaks out against the Nazis. This idea was further exploited in *Hitler's Children* (1943), directed by Edward Dmytryk, which combines the Nazi fascination with genes with masochism. Based on *Education for Death*, a novel by Gregor Ziemer, the film is about the methods used by the Nazis to indoctrinate the young. The primary goal of this education is the elimination of all compassion. When a pretty young girl (Bonita Granville) refuses to submit to the licentious Nazis (she does not want to bear illegitimate children for the Fuehrer's army), she is publicly whipped. Her boyfriend (Tim Holt), a Nazified youth, has maintained enough compassion to see the truth about the Nazis, and the two lovers die together defiantly. The movie includes scenes of efficient clinics where women are sterilized for such reasons as color blindness and undesirable political views.

Films about Hitler were popular, and an actor named Bobby Watson enjoyed a brief career portraying the Fuehrer in such films as *The Devil with Hitler* (Alan Mowbray plays the Devil), *Hitler—Dead or Alive*, and *That Nazty Nuisance Hitler*. Martin Kosleck became the preferred actor for the role of Goebbels, beginning in *Confessions of a Nazi Spy*. In *The Hitler Gang* (1944), directed by John Farrow, Watson as Hitler and Kosleck as Goebbels are joined by actors portraying other leading figures of Nazi Germany. Three of the actors were recent émigrés from Germany: Reinhold Schunzel as Ludendorff, Fritz Kortner as Otto Strasser, and Alexander Granach as Julius Streicher. The film, a newsreel-style fictional documentary of Hitler's career from 1918 to the beginning of World War II, was advertised as "The greatest gangster picture of them all!"

The fate of people living in countries occupied by the Nazis provided filmmakers with a better vehicle for portraying the enemy. Jean Renoir, in exile in Hollywood from occupied France, directed *This Land Is Mine* (1943). Set "somewhere in Europe," the movie tells the story of a timid schoolteacher (Charles Laughton) who, finally outraged by the actions of the German invaders, reads to his class from banned books and delivers an impassioned speech about the rights of free people before he is killed by the Germans.

Bertolt Brecht, who had fled Nazi Germany in 1933, wrote the screenplay for *Hangmen Also Die* (1943), directed by Fritz Lang. The subject of the film is the assassination in Czechoslovakia of Reinhard Heydrich, "the hangman of Europe." The assassin (Brian Donlevy) is sheltered by the underground and becomes a symbol of freedom to the Czech people, and although the Nazis take terrible reprisals, including the massacre of four hundred people, the Czech underground refuses to turn him in. Instead, they offer the Germans a scapegoat, a traitorous brewer, and to save face the Germans execute him for the crime. The film concludes with the words, "Not the End."

The Nazis avenged the assassination of Heydrich by killing all the male inhabitants of the town of Lidice, deporting all the women and children, and razing the town. This event, along with the assassination of Heydrich, is depicted in gruesome detail in *Hitler's Madman* (1943), the first American film directed by Douglas Sirk, a director who had fled Nazi Germany in 1937 and changed his name (Detlef Sierck) because of anti-German sentiments. The role of Heydrich is played by John Carradine; among the Czechs is Ava Gardner. Reviewers felt the depiction of Nazi brutality was exaggerated.

The world war involved the peoples of many lands, and to portray all these foreign nationals in faraway places, Hollywood scriptwriters resorted to stereotypes, drawn, of course, from Hollywood films. Czechoslovakia, Poland, Norway, and the Ukraine all seemed to be populated by hearty peasants who dined on dark bread and thick stew and, when not laboring in the fields, passed the time singing traditional folk songs and dancing, the women dressed in long skirts embroidered with floral designs. Most villages boasted a doctor (usually Walter Huston) and a local hero (a leading American actor). The theme of the majority of these films is the heroic resistance of the proud people, ordinary men fighting against overwhelming odds, and even though the characterizations of the locals seem hackneyed, many of these films have maintained an exhilarating spirit. Norway, invaded by the Germans in 1940, was the setting for several of them.

Commandos Strike at Dawn (1942), directed by John Farrow, stars Paul Muni as a Norwegian Resistance leader. When he discovers that the

Left: *Rosemary DeCamp fends off a German advance in* Commandos Strike at Dawn *(1942).*

Germans are constructing an airfield near his village, he escapes to England and returns as the guide for a British commando raid on the airfield.

Far more exciting is *Edge of Darkness* (1943), directed by Lewis Milestone, which begins with a rousing chorus of "A Mighty Fortress Is Our God" and ends with the words of President Roosevelt: "If there is anyone who still wonders why this war is being fought, let him look to Norway. . . . And if there's anyone who has doubts of the

democratic will to win, again I say, let him look to Norway." The leader of the Resistance movement in the Norwegian town of Trollness is Errol Flynn; his girl friend is Ann Sheridan, daughter of the local doctor (Walter Huston). With weapons supplied by the English, the townspeople rise up and kill the occupying Germans. All the Germans die, but so do all the Norwegians.

The people in another Norwegian town rise up against their German oppressors in *The Moon Is Down* (1943), directed by Irving Pichel. The screenplay for the film was written by Nunnally Johnson, based on the novel and play by John Steinbeck. Lee J. Cobb plays the local doctor; Cedric Hardwicke is the leading German. The Germans shoot and hang civilians as reprisals for acts of sabotage; with dynamite supplied them by the British, the townspeople blow up the town's coal mines.

The most remarkable films made by Hollywood during World War II are those that were made in support of America's ally the Soviet Union. The first of these, *Mission to Moscow* (1943), directed by Michael Curtiz, is the most famous. The philosopher John Dewey called it "the first instance in our country of totalitarian propaganda for mass consumption." In its effort to rally Americans to support the Soviet Union, the film made some drastic adjustments in recent Soviet history, falsifying, distorting, and omitting many facts.

The screenplay for the film was based on a book by Joseph E. Davies, who had served as ambassador to the USSR from 1937 to 1938; the screenplay was written by Howard Koch, who had just completed work on *Casablanca*. *Mission to Moscow* was produced by Warner Brothers, the same studio that, during World War I, had produced *My Four Years in Germany*, the film based on the memoirs of Ambassador Gerard. It was President Roosevelt who requested that a film be made of Davies's memoirs; Jack Warner claimed Roosevelt had asked him personally to do so.

The film begins with a prologue spoken by Davies in which he claims that what follows is true. The remainder of the film follows Davies (played by Walter Huston) on his mission to Moscow, where he and the audience are disabused of some misconceptions. The ambassador is taken to witness the famous 1937 purge trials (at which Stalin liquidated his opposition), and he learns that the Trotskyites are in league with the Germans and Japanese, who have already made plans for divvying up Russia. He also learns that the reason Soviet industry has problems is that

84

it is constantly being sabotaged by German and Japanese agents. The ambassador even gets to speak with Stalin (Mannart Kippen), a sage, pipe-smoking leader. The film skips over such matters as the Nazi-Soviet nonaggression pact and the Soviet invasion of Poland. Although many of the film's statements—including the oft-repeated notions that Americans and Russians are really very much alike and that communism and capitalism achieve the same ends—can be excused as exuberant, well-intentioned plati-tudes, the film stands as a landmark in Ameri-can filmmaking, a film made to spread lies for the government. The film was not an effective piece of propaganda and inspired more outrage than admiration. The people who worked on it found themselves in trouble when the House Un-American Activities Committee began its own purge trials in 1947. Koch was blacklisted in 1951.

That fate befell many of the people who worked on pro-Soviet films during the war. Lil-lian Hellman, who was an uncooperative wit-ness when she appeared before the HUAC, wrote the screenplay for *The North Star* (1943), directed by Lewis Milestone. The film is remarkable for its music, a score by Aaron Copland and songs with lyrics by Ira Gershwin. The first half of the film presents the gay life of Russian peasants, among them Anne Baxter, Dana Andrews, Farley Granger, Walter Brennan, and Walter Huston (as the village doctor), who sing and dance both at work and at play. Then the Germans come. Among the German invaders are two SS doctors (Erich von Stroheim and Martin Kosleck) who drain the blood from Russian children for trans-fusion into German wounded. The peasants stop singing and become guerrillas. In 1957, the film was reedited and rereleased under the title *Ar-mored Attack*. No longer pro-Soviet, the peasants were changed to freedom fighters battling the Communists.

Russian music was central to *Song of Russia* (1943), directed by Gregory Ratoff, the story of an American orchestra conductor (Robert Taylor) who goes to Russia on a concert tour and visits the birthplace of Tchaikovsky. While there, he falls in love with a cute piano-playing peasant (Susan Peters), and they marry. When the Ger-

mans invade, the newlyweds become guerrilla fighters; they are ultimately persuaded that they can serve the cause of Russia more forcefully by returning to America and spreading the song of Russia. The film's score includes music by Tchai-kovsky and modern Russian composers.

Gregory Peck made his screen debut in *Days of Glory* (1944), directed by Jacques Tourneur. Peck plays a Russian partisan leader named Vladimir. Russia's artistic heritage is not forgot-ten: Vladimir is in love with a ballerina (Tamata Toumanova, a ballerina with the Ballet Russe, also in her screen debut). They fight the Ger-mans together.

Whether Norwegian or Russian, Hollywood's freedom fighters were very much alike. Ethnic garb and stereotypical traits defined their na-tionalities, and their struggle against the Ger-

Opposite top: The Way Ahead *(1944)*.
Opposite bottom: *Raymond Massey* (top left) *and*
Humphrey Bogart (right) *in* Action in
the North Atlantic *(1943)*.

mans served to diminish any ulterior political motives. The fact that guerrilla bands can be composed of both sexes was rarely ignored by scriptwriters. One of the major appeals of all war movies is their heady mixture of romance and violence. When men and women are thrown together in perilous situations involving the threat of sudden death, the opportunities for poignant romance become endless. Films about guerrilla fighters have an advantage over films about servicemen in that the presence of the females does not need to be contrived. Rather than making their entrance as nurses or nightclub performers encountered on leave, the women are there to fight, arm in arm, with the men.

In America, the most talked-about film of 1943 was *For Whom the Bell Tolls,* directed by Sam Wood. The film version of Ernest Hemingway's novel had been awaited with the same level of excited anticipation that had preceded Margaret Mitchell's *Gone with the Wind.* Audiences were particularly eager to see how the filmmakers had handled a suggestive scene involving a sleeping bag. Those who had expected more than titillated imaginations were disappointed, as were those who had expected a political statement. The screenplay, by Dudley Nichols, avoided politics in favor of romance.

Like the first screen version of a Hemingway novel, *A Farewell to Arms, For Whom the Bell Tolls* stars Gary Cooper (Hemingway himself had requested him). Robert Jordan (Cooper) goes to Spain to fight with the Loyalists and is assigned the task of blowing up a strategic bridge. Among the guerrillas with whom he fights is Maria (Ingrid Bergman), who has been raped and tortured by the enemy. The two fall in love; he ultimately gives his life to save his compatriots. The film was assailed by many critics for turning the novel into a love story; great emphasis was placed on the fact that the names of the opposing sides were given as Republican (for Loyalist) and Nationalist (for Fascist). But the civil war in Spain was over. The movie had not been made to promote support for the heroic Loyalists—it had been made for entertainment.

Such films as *Song of Russia* and *Days of Glory* failed to do for the Soviet Union what *Mrs. Miniver* had done for Britain, but films promoting

the British cause had a great advantage over films promoting support of Russia: Americans were already sympathetic toward the British. Much of this sympathy was based on popular notions of what the British were like: polite, courageous, and sporting—they "played fair." The British themselves shared and perpetuated many of these dreamy notions. *The Life and Death of Colonel Blimp* (1943), another film made by Michael Powell and Emeric Pressburger, examines one of Great Britain's most popular mythical creatures, the professional military man. The title of the film is taken from a cartoon character created by David Low; in the film, the character's name is Clive Candy (Roger Livesey), but with his rosy cheeks and walrus mustache, Candy is the embodiment of a Colonel Blimp. A soldier all his life, Candy has fought in the Boer War and the Great War. He is too old for service in World War II, and his ideas of warfare are equally antiquated. He has nothing but blustering contempt for modern methods of warfare, and he believes the English should "play fair" with the Germans. He has as a friend a German officer (Anton Walbrook), a liberal-minded German who has fled Nazi Germany for Britain. The German tries to correct Candy's view of the war. Playing fair will not win the war; indeed, Candy (and the audience) is ultimately convinced that Britain will lose the war if it does not use the foul methods employed by its enemies. The film treats Candy-Blimp with the compassion due a figure fashioned of tradition and nostalgia.

We Dive at Dawn (1943), directed by Anthony Asquith, is another of the fictionalized documentaries popular with British filmmakers. The film recounts the sinking of the German battleship *Brandenburg* by a British submarine, the *Sea Tiger.* The drama is made compelling by understating the action and emphasizing instead the personalities of the men in the submarine (led by Eric Portman and John Mills).

Modern wars are fought by armies of conscripted soldiers, men who are drawn from all walks of life and put in identical uniforms to fight and perhaps die together. The men do not necessarily want to fight; nor do they choose to leave their homes and jobs to face an uncertain future. *The Way Ahead (The Immortal Battalion)*

(1944), directed by Carol Reed with a screenplay by Eric Ambler and Peter Ustinov, is about seven such men, men from diverse occupations and social classes who are drafted shortly after Dunkirk to serve in the British Army. The film follows them through their training and leaves them as they walk off through swirling desert sand to confront Rommel's tanks. By the end of the film, the seven separate individuals have been trained to work together as a fighting unit. Rather than "The End," the film concludes with "The Beginning."

Realism is not an obligatory ingredient of war movies. *A Guy Named Joe* (1943), directed by Victor Fleming with a screenplay by Dalton Trumbo, concerns a daredevil American pilot (Spencer Tracy) whose foolhardy approach to aerial combat finally gets him killed. The dead flier next finds himself in a special fliers' heaven, run by "The General" (Lionel Barrymore), who hands out new orders to the dead airmen. Tracy's orders are to return to earth and teach a novice flyer (Van Johnson) the traditions of the service. Things get complicated when the young flier falls for the dead man's girl (Irene Dunne), creating an unusual love triangle. The title of the film comes from a remark made by General Claire Chennault, leader of the Flying Tigers: "Boys, when I'm behind the stick, I'm just a guy named Joe."

Ordinary guys named Joe were to be found in every group of American servicemen. Humphrey Bogart, who plays a sergeant named Joe in *Sahara,* plays a member of the merchant marine named Joe in *Action in the North Atlantic* (1943), directed by Lloyd Bacon. A dramatic account of the perils faced by the merchant marine convoys taking supplies to Europe, the film was considered so realistic that the merchant marine used it as a training film.

Bogart serves aboard a Liberty ship commanded by Raymond Massey. The ship is torpedoed, the crew's lifeboat is rammed by the German submarine, and the surviving members of the crew spend eleven days clinging to a raft. They are rescued and almost immediately go back to sea in a new ship, part of a very international convoy taking supplies to Murmansk. Along the way they are attacked by both a submarine and a German bomber, and some of the crewmen are killed, including one boy from Kansas. "All the ocean he ever knew was in a mud hole," eulogizes Bogart as the boy is buried at sea. "A lot more people are going to die before this is over," he continues, "and it's up to the ones who make it through to make sure they didn't die for nothing." The ships make it safely into the Russian port, where the jubilant Russians shout, *"Tovarich!"* ("Friend"). The screenplay for the film was written by John Howard Lawson, known for his liberal politics; the scenes of the friendly Russians have been deleted from some prints of the film.

Corvette K-225 (1943), directed by Richard Rosson, is about Canadian Navy corvettes protecting convoys bound for Allied ports. To make

the film as realistic as possible, Rosson spent more than three months in the Canadian Navy and went on five transatlantic round trips aboard corvettes like the one in the title. He witnessed and filmed submarine and plane attacks on the ships, and much of this footage is used in *Corvette K-225,* giving it the feel of a documentary. The story of the film follows the maiden voyage of corvette *K-225.* While shepherding a convoy through the submarine-infested sealanes, the corvette confronts many dangers, including storms and enemy torpedoes. Applied to this account is a tale of heroism and romance: the captain of *K-225* is Randolph Scott, and aboard ship is the brother (James Brown) of the captain's sweetheart (Ella Raines, in her screen debut).

Thanks to a long-standing naval superstition, women rarely appear aboard ships at sea, but females can bring mariners calamity even when they are left behind on dry land. The love triangle is one of the most perilous situations a serviceman can face, far more dangerous even than battling the enemy: one of the two competing males almost always dies. In *Crash Dive* (1943), directed by Archie Mayo with a screenplay by Jo Swerling based on a story by W. R. Burnett, the two men are Tyrone Power and Dana Andrews; the woman is Anne Baxter. Andrews is the captain of a submarine, and Power serves alongside him. The sub goes through many exciting adventures, including an encounter with a German Q-boat (an armed vessel disguised as a merchant ship) and a raid on a German base,

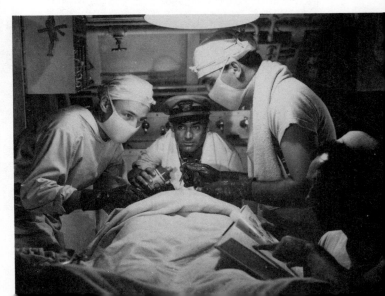

but it is the love triangle that propels the film.

Diminishing the love interest in a film leaves more room for action: in *Destination Tokyo* (1943), directed by Delmer Daves, the absence of a love story allows a submarine, the *Copperfin*, to experience a broad range of situations. Under the command of Cary Grant, the *Copperfin* leaves San Francisco with secret orders to pick up a meteorologist in the Aleutians and take him to Tokyo Bay. In the Aleutians, the submarine is attacked by Japanese planes, one of which drops a bomb on the sub. The bomb does not explode, however, and must be dug out of the hull. En route to Tokyo Bay, a pharmacist's mate is called upon to perform an emergency appendectomy. The sub makes its way through a minefield, surfaces within the harbor of Tokyo Bay, and sets the meteorologist ashore to collect weather information. Leaving, the submarine fights off a fleet of Japanese ships, sinking an aircraft carrier. The submarine is then attacked by destroyers, which drop depth charges on it. The *Copperfin* survives and makes it back to San Francisco.

The mission of the *Copperfin*—to deliver a meteorologist to Tokyo Bay—connects *Destination Tokyo* to one of the most celebrated events of World War II, for the weatherman is collecting data for the Doolittle raid, the historic "thirty seconds over Tokyo" during which sixteen American B-25s bombed the Japanese capital and four other cities. The Doolittle raid, which took place on April 18, 1942, did little damage to the Japanese but did wonders for American morale, which was then at a low ebb. The story of the raid was continued in two films during 1944: *Thirty Seconds Over Tokyo* and *The Purple Heart*. Both films reflect a change that had taken place in American war movies, a steady movement toward a more honest portrayal of war.

Mervyn LeRoy directed *Thirty Seconds Over Tokyo*. The screenplay, written by Dalton Trumbo, was based on a book by Ted Lawson, who had piloted one of the B-25s in Doolittle's raid. A semidocumentary, the film uses the real names of the participants in the raid: Lawson is played by Van Johnson; Doolittle is played by Spencer Tracy. The film covers the entire course of the raid as experienced by Lawson and the crew of his plane, the *Ruptured Duck*. All of the

fliers were volunteers, and the mission was kept secret—the fliers were forbidden to discuss it even among themselves. The training included learning to take off a B-25 in five hundred feet (the normal take-off distance being about fifteen hundred) because the plan involved ferrying the bombers to within striking distance of Tokyo on an aircraft carrier, the *Hornet*.

The sixteen planes successfully leave the pitching deck of the *Hornet*, fly low over choppy waves, and are soon above the roofs of Tokyo. Having dropped their bombs, the planes were supposed to have landed on an airstrip in occupied China; only one plane landed safely (in Russia); most of the others crash-landed in China; two came down in Japanese territory. Lawson and the crew of the *Ruptured Duck* crash-land on the coast of China and are aided by Chinese partisans. Lawson's leg, injured in

Right: *Robert Walker in* Thirty Seconds Over Tokyo *(1944).*

the crash, develops gangrene and has to be amputated by local medics. (Some viewers complained about the scene in which two nurses carry the wrapped-up limb down a corridor.) Lawson is ultimately reunited with his wife, and in his joy at seeing her, he forgets his missing leg and rises from his wheelchair, only to collapse to the floor.

The fate of the fliers downed over Japan in the Doolittle raid was covered in *The Purple Heart*, directed by Lewis Milestone. The film was very topical, for it was released shortly after the US government had issued reports of the Japanese torture of American prisoners of war. Darryl Zanuck, who wrote the screenplay under the pseudonym Melville Crossman, had little information to work with, but his account came close to reality: three of the captured fliers were executed by the Japanese in reprisal for the raid. In the film, eight fliers (among them Dana Andrews, Farley Granger, and Sam Levene) are captured by the Japanese after the Doolittle raid and are tried for murder. They are also mercilessly tortured. The Japanese want to know where the bombers came from (bombers had never before taken off from an aircraft carrier, and the use of the carrier was kept secret—President Roosevelt offered the explanation that the planes had come from Shangri-la). The men stubbornly recite their names, ranks, and serial numbers. The actual tortures are not shown; rather, terrible screams are heard coming from

behind closed doors. In the end, the heroic Americans are marched off down a hallway to be executed.

The grim brutality of *The Purple Heart* reflected a changing view of the war. By 1944, after more than two years of reading depressing headlines and seeing newsreels depicting the realities of combat, Americans were more aware than ever of the wide gulf between war movies and war. They were also becoming impatient. Although ultimate victory was supposedly within view, the casualty lists, most of them from faraway places Americans had never heard of, continued to lengthen. Like the soldiers overseas, Americans at home wanted escape from the war, and Hollywood complied by turning away from the battlefields to less traumatic areas. The most popular film of 1944 was *Going My Way*, directed by Leo McCarey, a sentimental tale of priests, starring Bing Crosby and Barry Fitzgerald. The film's tear-jerking theme of spiritual victory helped many Americans through difficult times. There was also *Four Jills in a Jeep*, directed by William Seiter, a silly story of actresses touring the battlefronts, starring Kay Francis, Carole Landis, Martha Raye, and Betty Grable. Grable also appeared in 1944's *Pin-Up Girl*, directed by H. Bruce Humberstone. Grable represented "the girl left behind" for millions of American servicemen, and the photo of her in a bathing suit, smiling over her shoulder, was the most popular pinup picture of the war.

Opposite: *Joseph Cotten and Claudette Colbert in* Since You Went Away *(1944).*

By 1944, the armed forces were able to make substantial contributions to films. For *Winged Victory* (1944), directed by George Cukor, the army provided more than a dozen technical advisers, the use of facilities at seven military bases, a cast of many hundreds, and unlimited equipment. (It was a good investment, for all the film's profits were given to Army Relief.) Based on a stage play by Moss Hart, the film deals with the training and testing of pilots—the title is the name of a Flying Fortress. A large portion of the film is devoted to the romantic lives of the cadets, the girl friends and wives they will leave behind.

The story of the women left behind was told in *Since You Went Away* (1944), written and produced by David O. Selznick and directed by John Cromwell. With millions of American men far from home and perhaps never coming back, the nation's heartstrings were painfully exposed, and *Since You Went Away* unerringly pulls them all. A tearjerker of awesome propor-

tions, the long, unabashedly emotional film was an enormous popular success. Set in 1943, the film tells the story of one "typical" American family, the Hiltons, and how it is affected by the war. Mr. Hilton (Neil Hamilton) has been drafted (he never appears in the film and is seen only in photographs), leaving behind Mrs. Hilton (Claudette Colbert) and their two daughters, Jane (Jennifer Jones) and Bridget (Shirley Temple). They live in "that unconquerable fortress—the American home." It is a very hotellike home, a dream culled from an illustrated magazine, and counts among its occupants a servant named Fidelia (Hattie McDaniel) and an old bulldog, who races from the lawn when the sprinklers are turned on. To make ends meet, Mrs. Hilton takes a boarder (Monty Woolley) and goes to work at a shipyard.

She and her busy family are visited by a crowd of people, including their boarder's grandson (Robert Walker), with whom Jane soon falls in love, and one of Mrs. Hilton's former suitors (Joseph Cotten). When her husband is re-

ported missing in action, Mrs. Hilton is heartbroken, but she bravely carries on. The grandson is drafted, and in one of the film's most famous scenes, Jane must say good-bye to him at a train station. News soon arrives that he has been killed in action. On Christmas Eve, with the absence of her husband more painful than ever, the telephone rings, and Mrs. Hilton learns that her husband is alive and well and coming home. It was exactly the victory millions of Americans prayed for.

I'll Be Seeing You (1944), directed by William Dieterle, is another tale of Christmas, 1943. A combat veteran suffering deep emotional damage (Joseph Cotten) meets and falls in love with a girl (Ginger Rogers). Both of them are home for Christmas. He is on a furlough from the army, and she has a ten-day pass from a penitentiary, where she has been doing time for manslaughter—she killed her boss when he made a pass at her. The girl's affection gives the soldier hope for the future; his does the same for her.

By 1944, films about the war had begun to exhibit the awareness that victory would not come through melodramatic heroics. To win the war, everyone would have to settle down and do his or her duty, no matter how disagreeable. Ordinary soldiers or sailors could not expect to understand "the big picture"; their role was to carry out their orders without questioning (not an easy thing for Americans). Officers, understanding the overall strategy and the necessity of sometimes losing in order to ultimately win, were faced with the agonizing responsibilities of sending men to their deaths. Winning the war was proving to be fully as traumatic as losing it: the heroic martyrs of *Bataan* and *Wake Island* were being replaced by men whose deaths, necessary for final victory, were less glorious.

The subtitle of *Wing and a Prayer* (1944), directed by Henry Hathaway, is *The Story of Carrier X.* The final credits explain that, for military reasons, the names of the carrier and the other ships could not be given. Of course, the produc-

ers could have used any invented names, but "X" served their purposes, lending a certain urgency to the film and involving the audience in the alleged secrecy. The film relates the day-to-day life of the members of a torpedo-plane squadron. Although full of exciting action and inserted battle footage, the film deals with a difficult situation: the carrier on which the action takes place is a decoy. Its job is to make appearances at various places throughout an area in the Pacific in an effort to mislead the Japanese about the actual location of the American fleet. The commander (Don Ameche) has to put up with the complaints of the crew, who want to fight the Japanese, not sail in circles. In one of the film's climactic scenes, the commander refuses to radio the location of the carrier to a lost pilot. Sometimes, seeming to retreat is an important tactic; sometimes, men must be sacrificed.

It wasn't enough just to get angry, grab a gun, and go shoot at Japs. Even John Wayne had to learn that lesson. *Fighting Seabees* (1944), directed by Edward Ludwig, begins with a team of civilian engineers returning from a mission on a Pacific island. Forbidden by international law to carry arms, the workers have been mauled by

the Japanese. "We're not fighting men anymore, we're fighting animals," explains a navy officer named Yarrow (Dennis O'Keefe). Wedge Donovan (Wayne), the man who organized the construction team, is eager to fight "Tojo and his bug-eyed pals." Donovan and Yarrow discuss the possibilities of creating a special battalion of trained and armed construction engineers. Yarrow also introduces Donovan to his girl friend, a red-haired newspaper correspondent (Susan Hayward), establishing a love triangle that proves fatal to one of the men. The impatient Donovan does not want to have his men trained: they already know how to fight. He goes on the next expedition and brings along a supply of rifles. When the Japs attack, he and his untrained civilians blunder into the middle of a battle, and their foolhardy heroism gets many men killed. Finally convinced that his men need training, Donovan assists in the formation of the navy's Construction Battalions (CBs, or Seabees). Back in the Pacific (on an island referred to only as X-371), Donovan and his men again tangle with the Japs. This time the result is more satisfying. The construction workers use their equipment well. Pushing a Jap tank over a cliff   93

Opposite: Fighting Seabees (1944).

with a bulldozer, Donovan declares, "That'll teach 'em to monkey with construction men!" It is Donovan who is finally killed, and the film ends with a speech commemorating the Seabees: "We build for fighters. We fight for what we build."

Fighting the ruthless Japanese demanded equally ruthless methods. One of the few films to deal with America's Chinese allies in the fight against the Japanese was *Dragon Seed* (1944), directed by Jack Conway. Based on a novel by Pearl S. Buck, the story concerns Chinese peasants in an area occupied by the Japanese. The stars of the film, including Katharine Hepburn and Walter Huston (almost inevitable in any film about an occupied land), were made up to appear Oriental (their eyes were stretched). Playing a character named Jade, Hepburn organizes the local peasants to fight the Japanese. She adopts the Russian "scorched-earth" tactic and has the farmers burn their crops to prevent them from falling into the Japanese hands. Then she prepares a surprise for a victory party given by the snarling Japanese officers: she puts poison in their food. They writhe in agony as they die.

What life was like in Japan itself before and during the war was a subject left untouched by American filmmakers, in large part because they had no material with which to work. Such was not the case with Nazi Germany, but the movies about life inside Germany succumbed to a sort of stasis: most were about prewar Germany, probably because most were based on

stories written before the war. The screenplay for *Address Unknown* (1944), directed by William Cameron Menzies, was based on a story that had first appeared in *Story Magazine* in 1938. The film begins in the summer of 1932, when Martin Schulz (Paul Lukas), a German who has been living in America for many years and is co-owner of a San Francisco art gallery, returns to Germany for business. While there, he embraces Nazi doctrines. When he betrays his son's fiancée, a Jewish actress, to the Nazis, his son (Peter Van Eyck) takes revenge by sending him letters in code. As the son anticipated, the letters are all opened by the Nazis, who accuse Schulz of espionage. His pleas of innocence go unheeded. The son knows he has achieved his end when his last letter is returned from Germany marked "address unknown."

Menzies was an art director and set designer before he was a director, and his vision of Nazi Germany is truly remarkable, a baroque world of extravagant proportions, enormous rooms with giant paintings of Hitler and huge swastikas hanging from the walls.

The Seventh Cross (1944), directed by Fred Zinnemann, is set in 1936. When seven men escape from the Westhofen concentration camp, the camp's commandant has seven trees stripped and made into crosses. As each of the men is caught, he is tortured and then tied to a cross and left to die of exposure. Eventually, six men are hanging from six trees: the seventh cross remains bare, for its intended victim (Spen-

The Seventh Cross *(1944).*

cer Tracy) escapes capture. He succeeds in reaching Mainz, his hometown, where he is helped by various people. In fact, his cynical view of mankind is changed by the courage of the people who risk their lives to hide him from the Gestapo. With their help, he eventually makes it to freedom.

The Seventh Cross is remarkable for its sympathetic portrayal of the German people. The fugitive finds a strong current of anti-Nazism, and the film implies that most Germans were not evil Nazis but merely allowed themselves to drift into Nazi rule. It was a little too late to make amends. The novel that the screenplay was based on had been first published, in German, in 1939; the English translation had appeared in 1942. Anna Seghers (the pen name of Netty Reiling Radvanyi), the author of the novel, was herself a German refugee from the Nazis. A member of the Communist party, she had fled Germany in 1933 and gone to live in Mexico City. She returned to Germany in 1947 and lived in East Berlin, where she died in 1983.

The terrifying psychology of the Nazis is abundantly evident in *Ministry of Fear* (1944), directed by Fritz Lang and based on a novel by Graham Greene. The film begins with Stephen Neale (Ray Milland) being released from an English asylum, where he has been serving a two-year sentence for murder, accused of the mercy killing of his wife. He wins a cake at a charity bazaar and soon finds himself in deep trouble, framed for another murder and chased by some very nasty characters. The cake contained microfilmed invasion plans, and the Nazis—of whom there is a large number in England—want them. The action takes place during the Blitz, with blackout curtains over every window and the occasional sound of sirens followed by a far-off rumble that only grows louder until buildings explode. Plagued by self-doubts and confronted by an inexplicable riddle, Neale becomes involved with such organizations as the Mothers of the Free Nations and the Ministry of Home Security. Fear is the Nazis' prime weapon, and before he can extricate himself, Neale meets some very ruthless Germans.

Even singly, Nazis were powerful enemies. *Lifeboat* (1944), directed by Alfred Hitchcock and based on a story by John Steinbeck, presents an allegory of the war in which one Nazi proves more than a match for eight representatives of the Allied cause. The action of the film takes place in a lifeboat in the North Atlantic. In the small boat are eight survivors of a torpedoed freighter and the captain of the German submarine that sank the freighter. The survivors include a vain female journalist (Tallulah Bankhead); a nurse (Mary Anderson); a tough stoker of Czech ancestry (John Hodiak); a radio operator (Hume Cronyn); a shipping magnate (Henry Hull); a distraught mother (Heather Angel), clutching her dead child; a black steward (Canada Lee); and a wounded crewman (William Bendix). Thrown together in the lifeboat, these representatives of democracy bicker constantly, indulge in self-pity, and reveal themselves as weak and miserably unprepared. Their divergent beliefs and opinions prevent them from agreeing on a concerted action. Far different is the German captain (Walter Slezak). He is determined and unemotional, prepared and resourceful. He has a compass, vitamins, and a chemical for making seawater potable. He is firm in his convictions and sure of what he must do. He also has a plan, and by taking advantage of the confused "allies," he nearly accomplishes his end.

Hitchcock meant the film as a warning: to defeat the Nazis, the world's democracies would have to forget their squabbles and join in a united effort. If they did not do so, the Nazis' dedication to their cause would triumph.

Hitchcock was fond of getting himself into his films, and with *Lifeboat* he was faced with a difficult situation: it would be impossible for him to suddenly appear in a lifeboat adrift in the middle of the ocean. He solved the problem handily by appearing as the "before and after" model in an ad for a weight-reduction product ("Reduco, the obesity slayer") on the back of a newspaper read by William Bendix.

Few war movies were released during the last year of the war. The public was weary of them, the efforts to make them realistic—they had to compete with newsreels—made them expensive to produce, and victory was in sight: 95

Left: *Walter Slezak* (left), *John Hodiak, Hume Cronyn, Henry Hull, Tallulah Bankhead, Mary Anderson, William Bendix, Heather Angel, and Canada Lee in* Lifeboat *(1944).*
Below: *Alan Hale* (left) *and Dennis Morgan in* God Is My Co-Pilot *(1945).*

foreseeing the end of the war, filmmakers did not want to be caught with unsalable products. The war movies released during the first six months of 1945 showed little change from previous films. *Counter-Attack*, directed by Zoltan Korda, praised the courage of the Russians: Paul Muni stars as the leader of a group of Soviet paratroopers dropped behind enemy lines to attack a German headquarters. *Objective, Burma*, directed by Raoul Walsh, deals with 50 American paratroopers dropped 180 miles behind enemy lines to destroy a Japanese radar station as preparation for the reinvasion of Burma. They succeed in blowing up the station, but the plan to airlift them out of the area has to be aborted,

forcing them to fight their way out through the Japanese-infested jungle. The atmosphere of the jungle, including the calls of native birds and the buzzing of insects, is made apparent, as is the brutality of the enemy, who torture and mutilate prisoners. Only a dozen of the original fifty survive the journey.

Objective, Burma was attacked by British critics for giving the impression that Americans alone had fought the Japanese in Burma. The outcry against the film led to its withdrawal in Britain. It was rereleased in 1952 with an explanatory introduction.

God Is My Co-Pilot, directed by Robert Florey, presents the biography of Colonel Robert Lee Scott, known to his comrades as "the one-man air force." An inspirational film full of religious overtones, *God Is My Co-Pilot* recounts Scott's (Dennis Morgan) love of flying, from his first attempts (jumping off the roof of a barn with an umbrella as a parachute) through his career flying the mail, his days at West Point, and, at the age of thirty-four, his membership in the Flying Tigers. (Raymond Massey plays Claire Chennault.) Although considered overage, Scott manages to wreak havoc on the Japanese, shooting down the notorious Jap ace, Tokyo Joe (Richard Loo), and twelve other Japanese planes. The fact that he has survived so many dangerous missions makes Scott believe that he is not alone when he takes off in his P-40. A missionary priest named "Big Mike" Harrigan (Alan Hale) agrees, telling Scott, "Son, you're not up there alone. You have the greatest co-pilot in the world."

There were victories to be celebrated, of course. *Back to Bataan*, directed by Edward Dmytryk, begins and ends with scenes of the rescue of American prisoners of war from the Japanese prison camp at Cabanatuan in the Philippines. Twelve of the men actually rescued are shown marching by (the raid on the prison camp took place in January 1945; the film was released in May). Between these scenes, the film recounts the history of the war in the Philippines, beginning with the fall of Bataan and ending with the American reinvasion of the islands. Following the Japanese attack, an American colonel named Madden (John Wayne) stays behind to organize a resistance movement. He is aided by a Filipino named Bonifacio (Anthony Quinn), whom he rescues from the Bataan "Death March." With a small band of insurgents, the two inflict great damage on the Japanese and prepare the way for the American return.

It is clear that the Japanese are cruel oppressors: when the principal of a local school refuses to lower the American flag, he is hanged. Talking about their "Greater East Asia Co-Prosperity Sphere," the Japanese try to win the Filipinos over to their side. According to the Japanese, it is the Americans who are the true invaders, beginning with the Battle of Manila Bay. The Filipinos are proud of their national heritage, but they have come to value the benefits of friendship with the United States, benefits that include hot dogs, baseball, and liberty (although one courageous boy has trouble spelling the word).

In the midst of its overdone action scenes, *Back to Bataan* shows the maturing of Hollywood war movies. Compared to the battle scenes in *Bataan*, those in *Back to Bataan* are noticeably more realistic, conveying a strong sense of fear and pain—wounded men scream. There is also some of the introspective philosophizing that characterizes later films. The farewell "I'll be seeing you" is used many times in the film and is made touching by frequent discussions of how in wartime people meet and then soon separate, never to see one another again. Victory celebrations were accompanied by memories of the dead.

A Bell for Adano (1945), directed by Henry King, celebrates another kind of victory. Based on a Pulitzer Prize-winning novel by John Hersey, the film tells a sensitive and moving story of the postwar reconstruction of a Sicilian fishing village. Major Joppolo (John Hodiak), a civil affairs administrator, and Sergeant Borth (William Bendix) approach the problems of the town in frequently unconventional ways, basing their decisions on the human and spiritual needs of the community even when doing so involves conflict with their bureaucratic superiors. The Americans manage to overcome the suspicions of the townspeople and teach them the meaning of democracy. They also help the town replace its cherished bell, the original having been melted down by the Fascists to make bullets.

Opposite: *Errol Flynn* (left) in Objective, Burma *(1945).*

The memory of those who died, the friends, lovers, and comrades known for a short but unforgettable time, provides the basis of *The Way to the Stars (Johnny in the Clouds)* (1945), directed by Anthony Asquith. One of the last British-made films of World War II, it was released after the war in Europe had ended. Indeed, by the time it appeared, the story of the war could be told in flashback and was becoming the source of nostalgia. The film begins with a deserted airfield, grass growing through the cement, debris scattered across the runway. It then moves back to the time, 1940, when the airfield was full of people and activity. The film does not stress aerial combat but centers, instead, on the lives of the airmen, particularly their romantic involvements. The British RAF pilots (including Michael Redgrave and John Mills) are joined by Americans (including Douglass Montgomery). The two groups bicker and then become friends; they have various relationships with the local women, and most of them die. The film evokes the atmosphere of the period, one of enormous tension mixed with humor and restrained courage. The nostalgia of the film is for more than just the unforgotten dead—it is also for the war itself, and its undeniable power to heighten every experience.

The best American films of World War II appeared as the war ended: *The Story of GI Joe* and *A Walk in the Sun*, both about infantrymen in Europe; and *They Were Expendable*, about PT boats in the Pacific.

Released just after the war in Europe had ended, *The Story of GI Joe* (1945), directed by William Wellman, is based on the news stories of war correspondent Ernie Pyle. Pyle was the most popular correspondent of the war, loved by American GIs because he wrote about the experiences of ordinary soldiers rather than about battles or generals. He was not concerned with the "big picture," but only with the close horizon of the plodding foot soldier. He traveled with fighting soldiers through the campaigns in North Africa, Europe, and the Pacific.

With his head shaved to imitate Pyle's baldness, Burgess Meredith plays Pyle (Pyle himself had requested him). The film begins with Pyle's arrival in North Africa and ends with him on the road to Rome; without a plot, the film follows incidents in the daily existence of an infantry unit. A sense of documentary authenticity is achieved through the use of actual battle footage, but far more important is the fact that the film has no contrived heroics and no inspiring speeches. All the same, it is an eloquent film, a powerful statement of the world of the infantryman, a small, uncomfortable world full of rain and mud, short tempers, sudden, unexpected violence, whimsical humor, and a lot of boredom.

The film is related from Pyle's point of view. When men that he has come to know and like go off to fight, he remains behind. When they don't come back, he knows they're dead. The group's lieutenant (Robert Mitchum), a strong, capable man, holds the soldiers together. At the end of the film, his dead body, laid over a donkey, is brought down a hill and without ceremony added to a row of dead bodies beside the road to Rome. The loss is shattering, both to the surviving soldiers and to the audience.

General Eisenhower called *The Story of GI Joe* "the greatest war picture I've ever seen." GIs who saw the film claimed it was true to life. More than one hundred veterans of the Italian campaign took part in the film as extras. When work on the film was completed, they were shipped off to the Pacific, where there was still a war on. Many of them died there, as did Ernie Pyle, killed by a Japanese sniper's bullet on Ie Shima.

They Were Expendable (1945), directed by John Ford, was released two months after the Japanese surrender. The screenplay for the film was based on a book by William L. White about John Bulkeley, the man who had pioneered the use of PT boats in the Pacific. Ford, who had risen to the rank of rear admiral in the navy, knew Bulkeley; in the film, Bulkeley's name is changed to Brickley, and the part is played by Robert Montgomery, who had commanded a PT boat in the Pacific. Also starring is John Wayne, as a fictional character named Rusty Ryan. Both men portray PT boat commanders.

The story concerns the heroic actions of PT boats in the Philippines following the attack on Pearl Harbor. Until Pearl Harbor, the PT boats were derided as a "splinter fleet," little more

than pleasure craft. But with the Japanese invasion, the tough, fast-moving boats became essential weapons. Against overwhelming odds, the crews of the boats stall the enemy, sacrificing themselves to buy time for the retreating Americans. The crewmen of the PT boats are the "expendables," and their heroism lies in their unquestioning—if fatalistic—determination to perform their duty. They go on suicidal raids against the Japanese and help in the evacuation of General Douglas MacArthur from Bataan to Australia. Their losses are always terrible.

The film is made compelling by its straightforward presentation of men at war, their respect for rank, acceptance of duty, and, above all, their firm belief in the cause for which they are fighting. It was a matter of "victory in defeat," and the film makes viewers painfully aware of what that meant to the men who died so that others could continue fighting.

The last of the wartime combat films, *A Walk in the Sun*, was released in December 1945. Directed by Lewis Milestone and based on a novel by Harry Brown, the film relates the events of one September morning as experienced by a platoon of American infantrymen who land at Salerno and take "a little walk in the warm Italian sun." The film begins with a landing craft approaching the beachhead. Before the boat reaches the shore, the platoon's young lieutenant is fatally wounded. The sergeant who assumes command is killed on the beach. The remaining members of the platoon, eventually led by Sergeant Tyne (Dana Andrews), move inland, following their orders to capture a farmhouse six miles from the beach. It takes most of the morning to reach their objective, and along the way they are strafed by German planes, encounter two enthusiastically surrendering Italian soldiers, and have a confrontation with a German armored car. However, most of the battle takes place beyond their view. The war seems to be going on somewhere over the next hill; there is the sound of distant gunfire, and shells screech over their heads—smoke curls up over the horizon. They finally reach the farmhouse, which is occupied by Germans. After a bitter fight, they take possession of the building at noon.

Like *The Story of GI Joe*, *A Walk in the Sun*

has no mock heroics. It is about the experiences of ordinary soldiers, and it evokes the atmosphere of anxious waiting mixed with boredom. The GIs are concerned only with what is directly in front of them, and their sole interest is to stay alive, to survive each encounter with the enemy. As one says, "Everything in the army is simple: you live or you die." There are no propaganda statements, no expressions of patriotic fervor. The soldiers are ordinary men far from where they want to be.

The platoon (introduced in the opening credits by Burgess Meredith) is a traditional American outfit, counting among its members a former boxing champ, a minister's son, a farmer, a slow southerner, an Italian-American, and a Brooklyn Jew. The Italian-American, Rivera (Richard Conte), and the Brooklynite, Friedman (George Tyne), man a machine gun. Whether walking along a road or crouching in a foxhole, they carry on a lively, at times significant banter. They are Captain Flagg and Sergeant Quirt in a new war, a war that isn't fun for anyone. There are no

nurses to quarrel over, no barroom brawls to relieve the tension. The only glory to look forward to is returning home in one piece.

There are hints of nostalgia in *A Walk in the Sun*, including a ballad that portrays the GIs as modern folk heroes. There is also the sense of despair over lost friends that characterizes films made near the end of the war. "It's a funny thing how many people you meet in the army and never see again," remarks Sergeant Tyne. But the story of the film is the GIs and their experience of the war. They treat one another with rough compassion and try to prove that regardless of the uniforms they are wearing they are still individual men. Their strongest weapon is irony. As Rivera says, several times, "Nobody dies." A lot of men die in the wheat field in front of the farmhouse. But not Rivera and his pal, Friedman. When the shooting stops, they are still alive. They enjoy a brief noontime rest, another opportunity to think about going home.

For most GIs, thoughts of going home were mixed with anxiousness about what was waiting

100

Opposite: *Fredric March in* The Best Years of Our Lives *(1946).*

for them. The veterans of World War II were well aware of what had happened to the veterans of World War I, who had returned home heroes only to find themselves without work. The Bonus Marchers of 1932 and onetime heroes selling apples on street corners were still vivid memories. Nor was getting a job the only concern of the returning veterans. They had been away from their homes and families for a long time, and they worried about whether their wives or girl friends still felt the same way about them. They were coming home changed men—how would they fit back into society?

These fears were compounded for those veterans who were coming home wounded. In an effort to allay some of their fears, the government financed a remake of *The Enchanted Cottage*. The 1945 version, directed by John Cromwell, begins with Robert Young and his bride (Hillary Brooke) about to leave on their honeymoon. Their plans are canceled when he is called off to war. He returns from the war disfigured by a wound. His wife wants nothing to do with him, but a homely maid (Dorothy McGuire)

falls in love with him. They go to a New England cottage that has been used by countless happy newlyweds. There is magic in the place, in the air, the flowers, the rooms, and the two are transformed in each other's eyes. Their love removes all ugliness.

The problems facing wounded veterans were dealt with more directly in *Pride of the Marines* (1945), directed by Delmer Daves. The screenplay, by Albert Maltz, was based on the true story of Al Schmid, a marine who was blinded by a hand grenade while heroically holding off the enemy on Guadalcanal. Schmid (John Garfield) is sent back to a hospital in the United States, where he and the other veterans discuss their worries about finding jobs, seeing former lovers, and fitting back into society. "It won't be like 1930 again," maintains one. "How do I know anyone will ever want me?" asks another. Schmid has a girl friend, Ruth (Eleanor Parker), but he doesn't want to go home to her, doesn't believe she could still love him, and doesn't want her pity. Schmid (and through him all other wounded veterans) is finally convinced that "no one was a sucker," that the war was one that had to be won, and that their sacrifices are appreciated by all Americans. Helped by Ruth's sincere love, Schmid regains his pride. He accepts the Navy Cross, a symbol of his heroism. He also learns that he can have his old job back. There is even the hope that he might someday see again. Getting into a taxicab with Ruth, he gives the cabbie their destination: "Home."

Veterans going home was also the theme of *The Best Years of Our Lives* (1946), directed by William Wyler, one of the most popular films of the postwar era and an enduring classic of American filmmaking. The screenplay, written by Robert Sherwood, was based on *Glory for Me*, a novel written in free verse by MacKinlay Kantor. It is the story of three returning veterans: Al Stephenson (Fredric March), an infantry sergeant; Fred Derry (Dana Andrews), a decorated air force captain; and Homer (Harold Russell), a sailor who has lost both of his arms below the elbow and has articulated hooks in place of hands. The three meet on their way home—they are all returning to the same town, Boone City, and with their experiences of the war separating them from the civilians around them, they become friends. Like all returning veterans, they take off their uniforms and resume their "real" lives: the middle-aged Al was a banker; Fred, in his twenties, was a soda jerk in a drugstore; Homer, just old enough to drink, was in high school. Al has a wife (Myrna Loy) and children; Fred has a wife (Virginia Mayo); Homer has his high school sweetheart (Cathy O'Donnell). Readjusting to civilian life is difficult for all three. Al rebels against the selfish business ethics forced on him: "Last year it was 'kill Japs'; this year it's 'make money.'" He finds his wife unchanged, but his children are strangers, his son full of enthusiasm for the atomic wars of the future. Fred, the air force hero, is woefully out of place behind the soda fountain, and he comes home to every serviceman's worst fear: an unfaithful wife. Homer's girl friend has remained loyal, but he has to endure the excessive pity of his family.

Without denying the very real problems facing all returning veterans, the film ends optimistically. Even Fred, who has lost his wife and his job, finds hope for the future. He has fallen in love with Al's daughter (Teresa Wright), and he finds new employment. Wandering through a junkyard full of discarded war planes, he is offered a job helping to convert the planes into homes for returning soldiers. Like the planes, Fred has a place in the postwar world.

The Best Years of Our Lives won seven Academy Awards, including best picture and best director. Harold Russell, a real amputee (he had lost both hands in the explosion of a grenade), was given two awards, one as best supporting actor and a special award "for bringing hope and courage to his fellow veterans." In 1964, he was made chairman of the President's Council on Hiring the Handicapped, and in 1980, he appeared in another film, *Inside Moves*, directed by Richard Donner.

The story of *The Best Years of Our Lives* was repeated, updated for another war, in *I Want You* (1951), directed by Mark Robson and starring Dana Andrews. The film relates the effects of the Korean War on a typical American family. In 1975, *The Best Years of Our Lives* was remade as *Returning Home*, a television movie directed by Daniel Petrie. The three returning veterans are played by Dabney Coleman, Tom Selleck, and James R. Miller. Like Harold Russell, Miller is an amputee—he lost both his hands in Vietnam attempting to throw back a hand grenade.

Till the End of Time (1946), directed by Edward Dmytryk and based on a novel by Niven Busch, *The Dream of Home*, tells the story of three marines and their problematic homecomings. Young Guy Madison comes home to find that his parents still treat him like a kid; Robert Mitchum returns with a silver plate in his skull that seems to induce wildness; Bill Williams, a former boxer, comes back with both legs amputated.

Homecoming (1948), directed by Mervyn LeRoy, deals with a different sort of problem. Clark Gable makes it home to his wife (Anne Baxter) without any visible wounds, but he has had a love affair while overseas (with Lana Turner) that he cannot forget. The "other woman" is dead, however, and he eventually confesses to his wife and begs her understanding.

Marlon Brando made his screen debut in *The Men* (1950), directed by Fred Zinnemann with a screenplay by Carl Foreman. Brando plays a paraplegic, paralyzed from the waist down by a sniper's bullet. Understandably embittered by his fate, he rejects the affection of his girl friend (Teresa Wright), insisting that they could never have a life together. Much of the film was shot in the Birmingham (Alabama) Veterans' Hospital, and forty-five actual paraplegics were given roles in the film, infusing it with a powerful sense of realism. To prepare himself for the role, Brando spent time living with the veterans in the hospital.

To make his performance as a blind veteran in *Bright Victory* realistic, Arthur Kennedy wore opaque contact lenses that rendered him sightless. Directed by Mark Robson, *Bright Victory* (1951) relates the treatment and rehabilitation of Sergeant Larry Nevins (Kennedy), a soldier blinded by a sniper's bullet. Like *The Men, Bright Victory* uses a veterans' hospital, Valley Forge General, for many of its scenes, and like most films about the rehabilitation of injured servicemen, Nevins is helped by the love of a girl (Peggy Dow).

Bright Victory deals with how Nevins over-

Marlon Brando and Teresa Wright in
The Men *(1950).*

comes his despair and finds the courage to face the future. The movie is also concerned with how he deals with another malady, one that he had even before the war: racism. Being blind, Nevins cannot see his fellow hospital inmates. He becomes very friendly with one man (James Edwards), only to be shocked when he finds out the man is black. This second form of blindness proves more curable than the first.

James Edwards and director Mark Robson had already worked together on a film about racism, *Home of the Brave* (1949). The screenplay for the film was written by Carl Foreman, based on a play by Arthur Laurents. The play is about

anti-Semitism; in the film, the subject is changed to racial bigotry. The film begins with an army doctor (Jeff Corey) trying to uncover the psychosomatic reasons for a soldier's (Edwards) paralysis. Although not physically wounded, the man cannot walk. Using drugs and some very straightforward talk, the doctor eventually induces the soldier to relate his story, which begins with a childhood full of hatred and segregation and ends with his participation in a dangerous patrol during which his best friend (Lloyd Bridges) is killed. It was his momentary sense of elation that it was his friend and not himself who was killed that brought on his

Below: *Leo G. Carroll* (right) *in*
The House on 92nd Street *(1945).*

breakdown. The realization cures him. (When it was first released, the film was banned in South Africa on the grounds that it might "disturb the peace.")

Home of the Brave was only one of several films about important social problems that were made during the late forties. Like Al Stephenson in *The Best Years of Our Lives*, Americans were reexamining their values and beliefs. The war had been won, but the victors were not all that their propaganda claimed. Along with liberty and justice, America was home to some very real inequities and prejudices. The experience of the war led American filmmakers to confront previously tabu subjects. Guided by the realistic wartime documentaries and by the starkly realistic films coming from postwar Italy, American filmmakers suddenly—and for a very brief period—demonstrated a powerful social consciousness.

Crossfire (1947), directed by Edward Dmytryk, is about anti-Semitism. An insanely bigoted ex-GI (Robert Ryan) murders a Jew and is eventually caught by the police (led by Robert Young). The screenplay for the film was based on a novel, *The Brick Foxhole*, by Richard Brooks. The victim in the novel is a homosexual, but ho-

mosexuality was still beyond the pale of American filmmakers, and the subject was changed to anti-Semitism.

In the same vein was *Gentleman's Agreement* (1947), directed by Elia Kazan, the story of a magazine writer who, assigned to write a story about anti-Semitism, pretends that he is a Jew and discovers anti-Semitism in every corner of society—in his office, among his friends, even in his fiancée.

Along with these so-called problem films were semidocumentaries, the first of which was *The House on 92nd Street* (1945), directed by Henry Hathaway, the story of FBI agents tracking down Nazi spies in New York City. This was the first major Hollywood production filmed on actual locations rather than on studio sets. The producer of the film was Louis de Rochemont, who had been responsible for the "March of Time" newsreels.

The House on 92nd Street inspired a cycle of semidocumentary films, including *13 Rue Madeleine* (1946), another film directed by Hathaway and produced by De Rochemont. This film relates the story of the Office of Strategic Services (OSS), the first US intelligence agency, and

deals with a secret mission to France (led by James Cagney). Foreshadowing the paranoia soon to grip the nation, the film begins and ends with an inscription outside the OSS headquarters: "What is past is prologue." The OSS was disbanded in 1945, but its intelligence-gathering functions were continued by the Central Intelligence Agency (CIA), established in 1947. One war was over; another, the Cold War, had already begun. Hollywood's liberalism was to be short-lived.

The realism of many of these postwar American films—particularly the use of nonprofessional actors, as in *The Men*—was compared to the neorealist films being made at that time in Italy. The experience of the war had had a profound effect on that nation's filmmakers, turning them away from contrived plots and professional actors to confront directly and as accurately as possible actual social situations.

It was *Open City (Rome, Open City)* (1945), directed by Roberto Rossellini, that established the postwar Italian cinema and gave neorealism its clearest expression. Rossellini and his associates (including Sergio Amidei and Federico Fellini) began working on the film immediately after the German evacuation of Rome. Using a camera stolen from the Nazis and shooting the scenes in natural light, Rossellini created a moving and sometimes shocking account of the underground movement during the German occupation of Rome. The film is so realistic that some viewers thought they were seeing a newsreel. The story involves real characters—the priest Don Pietro is based on Don Morosini, a priest executed by the Germans; the Communist partisan Manfredi is based on a Resistance leader named Celeste Megarville—and Rossellini shot many scenes at the actual sites of incidents. The stars of the film, including Aldo Fabrizi as Don Pietro, Marcello Pagliero as Manfredi, and Anna Magnani, worked for minuscule salaries and were joined by numerous nonprofessional actors, recruited from the streets, many of whom worked for nothing more than a good meal. The story follows actual events as closely as possible, including horrific torture scenes. These scenes accurately present the

connection between Nazi cruelty and sexual perversion. (From *Hitler's Children* to the sadomasochistic films of the seventies and eighties, such as *The Night Porter*, this aspect of Nazi cruelty has been a source of titillation. It was quite different for those who experienced it.)

Open City was enormously successful in most western countries, but not in Germany, where it was banned until 1961. Even then, the film was presented in a heavily cut version, the scenes of torture in particular being truncated. It was also felt necessary to add a prologue: "This film does not attack the German people. It does not attack the German soldier. It describes the fight of freedom-loving people against despotism and tryanny."

Rossellini followed the success of *Open City* with *Paisan (Paisà)* (1946), another film shot on actual locations with the use of nonprofessional actors. The film is composed of six episodes, each presenting a different aspect of the war in Italy. The episodes concern GIs in Sicily; Naples after its liberation by American troops; the liberation of Rome; street fighting in Florence; the visit of three American Army chaplains to a monastery in the hills near Bologna; and bitter fighting in the marshlands of the Po River delta. As with *Open City*, the power of *Paisan* is its intense humanism and its ironic optimism, which are the result not of a glorified view of people but of an intimate awareness of their weaknesses, an awareness that makes their acts of courage and self-sacrifice deeply moving.

For *Germany Year Zero* (1947), the last in this trilogy of war movies, Rossellini went to war-devastated Berlin. The story concerns a young boy who kills his father and commits suicide, his actions the result of Nazification and despair brought on by the German defeat.

Neorealism did not survive the period that had given it birth. Postwar Italy's improving economic conditions made its despairing attitudes unpopular, and it was suppressed by the Italian government, which looked with great disfavor on its depiction of the underside of Italian life (a potentially Marxist view).

Germany was in ruins and divided in 1945. During the immediate postwar years, several films were made about the war and its causes.

The majority of these films came from the Eastern Zone. Wolfgang Staudte (who, as an actor, had had a role in the infamous *Jud Süss*) directed *The Murderers Are Among Us* (1946), about the difficulties of tracking down Nazi war criminals, many of whom had managed to avoid detection and were becoming leading citizens in postwar Germany. This was the first of the so-called rubble films, films made in the ruins of Germany's cities. *Somewhere in Berlin* (1946), directed by Gerhard Lamprecht, is about German soldiers returning home, half-starved, to their war-torn homeland. Kurt Maetzig directed *Marriage in the Shadows* (1947), a recounting of the true story of the actor Joachim Gottschalk, who married a Jewish actress and, when the Nazis wanted to take her away, committed suicide with her rather than face separation.

These grimly realistic, soul-searching films came to an end during the early 1950s. As in Italy, improving economic conditions in Germany led to the desire for pleasant entertainment, not melancholy reminders of the past.

In the Soviet Union, the end of the war was followed by several large-scale, epic celebrations of victory, communism, and, in particular, Joseph Stalin. *The Battle of Stalingrad* (1950), directed by Vladimir Petrov, and *The Fall of Berlin* (1950), directed by Mikhail Chiaureli, were both so long that each had to be shown in two parts. These films present glorifications of the Soviet side of the war; Russia's former allies, the United States and Great Britain, are portrayed only slightly more sympathetically than are the Germans.

The end of the long, terrible war bequeathed filmmakers an inexhaustible subject: the legions of the dead could be made to arise and fight again and again, enemies could become friends and friends enemies, and generations yet unborn could experience some of the drama and spectacle of an entire world at war.

The grave of a German soldier, from
Stalingrad (1943), a Russian documentary.

107

THE
FIFTIES
AND
KOREA

Like the end of World War I, the end of World War II was followed by a brief respite from war movies, but the period following World War II was very short, lasting fewer than four years. *Battleground* (1949) is frequently credited with renewing the popularity of war movies, but it was only one of a group of films. Beginning in 1948, war returned to movie theaters, and it stayed there for the next thirty years.

One of the first postwar combat films was *Fighter Squadron* (1948), directed by Raoul Walsh. Edmond O'Brien stars as a veteran of the Flying Tigers who leads a squadron of fighters in Europe and argues with superior officers over tactics. The fliers, including Robert Stack and Rock Hudson (in his screen debut), are valiant in their attacks on the Nazis. One of them, strafing a train, happily radios his comrades, "Hey, I've been working on the railroad!" O'Brien is shot down during the D-day invasion, but his men assure one another that his spirit will live on.

Critics compared *Fighter Squadron* to a popular Broadway play by William Wister Haines, *Command Decision.* The play became a film in 1948, directed by Sam Wood. The theme of *Command Decision* is the pressures of leadership. Clark Gable stars as a brigadier general in command of a group of American bombers in England. Not only must he suffer the agonies of sending young men to their deaths, but he must also battle with superior officers, congressmen, and Defense Department officials about the strategies he employs, in particular, the daylight bombing of Germany.

Twelve O'Clock High (1949), directed by Henry King, is dedicated to the American fliers who pioneered daylight bombing. The beginning of the movie is reminiscent of the beginning of *The Way to the Stars*: Dean Jagger visits an abandoned airfield in England, where cows graze on the grass growing through cracks in the cement runway. As he looks out over the deserted airfield, he remembers the songs of the war and the sounds of bombers returning from a mission. In flashback, the film relates the story of the 918th Bomber Group of the Eighth Air Force and its commander (Gregory Peck). Peck takes over command of the bomber group when he decides that the acting commander (Gary Merrill)

is identifying too much with the men, creating a morale problem. A strict disciplinarian, Peck relentlessly drives the fliers to achieve their "maximum effort." He solves their morale problem with pride. Their initial resentment turns to respect, and he succeeds in making them into a powerful combat force, but at the expense of his own sanity. The responsibilities of leadership eventually bring him to an emotional and psychological collapse.

The responsibility of command is also the theme of *Sands of Iwo Jima* (1949), directed by Allan Dwan and based on a story by Harry Brown, author of *A Walk in the Sun.* The film is famous for its battle scenes and its ardent patriotism, and the image of John Wayne as Sergeant John M. Stryker made its way deep into the national imagination. The film has little of the serious reflection of *Twelve O'Clock High*: it is a rousing, "action-packed" tribute to America's fighting prowess, the kind of film that would fill the next decade. It is better than the films that followed it because it displays an honest affection for the marines. Tough Sergeant Stryker is a merciless taskmaster, and his men resent his brutal training methods. ("Saddle up!" yells Stryker, whenever he wants his men to move out.) Private Conway (John Agar) has a particular dislike for Stryker. Conway's father, a marine colonel, was killed on Guadalcanal. Stryker served under the colonel and has nothing but praise for the dead man; Private Conway has no fond memories of his father, who considered him "soft." Just as he rebelled against his father, Conway rebels against Stryker. The squad's opinion of their sergeant changes during their first encounter with the Japanese, on Tarawa, in which they learn the value of what he has taught them. On Iwo Jima, Stryker's squad takes part in the flag raising on Mount Suribachi, but Stryker is killed, shot by a sniper. His marines are ready to carry on without him. Private Conway proves that he has learned the truth about the Marine Corps by repeating Stryker's familiar command. "All right," he orders. "Saddle up! Let's get back to the war."

Sands of Iwo Jima was made with the full cooperation of the Marine Corps. For the flag-raising sequence, the actual flag was used, and

110

three of the men who had taken part in the event (Rene A. Gagnon, Ira H. Hayes, and John H. Bradley) repeated their actions for the film.

Such historical verisimilitude became an important feature of post-World War II war movies. America's film producers had access to an abundant supply of actual battle footage, which, properly inserted between reenactments, made it appear that stars like John Wayne were taking part in historic battles. Although the war was over, filmmakers were still offered technical assistance by the various military services. The air force wanted to see films made extolling the importance of their bombers; the navy wanted films presenting the case for sea power; the army sought films praising American infantrymen. All were competing for government funds, and each sought recognition as the most important component of America's defense.

Task Force (1949), directed by Delmer Daves, traces the development of the aircraft carrier. Gary Cooper and Walter Brennan star as two farsighted naval officers who struggle to convince their superiors of the importance of carrier-

Above: *Gregory Peck* (left) *and Millard Mitchell in* Twelve O'Clock High *(1949).*

Above and Beyond (1952), directed by Melvin Frank and Norman Panama, tells the story of one particular B-29, the *Enola Gay*, which let fall "Little Boy" on Hiroshima. The narrative centers on Colonel Paul Tibbets (Robert Taylor), his wife (Eleanor Parker), and how the secret mission affects them. The fearsome strains brought on by the secrecy lead to misunderstandings and nearly cause the break-up of their marriage.

Above and Beyond was followed by several movies about the air force, its planes, and "the bomb," purported to be the ultimate deterrent to war. These films were standard prewar preparedness films. *Strategic Air Command* (1955), directed by Anthony Mann, presents an animated catalog of SAC's aircraft. It stars James Stewart (it was Stewart's idea to make the film) as a former World War II B-29 pilot who has become third baseman for the St. Louis Cardinals. Just when he has a bride (June Allyson) and a new $70,000 contract, he is recalled for twenty-one months of active duty. He does a lot of griping until he gets a look at the new planes and has the importance of SAC explained to him. Frank Lovejoy, playing a character based on General Curtis LeMay, explains to Stewart, "We've got to be combat ready twenty-four hours a day, seven days a week." This preparedness involves constant tests and practice runs. Following one such test, in which an American city is "bombed" for practice, an incredulous bystander asks, "Do you mean this city has been destroyed . . . by a plane it has never seen?" "Sure," replies an officer. "One B-47 and a crew of three carries the entire destructive power of the B-29s we threw against Japan. We've been bombing cities all day and all night all over the United States without their knowing it." Stewart goes through rigorous training and ultimately decides to make the air force his career. As he says, "This is a kind of war. We've got to stay ready to fight so that we may never have to." His dedication brings on marital problems.

Bombers B-52 (1957), directed by Gordon Douglas and based on a screenplay by Irving Wallace, is about a career air force man (Karl Malden) who decides not to retire when he gets a look at the air force's newest bombers. Personally, he isn't pleased when his daughter (Natalie

launched aircraft. The film makes good use of combat footage and gave the navy the opportunity to show off its newest carrier, the USS *Franklin D. Roosevelt*.

Richard Tregaskis, author of *Guadalcanal Diary*, wrote the screenplay for *The Wild Blue Yonder* (1951), directed by Allan Dwan. Although the film includes a love triangle (pilots Forrest Tucker and Wendell Corey compete for nurse Vera Ralston; Tucker dies) and some odd humor provided by Phil Harris (who also sings a few songs, including "The Heavy Bomber Song"), it is about a plane, the B-29 Superfortress, used in the bombing of Japan.

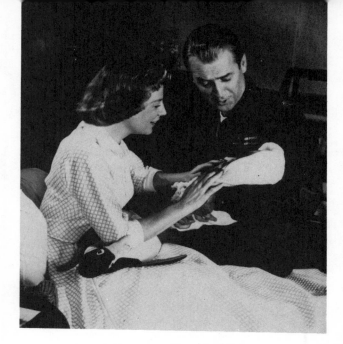

Wood) takes up with a "hotshot" captain (Efrem Zimbalist, Jr.), but all the problems are resolved after an exciting test flight in one of the monster planes. As one officer states, "The way to prevent wars is through long-range aircraft."

Along with the air force's displays of might, there were other conventional preparedness films, including *Take the High Ground* (1953), directed by Richard Brooks, a documentarylike chronicle of the training of infantry soldiers. Richard Widmark and Karl Malden star as a pair of sergeants saddled with the onerous chore of making fighting men out of American boys. Much of the film was shot at Fort Bliss, Texas, and the miseries of the rookies are presented as ofttimes comical.

The navy needed new aircraft carriers, the air force needed new planes, and the army and marines needed recruits because the end of World War II had been followed by the beginning of the Cold War. The new enemy was communism, and battling the "Red menace" had profound effects on both American society and American filmmakers. A conflict of ideologies, the Cold War demanded loyalty. The line was firmly drawn: Americans either were loyal or they weren't. For American society, this fear of subversion, of Commie spies and the even more insidious "fellow travelers," led to a decade of conformity and paranoia. For American filmmakers, it meant, beginning in 1947, an investigation by the House Un-American Activities Committee.

Hollywood was charged with being a center of subversive activity, as evidenced by the wartime films praising the Russians (the fact that these films had been made at the request of the government was overlooked) and the liberal-minded "problem" pictures and semidocumentaries. Screenwriters Albert Maltz (who was accused of putting too much "social consciousness" in *Pride of the Marines*) and John Howard Lawson (responsible for the friendly Russians in *Action in the North Atlantic*) were among the Hollywood Ten. Hundreds of other talented people were blacklisted, and an atmosphere of distrust descended over Hollywood. In its efforts to avoid further conflict with the government, the American film industry censored itself, canceling even the slightest manifesta-

tions of liberal attitude. The industry was facing tough challenges, particularly from television, and it was not about to risk disfavor with anyone. Banality triumphed—simplistic, "action-packed" war movies filled America's theaters.

The actions of the government, right-wing coercion, and economic uncertainty were not the sole causes of the film industry's anti-Communist stance. As they had been anti-Nazi, many filmmakers were anti-Communist. The late 1940s and early 1950s became another period of pre-war warning films. Like *Confessions of a Nazi Spy, The Iron Curtain (Behind the Iron Curtain)* (1948), directed by William Wellman, is about an

113

actual incident—the discovery of Russian spies in Canada. Igor Gouzenko (Dana Andrews), an employee in the Russian embassy in Ottawa, exposes a Russian spy ring and helps round up the operatives. Similar films include *The Red Menace* (1949), directed by R. G. Springsteen, and *I Married a Communist (Woman on Pier 13)* (1949), directed by Robert Stevenson. In *Conspirator* (1949), a British film directed by Victor Saville, Elizabeth Taylor is shocked when she finds herself wed to a Communist (Robert Taylor). Once again, American filmmakers were alerting the public to a growing danger.

Even *Battleground* (1949), directed by William Wellman, the best of the war movies made during the immediate postwar period, contains a Cold War preparedness message. When an army chaplain is asked if the war was really necessary, he responds, "Was this trip necessary? Thousands died because they thought it wasn't, till there was nothing left to do but fight. We must never let any kind of force dedicated to a super race or a super idea or a super anything get strong enough to impose itself on a free world. We have to be smart enough and tough enough in the beginning to put out the fire before it starts spreading."

A recreation of the Battle of the Bulge, *Battleground* was written by Robert Pirosh, who had taken part in the actual battle as an infantry sergeant. Dedicated to "the battered bastards of Bastogne," the film tells the story of the battle as it was experienced by one small group of men, a squad of Screaming Eagles (101st Airborne). There are no contrived heroics, and the fear and confusion of the soldiers are made clear. The little group of soldiers is cut off and surrounded. Bewildered, the men fight to survive. Like the infantrymen in *The Story of GI Joe*, they know only what is happening in their small sector: the war is reduced to a series of bitter contests for short stretches of snowy ground. And the war means irritating deprivations. One infantryman (Van Johnson) drags a dozen eggs through the fighting, forever hoping to find the time to whip up an omelet in his helmet.

Battleground was only the first of many films about the Battle of the Bulge, and it established most of the ingredients of such films, in-

cluding English-speaking German soldiers who, wearing American uniforms, infiltrate American lines; the historic reply—"Nuts"—given by General Anthony McAuliffe to the Germans requesting the surrender of Bastogne; the power of the German tanks; the massacre at Malmedy; and the influence of the weather on the outcome of the battle.

Hailed as the best Hollywood film about World War II, *Battleground* was compared to *The Big Parade* and *What Price Glory?* and was credited with the revival of war movies. Its sober view of war made it a singular film, however; most of its contemporaries were less low key.

Twenty years after directing *All Quiet on the Western Front*, Lewis Milestone directed *Halls of Montezuma* (1950), a film set firmly in the mold of *Sands of Iwo Jima*. Richard Widmark, Karl Malden, Jack Palance, and Richard Boone star as heroic marines fighting the Japanese on an island in the Pacific. The Marine Corps helped in the production of the film. For the scenes of the beachhead assault, the filmmakers used footage of real marines on training maneuvers. In Syracuse, New York, the mother of one of those marines went to see the film, hoping to catch a glimpse of her son. In the middle of the film, she was called out of the theater by the manager. Her husband had telephoned from home with word that they had received a telegram from the Defense Department: their son had been killed in action in Korea.

The Korean War began so suddenly that America's servicemen did not have time to change their taste in pinup pictures. When the war began, they were still toting around pictures of Betty Grable, Rita Hayworth, and Lana Turner (by the end of the war, Janet Leigh, Ava Gardner, and Shelley Winters had been added to the list). The new war melded with the old: it was all one nightmare from which Americans were not given a chance to awaken.

The first Hollywood production to incorporate battle footage from Korea was *Flying Leathernecks* (1951), a film about World War II. Directed by Nicholas Ray, the film relates the exploits of a marine fighter squadron. Its theme is air-ground support, the coordination of the fighter planes with the movements of the "mud" marines, the men fighting on the ground. The heroic exponent of the theories of close air-ground support is John Wayne. As always, he is a tough commander whose methods and morals are challenged, particularly by Robert Ryan. Wayne's ideas win out in the end. As one mud marine watching the fighter planes attack enemy emplacements on a nearby hillside exclaims, "Any closer and those guys will be using bayonets instead of propellers."

The producers of *Flying Leathernecks* were offered the use of one of the navy's aircraft carriers, the *Bataan*, but the offer had to be withdrawn when the carrier went on active duty off the coast of Korea. They had access to fresh combat film, however: Korean battle footage looked much like World War II battle footage. For the purposes of the film, the two wars were indistinguishable.

There were differences, however. The Korean War was the first war covered by television news. Television producers competed with the producers of newsreels for access to combat footage: the television producers eventually won out, leading to the demise of newsreels. The Korean War also saw an array of new weapons, including the jet plane and the helicopter, but the most distinctive feature of the war was the rampant

use of propaganda, which itself became an important weapon for the Chinese and North Koreans. They used loudspeakers to bombard entrenched GIs with popular songs from home and nagging questions about the US involvement in the war. Before attacking, the Chinese blew bugles—or played the sound over the ever-present loudspeakers. The enemy's most nefarious propaganda tool was brainwashing—forcible attempts to indoctrinate American prisoners. More than a proving ground for American arms, the Korean War was a test of American ideology.

Above right: Halls of Montezuma *(1950)*.
Below right: *Richard Boone* (center) *and Richard Widmark in* Halls of Montezuma.

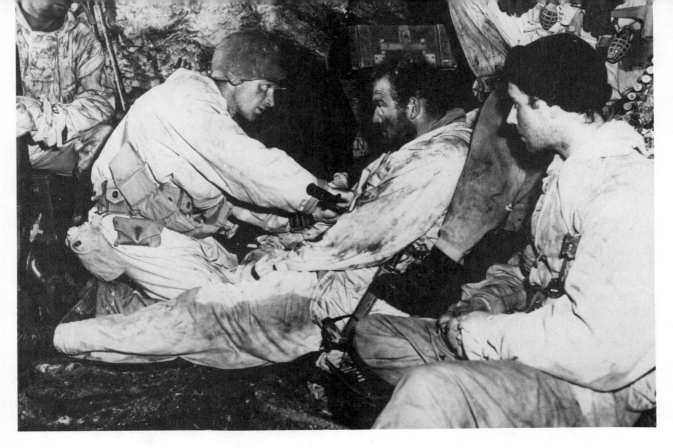

It had taken great efforts to push the United States into the two world wars, but the nation seemed to roll into Korea. There was no declaration of war in 1950, and Americans had no *Lusitania* or Pearl Harbor as an incentive to war. Even so, American soldiers (along with those of several United Nations countries) were fighting and dying. The Korean War was a very different kind of war, a war that was not being fought to be won. There was no dream of ultimate victory, but Americans were asked to believe that the war was necessary. It is understandable, then, that most films about the Korean War—among them the most dismal war movies ever made—are larded with strident propaganda.

The first important film about the Korean War was *The Steel Helmet* (1951), directed by Samuel Fuller. A veteran of World War II—he served in the infantry in North Africa and Europe and was awarded the Silver and Bronze stars and the Purple Heart—Fuller is one of America's most controversial filmmakers. His films are famous as celebrations of violence. His infantrymen are dirty and tired, burdened with weapons, packs, and assorted dangling objects. Bearded grumblers, they are not glamorous, but they are heroic, and Fuller's films are noisy paeans to the American foot soldier. Fuller loves his dogfaces, and he relishes their violence.

When on location, he signals his actors and crew to begin a scene by firing a pistol.

Fuller wrote, independently produced, and directed *The Steel Helmet*; it was made in twelve days on a budget of about $165,000. Dedicated to the US Infantry, the film begins with a close-up of a steel helmet. The helmet rises to reveal the wary eyes of Sergeant Zack (Gene Evans), a tough and resourceful noncom reminiscent of *The Immortal Sergeant*. The sole survivor of a massacre of American prisoners (their hands tied, they were machine-gunned), Zack is untied by a Korean boy (William Chun) who happens by. The boy, who is a devout Buddhist and speaks American Army slang, attaches himself to the coarse sergeant. Resigned to this unwanted companion, the sergeant dubs the boy "Short Round" and tells him to put on a "steel pot." The two are soon joined by a black medic (James Edwards).

This small group encounters an infantry platoon, among whom are a Nisei (Japanese-American) veteran of World War II's 442nd Combat Team (Richard Loo) and a World War II conscientious objector. A World War II veteran himself, Zack wants nothing to do with the platoon, but he (and the Korean boy and the medic) is inevitably forced to join it. They set up an artillery observation post in a Buddhist temple, in which

Gene Evans (center) in Fixed Bayonets *(1951).*

there are an enormous statue of Buddha and a cunning North Korean major. The Americans capture the North Korean, who speaks English and goes to work on the ethnic minorities among the Americans. "I just don't understand you," he says to the black medic. "You can't even eat with them unless it's during a war." "There are some things you can't rush," explains Edwards. "You've got the same kind of eyes as I have," the Communist points out to the Nisei. "I'm not a dirty Jap rat," responds Loo. "I'm an American." When a North Korean sniper shoots "Short Round," the North Korean major picks up a prayer to Buddha that the boy was writing and reads it aloud: "Dear Buddha, please make Sergeant Zack like me." The major makes a disparaging remark, enraging Zack, who shoots the unarmed prisoner (this mistreatment of a prisoner of war aroused criticism from a number of viewers).

The Americans direct artillery fire on advancing North Korean troops and are soon surrounded by hordes of enemy soldiers. In wonderfully absurd battle scenes, wave after wave of North Koreans rush the temple, only to be mowed down by the stalwart defenders. The fighting inspires the conscientious objector to explain his presence in Korea: "If a man lives in a house that's endangered and wants to keep on living in it, he fights to defend it." The battle ends quite suddenly. When another squad arrives to relieve the valiant defenders, it is greeted by Zack, the medic, the Nisei, and one other soldier. Surveying this ragtag group, one of the new arrivals inquires, "What kind of an outfit is this?" "US Infantry," snaps Zack.

The film does not end with "The End"; rather, the closing titles announce, "There is no end to this story."

Fuller continued his grim account of Korea in *Fixed Bayonets* (1951), the story of a platoon of American infantrymen fighting a rearguard action in a snowy mountain pass. The American soldiers are battle-hardened and thoroughly tough. "Morale is high, but ammo is low," explains a general. A man nearby asks the general about his wounded arm. "Still on," understates the commander. The general wants forty-eight men to feign being a regiment while the fifteen

thousand remaining GIs pull back. "Somebody's got to be left behind and get their bayonets wet," he says. Among the men chosen for this deadly assignment are Gene Evans, playing another bearded sergeant, and Richard Basehart, as a corporal who, because of an accident that occurred during his training, is afraid to assume leadership and has emotional difficulties shooting at the enemy.

The infantrymen grumble but accept their task. "They told me this was going to be a 'police action,'" says one. "Yeah, so why didn't they send cops?" asks his buddy. "Only three things you have to worry about in the infantry," says another. "Your rifle and your two feet." The small group takes up positions in a mountain pass and waits for the enemy, who soon arrive, blowing bugles. One by one, the leaders of the platoon are killed. As each man dies, the man assuming command gives the order to "Strip him of everything we can use, roll him in a blanket, and bury him—and mark it!" Finally, Gene Evans is killed, putting Basehart in command. But by now, the corporal has learned his lessons from Evans (whose voice returns to him, giving advice), and he takes over without difficulty, ordering the burial of his predecessor with the requisite phrase and successfully firing at an enemy soldier.

The fact that American soldiers, particularly marines, were being forced to retreat in Korea came as a blow to many Americans. Retreating was not a marine tradition. When, during World War I's bloody Battle of Belleau Wood, Captain Lloyd D. Williams had been asked if he planned to retreat, he had answered, "Retreat, hell! We just got here." His famous statement was echoed by Major General Oliver P. Smith, who, responding to a similar query about the marine withdrawal from the Chosin Reservoir, snapped, "Retreat, hell! We're not retreating, we're just advancing in a different direction." In *Retreat, Hell!* (1952), directed by Joseph H. Lewis, it is Frank Lovejoy who delivers the memorable retort. The film recounts the story of the First Marine Division in Korea, from its landing at Inchon and its fighting to regain Seoul to its advance north and its withdrawal in the face of Chinese hordes.

117

The Korean War was not without romance. John Hodiak and Stephen McNally find themselves in a love triangle with Linda Christian in *Battle Zone* (1952), directed by Lesley Selander. Robert Mitchum woos Ann Blyth in *One Minute to Zero* (1952), directed by Tay Garnett. (The army refused to cooperate in the production of this film because in one of its scenes, Mitchum orders mortars to open fire on a column of civilians. He gives the order because there are enemy soldiers among the civilians, but American soldiers were not supposed to be so brutally ruthless.)

The Korean War provided new opportunities for women to get near the fighting. The wives of many jet pilots lived with their husbands at air bases in Japan. While their husbands flew off to "work," the wives stayed home, anxiously awaiting the fliers' return. *Sabre Jet* (1953), directed by Louis King, concentrates on the lives of these women. Robert Stack is the squadron commander; he hasn't seen his wife (Coleen Gray) in two years, because she has a career of her own as a newspaper correspondent. He resents her career, however, and she doesn't understand his until she goes to Japan to write an article about the lives of the pilots' wives. She, too, endures the terrible hours waiting for the men to return from a mission, and she ultimately decides that her marriage is more important than her career.

The Korean War also witnessed the creation of a new location for romantic involvements, the Mobile Army Surgical Hospital, with its appropriate acronym for "meatball" surgery, MASH. *Battle Circus* (1953), directed by Richard Brooks, stars Humphrey Bogart as a battlefield surgeon who when not stitching up the wounds of GIs directs his attention to one of MASH 66's nurses, June Allyson. The wounded are brought to the field hospital in helicopters, and the hospital itself can be swiftly relocated thanks to the talents of a former circus worker (Keenan Wynn), who knows how to handle tents. The film sought to reassure Americans about the skilled treatment that wounded GIs were receiving while at the same time making an appeal for blood donations, always an important matter during a war.

After three years of bloody fighting, the war "ended" (there was no formal peace treaty). However, the cessation of hostilities was not followed by a respite from war movies. In fact, the Korean War went right on in movie theaters straight through the 1950s into the 1960s, joined to a flood of films about World War II. Perplexed theater patrons, uncertain as to which war was being fought in a particular film, could always hope for the sound of Chinese bugles or the sight of a jet plane as a clue.

The Fighting Lady (1945), directed by William Wyler, is a World War II documentary about life aboard an aircraft carrier. *Men of the Fighting Lady* (1954), directed by Andrew Marton, is a documentarylike account of naval action off the coast of Korea. The story deals with a squadron of jets and their attacks on North Korean railway junctions and military installations. In one of the

118

Left: *Helicopter rescue of a downed fighter pilot in* Men of the Fighting Lady *(1954).*

Robert Mitchum plays a World War II veteran pilot serving in Korea in *The Hunters* (1958), directed by Dick Powell. Mitchum is the leader of a squadron of jet planes stationed near the Yalu River in January 1952. Known to his cohorts as "The Iceman" because of his fearlessness, Mitchum becomes involved with the wife (May Britt) of one of the young fliers (Lee Philips) in his command. When Philips is shot down, Mitchum crash-lands his plane to save him; they are joined by a cocky young pilot (Robert Wagner) and, with the aid of friendly locals, they make their way back to their lines.

Most depictions of the ground war in Korea

film's climactic scenes, a blinded pilot (Dewey Martin) is guided safely back to the carrier by another flier (Van Johnson). This incident was taken from a story by Commander Harry Burns, "The Case of the Blind Pilot"; the rest of the screenplay was adapted from a magazine story, "The Forgotten Heroes of Korea," by James A. Michener.

Michener wrote two novels about the air war in Korea, and both were made into films. *The Bridges at Toko-Ri* (1954), directed by Mark Robson, is about the destruction of some strategically important bridges by carrier-based jets. William Holden stars as a World War II veteran who returns to service in Korea. Mickey Rooney (wearing a green top hat and matching scarf) plays the pilot of a rescue helicopter. When Holden must ditch his plane after destroying the bridges, it is Rooney who tries to rescue him. *Sayonara* (1957), directed by Joshua Logan, is also about jet pilots. Having shot down seven enemy planes, ace pilot Marlon Brando goes on leave in Japan and falls in love with a Japanese woman (Miiko Taka).

Battle Hymn (1956), directed by Douglas Sirk, relates the true story of Colonel Dean Hess (Rock Hudson). After service as a pilot during World War II, Hess becomes a minister, but he leaves his pulpit to serve as a training instructor in Korea. While there, he rescues more than four hundred war orphans. The film has a pronounced religious feel, as Hess shepherds his flock away from the impious Communists.

Right: *Marlon Brando and Miiko Taka in* Sayonara *(1957).*

Left: *Lee Philips in* The Hunters *(1958).*

are strikingly grim. The fighting is relentlessly brutal, and the enemy is both treacherous and alien. Many brave men die horrible deaths far from home. These films are not antiwar, however, and the severity of the combat and the bestiality of the enemy serve only to reinforce the necessity of the conflict. One of the trademarks of these films is the presence in Korea of weary but tough World War II veterans, men who are determined to serve their country regardless of circumstances. Their calm acceptance of their fates mirrors America's acceptance of its role as the ever-ready defender of freedom. GI Joe, the Brooklyn taxicab driver who is willing to wear khaki and follow orders for the "duration," was being replaced by professional soldiers. War

120

was no longer an interruption of "real" life; it was becoming an unavoidable feature of the modern world.

Soldiers from fifteen United Nations countries were present in Korea, but few films have been made about their activities: Americans did most of the fighting, and Americans made most of the films. An exception is *Hell in Korea (A Hill in Korea)* (1956), a British-made film directed by Julian Amyes. The theme of the film is the relationship between National Servicemen (civilian soldiers) and Regular troops. Sixteen soldiers (ten of whom are National Servicemen) are sent on a mission to see if a Korean village has been occupied by the enemy. They end up in a Buddhist temple (with a giant statue of Buddha) on a hill, surrounded by Chinese. The Chinese blow their bugles and charge; the British soldiers mow them down ("They seem to want to die," comments one Briton). Led by an aloof but competent officer (George Butler), seven of the men (including Stephen Boyd, Robert Shaw, and Michael Caine, all looking astonishingly youthful) make it to safety. There are no reflections on the war. The men complain about the size of the local flies, and, with the exception of a slacker who throws away their radio when carrying it becomes onerous, they do their duty.

Men in War (1957), directed by Anthony Mann, is about another bitter contest for the possession of a hill. The story is set in Korea in 1950 during an American retreat; all the action takes place in one day (the screenplay was based on a novel by Van Van Praag, *Day without End*). Cut off and surrounded by the enemy, a patrol (led by Robert Ryan) makes a fifteen-mile trek to its battalion headquarters. Mortar barrages, snipers, and land mines constantly reduce their number. They encounter a tough sergeant (Aldo Ray), who is trying to get a shell-shocked colonel (Robert Keith) to safety. When they reach the hill—Hill 465—they find that the North Koreans have occupied it. Only Ryan and Ray survive the effort to retake the hill.

The best movie about the Korean War concerns the battle for still another hill, *Pork Chop Hill* (1959), directed by Lewis Milestone. While truce negotiators at Panmunjom haggle over petty details, several hundred GIs (led by Gre-

Opposite: *Gregory Peck in* Pork Chop Hill *(1959).*

gory Peck) attempt to recapture a hill. The hill (its name refers to its shape) has no strategic value, but as the negotiations drag on, its possession assumes symbolic importance. The side that possesses the hill has an edge in the peace talks, but what is more, the hill's very unimportance makes it a symbol of America's determination. The fighting takes place in a series of trenches running across and around the hill, and the film is unusually realistic in its creation of the atmosphere of battle. The terrain is flat and treeless, and the GIs, encircled by swirling dust and smoke, can rarely see farther than a few yards in any direction. Scores of men die for each section of trench. After each short and bloody fight, Peck stops to assess the losses. "Had your iron today?" he asks, extending a box of raisins to those nearest him. Among the men are a Japanese-American, who has the task of leading a bayonet charge, two black GIs (James Edwards and Woody Strode), and a machine-gun team led by Harry Guardino. The Chinese blow bugles and harangue the GIs with loudspeakers. The Americans ultimately succeed in taking the dugout on the top of the hill, and they are saved from slaughter by the last-minute arrival of reinforcements.

The battle would seem to be a dramatic example of the futility of war. After the loss of so many lives, the hill, again a valueless piece of real estate, becomes part of the neutral zone between North and South Korea. But as Peck and the few surviving men stumble down the barren hill, a narrator explains, "Victory is a fragile thing, and history does not linger long in our time. But those who fought there know what they did . . . and the meaning of it. Millions live in freedom today because of what they did."

The survivors of Pork Chop Hill could return home heroes (the film points out, however, that there are no monuments to their valor). But a different fate awaited those GIs unfortunate enough to be taken prisoner. They had to face torture and brainwashing while captive, and when repatriated, they frequently had to face accusations of collaborating with the enemy. In *The Bamboo Prison* (1954), directed by Lewis Seiler, a sergeant (Robert Francis) poses as an informer in a North Korean prison camp only to find himself accused of complicity with the en-

emy. In *Prisoner of War* (1954), directed by Andrew Marton, Ronald Reagan parachutes behind enemy lines and sneaks into a column of captured GIs in an effort to investigate the treatment received by Americans in Communist prison camps (how he intends to make his way back to deliver his report is unclear). "Every man has his breaking point," remarks Reagan, and he witnesses American POWs being pushed toward theirs, through cruel beatings and torture and cunning lectures by Russian and North Korean officers (Oscar Homolka and Leonard Strong).

The Rack (1956), directed by Arnold Laven and based on a teleplay by Rod Serling, is about a decorated Korean War hero (Paul Newman) who returns home after two and one-half years in a POW camp to find himself accused of treason by a fellow prisoner (Lee Marvin). Broken by his Communist captors, he made speeches charging the United States with capitalistic aggression. The reason for his failure to withstand the Communists is revealed to be his loveless relationship with his military father (Walter Pidgeon). He is defended at his trial by Edmond O'Brien; Wendell Corey acts for the prosecution.

Time Limit (1957), directed by Karl Malden and based on a Broadway play by Henry Denker and Ralph Berkey, is about a distinguished army major (Richard Basehart) who is accused of collaborating with the enemy. He has signed a confession charging the United States with germ warfare and has given propaganda lectures. He refuses to say anything in his defense. A colonel (Richard Widmark) assigned to investigate the charges interviews other POWs from the camp and assumes the role of a detective piecing together a murder mystery.

The theme of brainwashed POWs made its way into the political thriller *The Manchurian Candidate* (1962), directed by John Frankenheimer. The film begins with an American Army patrol taken prisoner by Chinese Communists. The men are brainwashed. One of them (Laurence Harvey) is so completely brainwashed that, at the behest of his amiable Chinese lecturer, he strangles one of his fellow prisoners and shoots another. He is then sent back to the United States to commit a political assassination.

122

Lee Marvin plays a Korean War veteran ac-

cused of collaborating with the Chinese Communists in *Sergeant Ryker* (1968), directed by Buzz Kulik. Based on a 1963 television movie, *The Case Against Paul Ryker*, the film covers Ryker's court-martial. The sergeant claims that he has not collaborated with the Chinese, but that he was on a secret mission behind enemy lines. He has no proof, however, for the colonel who had sent him there has been killed, and there is nothing in writing to substantiate his claim. He is defended by Bradford Dillman.

This interest in brainwashing and defection to the enemy reflects the ideological nature of the Korean War: were Americans strong enough, firm enough in their beliefs, to withstand Communist propaganda? There is another aspect to these films, an aspect that reflects America's frustration with a war that did not end in brilliant victory. Association with such a war could prove perilous for American servicemen.

Perhaps not surprisingly, the most popular war of the 1950s was World War II. The cycle of

Right: *Wendell Corey* (left), *Edmond O'Brien, and Paul Newman in* The Rack *(1956).*

films begun during the immediate postwar years continued unabated through the decade, fueled by popular novels, stories by veterans, disclosures of previously unknown incidents, biographies of the leading participants, and an international market for exciting action films. Among the most popular of these films were those about Allied prisoners of war in German prison camps.

The first World War II POW film was *The Captive Heart* (1946), a British film directed by Basil Dearden. The first film made in occupied Germany, it was filmed in an actual prisoner-of-war camp, Marlag Nord, in the British zone of occupation near Hamburg. Unlike the host of POW films soon to come, *The Captive Heart* presents life in a prison camp as grim and without glamour. The screenplay was written by Guy Morgan, who had been a prisoner in the camp during the war. Michael Redgrave stars as a Czech escapee from a concentration camp who assumes the identity of a dead British officer and falls in love with the dead man's wife (Rachel Kempson) through correspondence.

The publication in 1950 of *The Great Escape*, by Paul Brickhill, provided filmmakers with another view of POW life. Although the book was not made into a film until 1963, some of its spirit made its way into earlier films. *The Wooden Horse* (1950), a British film directed by Jack Lee, provides a more lighthearted version of the POW's life than that presented in *The Captive Heart*. The British prisoners in Stalag Luft III are having difficulty digging tunnels long enough to reach beyond the wire. Two prisoners (Leo Glenn and David Tomlinson) hit upon the idea of using a vaulting horse to conceal the digging of a shorter tunnel. They get the official okay for their plan from the camp's escape committee (a prestigious group encountered in most POW stories) and convince the Germans that the men need the vaulting horse for exercise. While other prisoners leap over the hollow, wooden structure, digging goes on beneath it. The horse is put back in the same place each day, and the digging resumes. Three men (Anthony Steel joins

Above: *Peter Graves* (left) *and William Holden* (right) *in Stalag 17 (1953).*

the original two) eventually escape. One goes off on his own, and the other two have various encounters with French workers and friendly Danes on their journey to Sweden, where they are reunited with the third man.

As sergeants in the US Air Force, Donald Bevan and Edmund Trzcinski spent two years in a German POW camp. They used their experiences as the basis for a popular play, and in 1953, the play was made into a film, *Stalag 17*, directed by Billy Wilder. Sardonic and sometimes very funny, the story concerns a cynical loner (William Holden) who is interested only in survival and self-aggrandizement. "Always hustling, always scrounging," he is adept at bribing the guards and runs a bar for the other prisoners. When it becomes clear that there is an informer in the barracks tipping off the Germans to escape attempts, Holden is the obvious choice, and in his own defense he exposes the real culprit. Otto Preminger plays the camp commandant; Sig Ruman is the buffoonish barracks guard Shultz; even Trzcinski was given a role, as

himself, a character named Triz.

The film was initially banned in Germany because of its unfavorable portrayal of the German prison guards. It was wildly popular elsewhere and led, in 1965, to a television series, "Hogan's Heroes," starring Bob Crane, which manifested none of the film's powerful bite.

Another former POW, Pat R. Reid, used his experiences as "escaping officer" in Germany's Colditz Castle as the background for *The Colditz Story* (1957), a British film directed by Guy Hamilton. Located deep in Saxony, four hundred miles from any neutral border, Colditz Castle was considered escape proof. The Germans had used it as a prison during World War I, and no one had escaped, so they used it during World War II to house those officers who had tried to escape from other camps. The film relates the escape attempts, some of them successful, of a mixture of British, French, Dutch, and Polish officers imprisoned in this dank but roomy castle. The senior British officer (Eric Portman) establishes the necessary escape committee, and

124

each of the four nationalities has its escaping officer; John Mills plays the part of Pat R. Reid, the British escaping officer. The mood is sometimes comic, the prison is like a boarding school (with the same deprivations), and the inmates have schoolboy fun trying to fox the Hun (most of whom are pig-eyed and pudgy). The film ends with the statement that more POWs escaped from Colditz than from any other German POW camp: there were 320 attempts, and 56 men got away.

The enormous popularity of *The Colditz Story* led to a BBC television series. In 1977, the television series was used in the creation of *Escape from Colditz*, directed by W. Slater and P. Gregreen, in which the prisoners include Robert Wagner and David McCallum. Once again, an intricate escape plan is put into effect. Four men make it out, bound for the Swiss border with falsified papers identifying them as Flemish concrete workers. Catching their breaths in a German movie theater, two of them are treated to scenes from *Triumph of the Will*. With remarkably little unpleasantness, they make it safely across the border.

Breakout (Danger Within) (1959), a British film directed by Don Chaffey, relates another true story of escaping POWs (the film's producer, Colin Lesslie, participated in the 1943 escape presented in the film). The escape plans of the British officers in another "escape-proof" prison, this time in northern Italy, are constantly foiled by an informer, but the traitor is identified in time for the mass exit of the POWs; on the day Italy capitulates (September 8, 1943), more than four hundred of them escape.

The One That Got Away (1957), a British film directed by Roy Baker, relates the true story of the only German POW to escape from a British camp during the war. Hardy Kruger plays the wily Luftwaffe lieutenant who manages to get away from his British captors and make it to the neutral United States.

The British and American films about Allied POWs in German camps display a mixture of high spirits and schoolboy high jinks. Just over the wall, just beyond the wire, is Germany, which, after all, is not such a strange place. No one asks too many questions in the local beer

halls, and riding on trains disguised as foreigners speaking some arcane language (such as Flemish) is great fun, made even more exciting by chance encounters with inquisitive Gestapo agents. This cycle of films reached its apex in 1963's *The Great Escape*.

The most remarkable aspect of the war movies of the 1950s was the changing image of Germany and the Nazis. German soldiers were cleansed of the taint of Nazism (which, it seemed, had been the exclusive madness of one man and his coterie of maniacs) and made to shine as perfect examples of the dedicated soldier. Although Germany had been defeated, Germany's propaganda remained intact: Germans were the best soldiers in the world. American filmmakers accepted the idealized view of the German soldier and perpetuated it. Until the late 1970s, the Germans in American war movies are always clean shaven, with every button of their tunics neatly closed. And they never even flinch during battle.

The Soviet Union was the new enemy of the United States, and Germany was a valued ally (West Germany entered NATO in 1955): all those wonderful tanks, marvels of engineering, were on our side. Furthermore, American filmmakers catered to a worldwide audience. War makes great international entertainment; bitter indictments don't. Shorn of entangling political or moral concerns, the war became pure, exciting action.

Decision Before Dawn (1951), directed by Anatole Litvak, was made amid the ruins of sixteen German cities. A spy thriller, the film presents a grim view of the collapse of the Third Reich. The story takes place in December 1944, when the Office of Strategic Services decides to use German prisoners as spies. They are to return to Germany and, in a patriotic effort to hasten the inevitable end of the war, do espionage work for the Allies. Oskar Werner stars as one of the prisoners chosen, a disillusioned Luftwaffe medic. He is forced to choose between loyalty to Hitler and loyalty to his homeland.

The German field marshal Erwin Rommel, famous as "The Desert Fox," was forced to make a similar choice. *The Desert Fox (Rommel—*   125

The Colditz Story (1957). The easiest way to escape from Colditz: dress up in German uniforms and walk out the gate.

Desert Fox) (1951), directed by Henry Hathaway, presents the German commander in a very sympathetic light—he is made into a hero. Based on a best-selling biography, *Rommel*, by Desmond Young, the film portrays Rommel (James Mason, who had read Young's book and wanted to play the part) as a wise, professional soldier, a man dedicated to his duty and his country. It is Hitler (Luther Adler) who is the villain. He sends Rommel insane directives, orders that lead to the defeat of the Afrika Korps. Convinced that Hitler is leading Germany to ruin, Rommel becomes involved in a plot to kill him. His involvement is discovered, and he is forced by the Nazis to commit suicide.

Although popular, the film was not well received in all quarters. It was boycotted by American veterans' groups and was withheld from circulation in West Germany for nearly a year. When it was finally shown there, the scenes of Hitler evoked hisses and nervous laughter. Local Communists tossed stink bombs into theaters showing the film. Far away in Argentina, Wilfred von Oven, Goebbels's former secretary and proud author of *With Goebbels to the End*, registered his complaints about the traitorous portrayal of the immortal general. There were fears that the film might lead to a revival of German militarism. A few calm reviewers pointed out that, according to the film, had it not been for Hitler, Rommel would have won the war in the desert, and how desirable was that? Whitewashing former enemies can be perilous.

James Mason repeated his impersonation of Rommel in a few short scenes of *The Desert Rats* (1953), directed by Robert Wise. The film is about the siege of Tobruk; the "desert rats" are the Australian defenders. One group of these, led by a strict British officer (Richard Burton), goes on a daring mission behind enemy lines to blow up an ammunition dump and then, isolated on a hilltop outside the defensive perimeter, holds off repeated German attacks until relief arrives. In one scene, Burton (temporarily prisoner of the Afrika Korps) has a sharp exchange with Rommel; in another, the field marshal is shown dining alone to the strains of classical music.

The heroic stature of the anti-Nazi German was confirmed in *The Sea Chase* (1955), directed by John Farrow, in which John Wayne plays a German sea captain, a detester of Hitler and all he stands for, but a German nonetheless. Wayne and his tramp steamer, the *Ergenstrasse*, are in Sydney, Australia, when war breaks out. His crew composed of a spy (Lana Turner), a Nazi fanatic (Lyle Bettger), and a good mate (Tab Hunter), Wayne sneaks his ship out of the harbor. They are pursued by a British warship, the

126

Above: *Oskar Werner (seated) being questioned by American Intelligence officers, including*

Gary Merrill (second from right) and Richard Basehart (right), in Decision Before Dawn *(1951).*

Above right: *James Mason* (center) *as Rommel and Richard Boone* (second from left) *as a German officer in* The Desert Fox (1951).
Below right: *James Mason* (center) *repeats the role of Rommel in* The Desert Rats (1953).

Rockhampton, commanded by a friend of Wayne's (David Farrar). They reach Valparaiso, Chile, safely, refuel, and set off toward Hamburg disguised as a Panamanian banana boat. The *Rockhampton* catches them, is not fooled, and sinks the *Ergenstrasse*, but Wayne and Turner survive the fray.

The friendly attitude toward the Germans spread even to Britain. Michael Powell and Emeric Pressburger, responsible for so many excellent war movies, wrote, produced, and directed *The Pursuit of the Graf Spee (The Battle of the River Plate)* (1956). This is a recreation of the last days of one of Germany's greatest battleships, the *Graf Spee*, which was hunted down by British cruisers and ultimately forced to take shelter in the neutral port of Montevideo, Uruguay. Rather than allow the ship to be captured or destroyed, its captain, Hans Langsdorff, had the ship scuttled. Langsdorff (Peter Finch) is the most sympathetic character in the film, an honorable man who plays fair and treats prisoners well. (Some of this was based on fact. Although the *Graf Spee* sank numerous unarmed merchant ships, no one was ever reported killed. Langsdorff himself felt obligated to commit suicide after ordering his ship scuttled, but this unpleasantness is omitted from the film.)

Curt Jurgens portrays an anti-Nazi German commanding a submarine in *The Enemy Below* (1957), directed by Dick Powell. His opposite number, the commander of an American destroyer searching the South Atlantic for enemy subs, is Robert Mitchum, a would-be pacifist who harbors no hatred for the Germans. The two men, both seasoned veterans, become involved in a chesslike duel of wits, the destroyer chasing the sub, the sub chasing the destroyer. In the end, with both vessels destroyed, the two commanders are pleased to have the opportunity of meeting.

In *Bitter Victory* (1957), directed by Nicholas Ray, Jurgens plays a less likable character—a British officer. Major Brand (Jurgens) hates Captain Leith (Richard Burton). The captain has had an affair with the major's wife (Ruth Roman) and knows of the major's cowardice. These two officers lead a commando raid on a German headquarters in Benghazi, Libya. On the way back,

Major Brand succeeds in killing his rival (he allows a scorpion to bite him) and leads the commandos back. He is awarded a medal for his heroism, but he loses the respect of his wife as well as that of his men. He pins the medal on a dummy used for bayonet practice.

The use of popular actors in the roles of sympathetic, anti-Nazi Germans blurred the line between friends and enemies. Good or bad did not belong exclusively to either side. In *The Young Lions* (1958), directed by Edward Dmytryk and based on a best-selling novel by Irwin Shaw, Marlon Brando, one of the decade's most popular actors, plays a German. In the beginning of the film, he believes that Hitler will bring the Germans a better life, and he enlists to fight for his country; by the end of the film, he has become disillusioned with Nazism. His story is paralleled by that of two American GIs, Montgomery Clift and Dean Martin. Clift enlists to fight Nazism and encounters anti-Semitism among his fellow American soldiers.

While Clift fights to maintain his pride, Brando fights the British in North Africa. He rebels against the cruel tactics of his superior officer (Maximilian Schell, in his first Hollywood film as a German officer, a role he repeated many times). The separate stories intersect near a concentration camp during the last days of the war. The camp brings Brando to the final realization of his country's crimes. After listening to the camp commander's complaints that he does not have enough men to kill his assigned quota of prisoners, Brando leaves the camp and smashes his gun against a tree stump. The camp is liberated by American soldiers, among whom are Martin and Clift. Walking down a road near the camp, the two GIs come upon the German. It is Martin who shoots him.

By the end of the decade, German soldiers—caught between duty to their country and the barbarity of the Nazis—had become heroic figures. Erich Maria Remarque, author of *All Quiet on the Western Front*, wrote a similar novel about World War II, *A Time to Love and a Time to Die*. The novel was made into a film in 1958, directed by Douglas Sirk. The story begins on the Russian front in 1944, where an idealistic young German soldier (John Gavin) is shocked by the cruelty of Nazi zealots. He is not alone: one soldier commits suicide when forced to execute a group of Russian civilians, including a cursing girl. Gavin is sent home to Berlin on a furlough and finds his family's house a pile of rubble. He is

reunited with his sweetheart (Lilo Pulver), and they marry. Her father, a doctor, has been sent to a concentration camp for making defeatist statements. A Gestapo officer gives Gavin a gift, a cigar box containing the dead doctor's ashes.

Most of the film takes place in war-torn Berlin, where civilians suffer both the falling bombs and the corruption of Nazi officials. In the midst of deprivations, SS officers enjoy an ongoing party. Remarque himself appears in the film, in the role of a Nazi-hating professor. "Isn't there a place where taking orders stops and personal responsibility begins, where duty turns into crime and can no longer be excused by blaming the leaders?" asks Gavin. "Each man has to decide for himself," responds the professor.

Back at the Russian front, Gavin comes upon a German soldier about to kill three Russian peasants. He kills the German and sets the Russians free. They are preplexed for a moment, but then one turns and shoots Gavin. He dies beside a small brook, a letter from his bride falling from his hand and floating away.

In 1949's *Battleground*, Van Johnson plays a weary GI trying to find the time during the Battle of the Bulge to cook some eggs. In 1958's *The Last Blitzkrieg*, directed by Arthur Dreifuss, he plays a German officer, one of the English-speaking Germans who, during the Battle of the Bulge, infiltrate American lines. When cruel Nazis order the slaughter of American prisoners, Johnson decides he's on the wrong side.

The change in the image of the German soldier reflects the short memory of motion pictures. The war against the Germans was over, and in the search for exciting entertainment, filmmakers did not concern themselves with any lingering memories of the horrors of the war. The war films of the fifties are related less to the war than to movies about the war: they continue themes begun on film, not in history. The soldier on film had taken on a life and history of his own. The war movies of the forties sang the praises of the American GI; in the films of the fifties, there is a commonality among soldiers, both American and German: they form one group, a group that is opposed to the group composed of corrupt politicians and civilians. On film, the military was coming unglued from history and politics (never a very firm connection), preparing an opening for the members of *The Dirty Dozen*, who fight for their own reasons, and the men in *Uncommon Valor*, who go against their government out of loyalty to their friends.

The Japanese did not receive similar sympathy from filmmakers. Throughout the 1950s, the war in the Pacific was loudly and patriotically reenacted in a cycle of films very much like *Sands of Iwo Jima. American Guerrilla in the Philippines (I Shall Return)* (1950), directed by Fritz Lang, recounts a familiar tale of seven Americans (including Tyrone Power) who are left behind when the Americans evacuate Corregidor. They form a resistance movement, spy on the Japanese, and prepare the way for MacArthur's triumphant return. The decade ended with *Surrender—Hell!* (1959), directed by John Barnwell, the story of Colonel Donald Blackburn, who refused to surrender to the Japanese when they occupied the Philippines and created a band of guerrilla fighters that came to be known as "Blackburn's Headhunters." Blackburn (Keith Andes) and his men (among whom are a few native headhunters) harry the Japanese and help pave the way for MacArthur.

One group of Japanese did receive some long-overdue respect: the veterans of the 442nd Regimental Combat Team, an American Army unit composed (except for officers) of Nisei from the United States, Hawaii, and Alaska. All of the men were volunteers, and they fought hard to prove themselves (many of their relatives were in "relocation centers" in the United States), receiving more individual and unit awards than any other unit in the US Army. Their battle cry was "Go for broke!" (a phrase popular with Hawaiian crapshooters).

Written and directed by Robert Pirosh (author of *Battleground*), *Go for Broke!* (1951) stars Van Johnson as a non-Nisei officer in command of the Nisei soldiers and uses actual veterans for the roles of most of the soldiers. Johnson is initially disappointed by his assignment, but he comes to admire the courageous Nisei during their fighting in Italy and France.

In the tradition of *Sands of Iwo Jima* and *Task Force*, most films about the war in the Pacific stressed the importance of the navy while providing audiences with exciting action. *Okinawa* (1951), directed by Leigh Jason, is about a destroyer, the USS *Blake*, stationed off Okinawa in 1945. During the invasion of the island, the destroyer fights off repeated kamikaze attacks.

Viewers were particularly impressed by the scenes, taken from Japanese newsreels, showing the ceremonies performed by the kamikaze pilots before taking off on their suicidal flights.

Away All Boats (1956), directed by Joseph Pevney, is a sort of *In Which We Serve*, recounting the story of one attack transport (a ship that ferries landing craft), the *Belinda*. "This is the way it was," announces a narrator, and the film begins with the *Belinda*, a brand-new ship, ready for service. With the exception of the officers, the ship's crew is composed of inexperienced sailors who, like the United States, are not ready for the war. ("Failing to remember the past, we seem doomed to repeat it," recites one officer.) The captain (Jeff Chandler) is a cold, strict man, and he pushes his men through endless drills. Like the commanders in many films of this period, he accepts the men's hatred and his own loneliness as necessary adjuncts to leadership. When they are barely prepared, they are sent to Makin for their first battle. From there, the *Belinda* goes to Kwajalein, Saipan, Guam, and Guadalcanal, the names flashing by like newspaper headlines. Finally, on Okinawa, the *Belinda* is struck by a kamikaze plane. The damaged vessel is towed by its landing craft, and its captain, wounded in the attack, stays alive long enough to make certain it is safe. As he says, "If a man has to die in war, it doesn't matter where."

Hellcats of the Navy (1957), directed by Nathan Juran, begins with a prologue spoken by Admiral Chester Nimitz and goes on to relate the adventures of an American submarine operating in the Tsushima Strait in 1944. The commander of the sub (Ronald Reagan) is in love with a nurse (Nancy Davis), but he isn't sure he wants to marry her. The outcome is obvious. (Reagan already was married to Davis. They were married in 1952; this was their only screen appearance together.)

Revenge is the theme of *Torpedo Run* (1958), directed by Joseph Pevney. Following the attack on Pearl Harbor, the American submarine *Grayfish*, commanded by Glenn Ford and his loyal executive officer, Ernest Borgnine, goes hunting for one of the aircraft carriers that launched the attack, the *Shinaru*. When the *Grayfish* catches

Glenn Ford (left) *and Ernest Borgnine*
in Torpedo Run *(1958).*

up to the *Shinaru*, the Japanese carrier is using
a transport ship as a shield. Aboard the transport ship are twelve hundred American POWs
being taken from Manila to Tokyo, and among
these captives are Ford's wife (Diane Brewster,
met only in flashbacks) and daughter—he has
this information from the Swedish Red Cross.
Ford takes a shot at the carrier, misses, and
sinks the transport. His subsequent search for
revenge takes him to the limits of his duty and
his sanity.

Personal conflicts outweigh the war in *Tarawa Beachhead* (1958), directed by Paul Wendkos. A young marine (Kerwin Mathews) sees his
commanding officer (Ray Danton) murder a fellow marine. The young marine then falls in love
with the dead man's widow (Julie Adams); the
commanding officer marries her sister (Karen
Sharpe). Their next stop is Tarawa, where the
war provides its own justice.

Like *Destination Tokyo, Destination Gobi*
(1953), directed by Robert Wise, is about the observation of weather conditions, in this case, in
the Mongolian desert. Seven sailors with sixty
saddles are sent to Gobi to report on the weather.
The saddles are meant to be used as gifts for the
Mongolians. There are plenty of Japanese to
fight, and the seven sailors become involved in
several humorous incidents.

Never So Few (1959), directed by John
Sturges, finds Frank Sinatra leading a force composed of Kachin guerrillas and British and
American soldiers against the Japanese in northern Burma. Between battles against the Japanese and incidents with the Nationalist Chinese
(some of whom are more interested in plunder
than in fighting the Japs), Sinatra woos and ultimately wins Gina Lollobrigida. She forsakes a
millionaire to be with the rugged, iconoclastic
captain (who, in "real" life, is a hardware dealer
in Indianapolis). "I kiss you," she says, "and the
bells ring wildly in my temples."

The Young Lions was only one of a series of
films based on popular plays and novels. Although some of these films were hailed as being
antiwar, they are not really against war, only
antimilitary.

From Here to Eternity (1953), directed by Fred
Zinnemann and based on a novel by James
Jones, won eight Academy Awards and is credited with salvaging the career of Frank Sinatra.
The setting of the story is an army barracks in
Honolulu; the film begins in the summer of 1941
and ends with the Japanese attack on Pearl Harbor. The Jap Zeros "resolve" the complicated personal stories of the men and women of the
barracks. Montgomery Clift stars as the sensitive, individualistic, bugle-playing Private
Prewitt, who undergoes vicious mistreatment for
refusing to join the captain's boxing team. Sinatra plays his friend, Maggio, a role originally set

131

for Eli Wallach. The film's unforgiving depiction of army life—the setting for illicit affairs and mindless cruelty—led to its being banned on navy bases as "derogatory to a brother service" (the army, however, okayed the film).

Battle Cry (1955), directed by Raoul Walsh, was based on a novel by Leon Uris. The film begins with a train leaving Baltimore full of fresh marine recruits, among them "a slum kid, an all-American boy, a farmer, a lumberjack, and a practical joker." There is even a "bookworm"—he passes the time reading Plato. Although these stereotypical American boys do see some action against the Japanese, they spend most of their time falling in love on long leaves in New Zealand. Even tough Aldo Ray (the lumberjack) finds a woman who appreciates his special coarseness (Nancy Olson). Tab Hunter (the all-Amerian boy) creates his own love triangle by becoming involved romantically with two women (Mona Freeman and Dorothy Malone).

Another novel by Leon Uris served as the basis for The Angry Hills (1959), a British film directed by Robert Aldrich. The story is set in Greece. When an American war correspondent (Robert Mitchum) gets his hands on a list of the leaders of the Greek Resistance, he finds himself pursued by both the local Gestapo chief (Stanley Baker) and a Greek traitor (Theodore Bikel). The Gestapo man is by far the more likable of the two.

The Caine Mutiny (1954), directed by Edward Dmytryk, addressed the two most important is-

sues of the decade: the responsibility of command and the limits of loyalty. Based on a Pulitzer Prize-winning novel by Herman Wouk, the film recounts the downfall of Captain Queeg (Humphrey Bogart), commander of the minesweeper Caine. The emotionally unstable Queeg rolls steel balls in his hands and metes out demonic punishments for imagined offenses to his meticulous sensitivities. His loyal executive officer (Van Johnson) is ultimately court-martialed for mutiny.

In Mister Roberts (1955), directed by John Ford, another neurotically meticulous sea captain is the source, instead, of comedy. The screenplay for the film was based on a play by Thomas Heggen and Joshua Logan. Beginning in 1948, Henry Fonda appeared in the title role in more than a thousand performances of the play, and he repeats his role in the film. The story takes place in a navy cargo ship ferrying supplies through the "safe" areas of the Pacific. James Cagney plays the neurotic captain who treasures above all things his palm tree, a gift from an admiral for "delivering more toothpaste and toilet paper than any other ship in the safe area of the Pacific." Mr. Roberts wants only to fight the enemy, but his letters requesting transfer to combat duty are marked "disapproved" by the captain.

Run Silent, Run Deep (1958), directed by Robert Wise, was based on a novel by Edward L. Beach, a decorated navy officer who served on President Eisenhower's staff and, in 1960, com-

132

Opposite: *James Whitmore* (second from left) *and Aldo Ray* (right) in *Battle Cry* (1955).
Below: *Montgomery Clift* (center) *and Frank Sinatra* in *From Here to Eternity* (1953).

manded the USS *Triton* on its historic submerged circumnavigation of the earth. Clark Gable stars as a submarine commander out for revenge (the last sub he commanded was sunk by a Japanese destroyer). He is given the command of the *Nerka*, which displeases Burt Lancaster, who was scheduled to take command of the sub, and the sub's crew. With Lancaster as a less than loyal executive officer and a crew that grumbles about his incessant drills, Gable steers the *Nerka* toward the dreaded Bungo Strait, graveyard for American submarines. The crew, among whom is Don Rickles, supplying cynical humor, nearly mutinies.

In 1958, ten years after its original publication, Norman Mailer's *The Naked and the Dead* was made into a film, directed by Raoul Walsh. A lot was lost transferring the novel to the screen: the characters lost dimension and the war lost its horror. What remained was a familiar tale about loyalty and leadership. With few exceptions (including character-explaining flashbacks), the action takes place on a Japanese-held island in the Pacific. The commander of the American invasion force (Raymond Massey) is a cynical manipulator of men. "The only morality of the future is a power morality," he says. Explaining his theory of command, he lectures, "Make the men hate and fear you. There is no other way." A young, inexperienced lieutenant (Cliff Robertson) disagrees: "The men must love you." The lieutenant gets the opportunity to prove his point when he is made the leader of a reconnaissance patrol sent behind enemy lines. The patrol's sergeant (Aldo Ray) is a sadistic killer who pries the gold out of the teeth of dead Japanese (flashbacks provide the explanation for his meanness: he came home early one rainy afternoon to find his wife in bed with a representative of a finance company). Most of the men in the patrol are killed, including the vicious sergeant. The lieutenant, wounded, is carried out of the jungle to safety by two of the remaining men. This action proves the lieutenant's theory: "There's a spirit in man that will survive all the reigns of terror . . . the spirit in man is godlike, eternal, indestructible."

The screenplay for *To Hell and Back* (1955), directed by Jesse Hibbs, was based on the auto-

biography of Audie Murphy, the most decorated GI of World War II (he was awarded twenty-four decorations, including the Medal of Honor). After the war, Murphy became an actor and starred in several low-budget westerns, but when the idea arose to make a film of his autobiography and the producers went looking for someone to play the leading role, they overlooked the boyish Murphy—he just didn't look like a war hero. He finally got the part, however, making *To Hell and Back* an unusual war movie, one in which a real war hero reenacts his heroic actions. Murphy also served as an adviser on the film, making certain all the details were correct.

Perhaps to explain his future heroism, the film begins in northeast Texas in 1937, where the diminutive Murphy has the responsibilities of caring for his siblings and ailing mother thrust upon him. When his mother dies, his brothers and sisters are put in an orphanage, and the underage, under-size Murphy tries to enlist. The marines turn him down, the navy turns him down, but the army accepts him. From North Af-

Right: *Richard Todd* (left) *and Robert Taylor in* D-Day the Sixth of June *(1956).*

rica to Sicily to Italy and finally to France, the shy Murphy proves himself a hero and is promoted, against his wishes, from corporal to lieutenant. He is driven by his powerful sense of responsibility and his affection for his friends. Indeed, his feats of courage always follow the death of a friend, as though there were a certain moral justice to his actions. His final act of courage takes place in the Colmar region of France. Standing on a burning tank, he uses a machine gun to single-handedly hold off 250 Germans and 6 tanks. That is what he actually did during the war, and that is what he does in the film. As a general says in the prologue, this is "the true story of the foot soldier."

The screenplay for *Between Heaven and Hell* (1956), directed by Richard Fleischer, was written by Harry Brown, based on a novel, *The Day the Century Ended*, by Francis Gwaltney. Like many war movies, this is a story of regeneration in battle. A wealthy and arrogant southerner (Robert Wagner) is drafted into the army. Also drafted are some of his poor tenant share-croppers. Fighting the Japanese on an island in the Pacific, the southerner overcomes both his fear and his prejudice.

Harry Brown also wrote the screenplay for *D-Day the Sixth of June* (1956), directed by Henry Koster, a film that uses the Normandy invasion as a backdrop to a love triangle. An American officer stationed in London (Robert Taylor) falls in love with the fiancée (Dana Wynter) of a British officer (Richard Todd). Both men participate in the D-day landings; the Briton solves the personal conflict by purposely walking off into a minefield.

Other personal problems are solved in *Screaming Eagles* (1956), directed by Charles Haas. Also a story of D day, this one involves the men of the first platoon, Company D, 101st Airborne Infantry Division (whose shoulder-patch insignia is a "screaming eagle"). Tom Tryon stars as a churlish replacement soldier who has trouble fitting into the platoon—the experience of combat, of fighting side by side with the other men, facilitates his integration into the unit. The

135

platoon is dropped in France behind enemy lines with the assignment of securing a bridge over the Douve River. En route, they rescue a French girl (Jacqueline Beer) from her German captors. The girl proves herself a valuable asset to the platoon, even though she speaks only French and German.

It took all kinds of men to make an army, of course, and *The Bold and the Brave* (1956), directed by Lewis R. Foster, is about three possible types: an irrepressible youth (Mickey Rooney), a religious bigot (Don Taylor), and a pacifistic idealist (Wendell Corey). Each responds to the war in his own way. Rooney wins $30,000 in a crap game and declares that he is going to open "the most beautiful restaurant in Jersey." The other men have other dreams, and the action of the film is mixed with comedy.

James Garner stars as Major William Darby in *Darby's Rangers* (1958), directed by William Wellman. The film covers the creation of a special force, its training, and its action in North Africa, Sicily, and Italy. Inevitably, the film also covers the love lives of the Rangers. One of them (Edward Byrnes) falls in love with an Italian girl (Etchika Choureau, a French actress in her first American film).

Only one film of the decade sought to present an alternative view of the war in Europe. *Attack!* (1956), directed by Robert Aldrich, brings together the major themes of the 1950s—loyalty and the responsibility of command—and combines them with the cynicism of the Cold War. Like *Battleground*, *Attack!* is about the Battle of the Bulge, but all similarities end there. *Attack!* is not a celebration of the courage of American GIs; rather, it is a bitter indictment of cowardice and corruption among the commanding officers (this film was made without the customary assistance of the armed forces). When a cowardly captain (Eddie Albert) is responsible for the deaths of a squad of soldiers, an enraged lieutenant (Jack Palance) wants the captain removed. The colonel in command (Lee Marvin) has no intention of offending the captain—the captain's father is the head of the political machine in his hometown and can be very useful to his career after the war. Rather than remove the captain, the colonel puts him and his men in an out-of-the-way area. It is there that the German surprise attack falls. The colonel orders Albert to capture a farmhouse; Albert orders Palance to carry out the mission. Before going, Palance threatens Albert that he will kill him if he again fails to bring support. Once again, Albert's cowardice leads to the deaths of American soldiers. The few remaining men make their way back, but Palance is killed before he can fulfill his threat. The panic-stricken captain wants to surrender to the Germans, but another lieutenant (William Smithers) shoots him, and the rest of the GIs fire into the captain's body to save the lieutenant from a court-martial.

The brutal violence of *Attack!* anticipates Aldrich's later films, particularly *The Dirty Dozen*, and the film's cynical view of American officers, with their mindless bureaucracy and corrupt politics, foreshadows *Catch-22*. But the most important aspect of the film is its nihilism—loyalty to a cause is replaced by loyalty to a group. It doesn't matter which uniform the group wears: Aldrich's next war movie, *Ten Seconds to Hell* (1959), stars Jack Palance and Jeff Chandler as two tough, courageous men who, when not competing for Martine Carol, risk their lives defusing unexploded bombs dropped by Allied planes on Berlin. The two heroes are, of course, Germans.

The British-made war movies of the 1950s reflect a clear conscience. While their American counterparts struggled with the moral and psychological problems of winning the war, British filmmakers reveled in the victory. Along with the entertaining films about POW escapades, there were several films celebrating historic incidents. *Above Us the Waves* (1955), directed by Ralph

Thomas, is about the sinking of the German battleship *Tirpitz* by midget submarines. *The Dam Busters* (1955), directed by Michael Anderson with a screenplay by R. C. Sherriff, is about the destruction of the Ruhr dams by bombers using special "bouncing" bombs. The bombs are devised by a scientist (Michael Redgrave); Richard Todd plays Guy Gibson, the mission's leader.

Feats of British espionage were also celebrated. *Night Ambush (Ill Met by Moonlight)* (1957), another film by Michael Powell and Emeric Pressburger, stars Dirk Bogarde as the leader of a team of British commandos who kidnap a German general (Marius Goring) on Crete. *The Man Who Never Was* (1956), directed by Ronald Neame, is about Operation Mincemeat. A corpse, supplied with forged documents intended to mislead the Germans about an Allied invasion, is planted where the Germans will find it. *I Was Monty's Double* (1958), directed by John Guillermin, is about another clever British deception, involving an actor who bore a striking resemblance to Field Marshal Montgomery. The screenplay for the film was adapted from a book by M. E. Clifton-James, the man who had actually impersonated Montgomery during the war. In the film, Clifton-James plays both himself and Montgomery.

Dunkirk (1958), directed by Leslie Norman, recreates the evacuation of the British Army from France in 1940. *Sink the Bismarck!* (1960), directed by Lewis Gilbert and based on a book by C. S. Forester, recounts the efforts to track down and sink Germany's greatest battleship. Although the battle is fought at sea, it is directed from the underground offices of the Admiralty. The man in charge is a very businesslike Kenneth More, described by one of his colleagues as "cold as a witch's heart." More calmly directs the movements of the British ships, shuffling models across a large map. The commander of the *Bismarck* calls the engagement "a most interesting chess game." The opposing sides seem at ease in their roles. They are differentiated most clearly by their choice of tobacco: the British smoke pipes, the Germans cigars.

A novel by Nicholas Monsarrat provided the basis for *The Cruel Sea* (1955), directed by Charles Frend. A grim account of the Battle of the Atlantic, the film focuses on the psychological effects of battling submarines. Jack Hawkins stars as the captain of the *Compass Rose,* a corvette protecting Atlantic convoys. In the five years covered by the film, Hawkins and his men sink only two German submarines, but there is no letup in the agonizing tension. The film begins with the statement that this is a story of the sea: "The men are the heroes—the heroines are the ships."

A magazine story by Monsarrat served as the inspiration for a film about one of those "heroines," *The Ship That Died of Shame* (1955), directed by Basil Dearden. This film provides a logical, if fantastic, extension of the proclivity of war movies to attribute personalities to ships. After proud wartime service, motor gunboat *1087* is retired and scheduled to be made into scrap. The ship's former crew saves it from this undeserved fate. The former sailors want to use the ship in their new line of work, cross-Channel smuggling. The ship rebels against this shameful activity and ultimately sinks itself.

The best British war movie of the 1950s was *The Bridge on the River Kwai* (1957), directed by David Lean. Although the setting of the film is a Japanese POW camp in Siam, it is not a film about escape attempts. Rather, it is about individual pride, group spirit, and the mocking futil-

ity of war. The commander of the camp, Colonel Saito (Sessue Hayakawa), wants the British prisoners to help in the construction of a bridge. The leader of the prisoners, Colonel Nicholson (Alec Guinness), refuses to cooperate when Saito demands that the British officers work alongside the enlisted men. That, according to Nicholson, would be against the rules set forth in the Geneva Convention, and, as he says, "Without law, there is no civilization." The Japanese colonel, a representative of another version of civilization, has his own code of honor and cannot understand the British: "You are defeated, but you have no shame."

Saito is finally forced to accept Nicholson's rules, and work on the bridge begins. It is a peculiar situation: the British are building a bridge for their enemy. In fact, Nicholson is determined to build a very good bridge, a "proper bridge," a bridge that will be an enduring monument to the superior skills of the British soldier. Saito is determined to complete the bridge on schedule. The two colonels, each following his duty as he perceives it, share a goal.

As the work on the bridge nears completion, a group of commandos, including an American escapee from the camp named Shears (William Holden), makes its way toward the bridge to blow it up. Each of the three groups—the British prisoners, the Japanese, and the commandos—has a perfectly valid reason for what it is doing. In the final confrontation, the bridge is destroyed, and Saito, Nicholson, and Shears die. The British doctor of the camp (James Donald), watching this spectacle of self-destruction, mutters, "Madness, madness."

In the novel by Pierre Boulle on which the film was based, the bridge is not destroyed. (Boulle, who was himself a prisoner of the Japanese during World War II, based his novel on the building of a real bridge, part of the notorious "death railway" in Thailand: there is a real river Kwai, and the bridge, still standing, has become a popular tourist attraction, although it is very hard to reach.) Although it is credited to Boulle, the screenplay for the film was actually written by Carl Foreman and Michael Wilson, but both men were at that time blacklisted and received no screen credit. The music for the film, composed by Malcolm Arnold, is a combination of two tunes, "Colonel Bogey," a British song written in 1916, and "The River Kwai March," which was written for the movie.

The first of the great "outdoor epics," *The*

138

Above: *Jack Hawkins* (right) *in* The Cruel Sea *(1955).*

Bridge on the River Kwai led to the enormous spectaculars of the 1960s, including Lean's *Lawrence of Arabia* and *Doctor Zhivago* and such films as *The Longest Day*. The film industry was becoming international, with the war (freed of any lingering animosities) its favorite topic.

The United States and Great Britain were the major producers of films about World War II during the 1950s. However, the war had been a world war, fought in many languages, and it was remembered by each of its participants.

The war was not a popular topic in Germany in the 1950s, and the few German-made films about the war were antiwar and anti-Nazi. G. W.

Pabst directed two films about Hitler and the Nazis, *The Last Ten Days* and *The Jackboot Mutiny*.

The Last Ten Days (Ten Days to Die) (1954) is a documentarylike account of Hitler's final days in his bunker beneath the Reich Chancellery. The screenplay for the film was based on a book by Michael A. Musmano, a judge at the Nuremberg trials; the original scenario was written by Erich Maria Remarque. The film is the story of Hitler (Albin Skoda) and his personal *Goetterdaemmerung*. As the Russians advance through the streets of Berlin, Hitler consults astrologers, sends imperatives to armies that have ceased to exist, tries to destroy everything (he orders the flooding of the Berlin subways, which were

139

Above: *Dana Wynter (left) and Kenneth More in* Sink the Bismarck! *(1960).*

being used as emergency shelters), and condemns everyone, even those few who have remained loyal to him. Deciding that the German people no longer deserve him, he commits suicide. Oskar Werner plays an intensely sane German major, a representative of Germany's human conscience. Trying to convince a Hitler Youth to surrender, he says, "Never say *jawohl* to anyone again. That's how it all began."

The Jackboot Mutiny (It Happened on 20th July) (1955) is about the abortive attempt to kill Hitler led by Colonel Klaus von Stauffenberg. This event has come to take on inordinate importance in films about the Nazis, providing proof that some of Germany's generals were against Hitler.

Helmut Kautner directed *The Last Bridge* (1954), the story of a German nurse (Maria Schell), serving with a Wehrmacht unit in Yugoslavia, who is taken prisoner by partisans (led by Bernhard Wicki). Her hostility toward her captors slowly turns to admiration for their courage and dedication, and she ultimately decides that "suffering is the only enemy." She is killed bringing medical supplies across a bridge.

Kautner also directed *The Devil's General* (1956), which stars Curt Jurgens as a World War I German ace who becomes a Luftwaffe general during World War II and, disillusioned with Hitler and Nazism—"I can't eat as much as I want to vomit," he says—commits suicide by crashing his plane. (The film was based on the true story

140

Gunther Hoffman, the youngest of the seven boys and the first to die defending The Bridge *(1959).*

of Ernst Udet, who committed suicide, but in a less dramatic way: he shot himself.) The film made Jurgens, who had spent the last years of the war in a concentration camp, an international star.

Bernhard Wicki, who plays the partisan leader in *The Last Bridge*, made his debut as a director with *The Bridge* (1959), one of the best German films of the postwar period and one of the most powerful antiwar films ever made. The story begins on April 27, 1945: Germany is collapsing, the Allied armies are closing in. Desperately in need of soldiers, the Wehrmacht is drafting schoolboys. Seven boys, all aged sixteen, are drafted together. They are taken out of their schoolroom and put into ill-fitting uniforms (taken off corpses) and given brief training. They are then put into a truck and sent toward the front. Hoping to save their lives, a colonel orders the seven boys off the truck and gives them the job of guarding a bridge on the outskirts of their hometown. The bridge is of no military importance and has already been set for demolition. The colonel expects the boys to run away, but they stay, and then the Americans arrive. The boys die agonizing deaths defending the useless bridge—and two days later the war in Europe ends.

Three films were made about German POWs in Soviet prison camps. *The Doctor of Stalingrad* (1958), directed by Hungarian Geza von Radvanyi, is about a German doctor in a Russian POW camp who performs operations with a pocketknife. He gains the trust of his captors when he successfully removes a brain tumor from the camp commander's son. *Until Hell Is Frozen (The Devil Played the Balalaika)* (1960), directed by Leopold Lahola, is set in 1950 in a POW camp in Siberia full of German and Japanese prisoners anxiously awaiting repatriation. The men formulate escape plans, all of which prove futile. (The film's producer, Peter Bamberger, had himself spent many years in a Russian camp.) *Taiga* (1961), directed by Wolfgang Liebeneimer, is also about Germans in a Siberian camp. The prisoners, starving to death, have lost all hope of returning home. Their spirits are revived by the arrival of a female German doctor, who becomes the symbol of home—the reason for staying alive—for each of the three hundred prisoners.

These three films are remarkable for their ambivalent attitudes toward both the captors and the captives. There are good men on both sides, and the reasons for the war become unclear and meaningless.

The Japanese films about the war are strikingly different from their American counterparts. There was a powerful antiwar movement in Japan following World War II, and Japanese films reflected these sentiments: war was the scene of suffering, not heroics. Two of the best of these films were directed by Kon Ichikawa. *The Burmese Harp (Harp of Burma)* (1956) is a poetically haunting film about a young Japanese soldier in Burma (Shoji Yasui) who is captured by the British. He volunteers to persuade a garrison of Japanese soldiers to surrender, but they refuse and are killed. The lone Japanese soldier wanders the corpse-strewn battlefields and, donning the robes of a Buddhist monk, assumes the responsibility of burying the dead. The soldier is a harpist, and the tune he plays is "Home Sweet Home" (a popular song in Japan even before the war). He plays the song alone, the song is sung by Japanese soldiers, by the British, and then by all of the soldiers together, all of whom want to return home.

Fires on the Plain (1959), set in Leyte in 1945 during the last days of the fighting there, is a far more brutal film. The Japanese Army has ceased to exist, and small groups of stragglers fight only to survive. Starving, they eat the enemy dead and, eventually, they begin to kill one another for food. A tubercular soldier (Eiji Funakoshi), rejected by his unit, wanders alone, witnessing scenes of murder and cannibalism.

The death of Joseph Stalin in 1953 led to greater freedom for filmmakers in the Soviet Union and in those countries under its rule. The strictures of propaganda and party dogma were loosened, and the massive, heroic epics gave way to smaller films characterized by a romantic sentimentality. *The Cranes Are Flying* (1957), directed by Mikhail Kalatozov, was one of the first films to display this new, more personal view of the war. The story concerns two lovers (Alexei Batalov and Tatyana Samoilova) who are sepa-

141

rated by the war. The film has an unhappy ending—he is dead, she is married to another man—and in the place of propaganda, there is an honest depiction of the effects of war.

Ballad of a Soldier (1959), directed by Grigori Chukhrai, is a lyrically beautiful film about a young soldier (Vladimir Ivashov) who, as a reward for heroism, is given a six-day pass to go home. He wants to see his mother and fix the roof of her house. His journey home is long and complicated. He meets and falls in love with a girl (Shanna Prokhorenko); he becomes involved in the emotional homecoming of a one-legged soldier; he dutifully brings two bars of soap to the home of a fellow soldier, only to find that the man's wife is living with another man. When he finally reaches his home, he has only enough

time to embrace his mother before turning around to go back to the war.

In Poland, the mid-1950s was a period of dynamic vitality, as a new generation of filmmakers sought to examine the war and its effects on the political and social beliefs of Poles. Among the leaders of this movement was Andrzej Wajda, who directed a trilogy of war movies, beginning with *A Generation* (1954). *A Generation* is about a group of teenagers who become Resistance fighters during the German occupation and are hunted down by the Gestapo. The generation was Wajda's—he had become a Resistance fighter at the age of sixteen. Among the actors in the film is Roman Polanski, who, at the age of eight, had been separated from his parents (his mother died in Auschwitz) and had sur-

vived the destruction of the Krakow ghetto.

Kanal (They Loved Life) (1956) recounts the final days of the Warsaw uprising of 1944. To escape the Germans, a small group of Home Guard soldiers and Resistance fighters goes down into the city's sewers. The Germans know they are there: all the exits are either blocked or booby-trapped. The partisans wander through the maze of stinking excrement and sewage. Some drown, some go insane, and some manage heroically to hold onto hope.

Ashes and Diamonds (1958), the last film of this trilogy, takes place in a small provincial town on May 9, 1945, the first day of the new peace. As the town prepares for a victory celebration, two members of the nationalist underground arrive with orders to kill the newly arrived district secretary, a Communist. One of them (Zbigniew Cybulski) succeeds in killing the

man but is himself killed. With peace comes only renewed strife.

The title of the film is taken from a poem by Cyprjan Norwid, a nineteenth-century Polish poet. The poem asks the question of what will remain when all the blazing flames are gone—will there be only ashes and chaos, or will there remain beneath the ashes a diamond? Wajda hoped to find a diamond in Poland after the flames of World War II. He based *Ashes and Diamonds* on a novel by Jerzy Andrzejewski. In 1976, Andrzejewski helped in the formation of the Workers' Defense Committee, an organization that played an advisory role in the formation of the independent Solidarity labor federation in August 1980.

Very few films about the war were made in France during the 1950s, but one, *Forbidden Games* (1952), directed by René Clement, is out-

143

Opposite: *Rentaro Mikuni leads his men in a chorus of "Home Sweet Home" in* The Burmese Harp *(1956).*

Below: *Vladimir Ivashov takes aim at a German tank in* Ballad of a Soldier *(1959).*

standing. The film begins with truly terrifying scenes of a German fighter strafing a column of refugees. The parents of a six-year-old girl are killed in the attack, and the girl (Brigitte Fossey) wanders alone until she is taken in by a family of peasants. She becomes the close friend of the family's nine-year-old son (Georges Poujouly), and the two children imitate the cruel adult world around them by creating a private cemetery for dead animals. They begin by burying the girl's dead puppy. They find other dead animals

to bury, steal crosses, and devise special funeral rites. When the adults discover this forbidden game, they send the girl away. She ends up alone and abandoned.

Hiroshima, Mon Amour (1953), directed by Alain Resnais, is about rebirth in the aftermath of war. A French actress (Emmanuele Riva) goes to Hiroshima to make a movie about peace. While there she has an affair with a Japanese architect (Eiji Okada). The woman is tormented by her past—she lost her lover, a German sol-

144

dier killed by the Resistance, during the war; the man lost his family to the atomic bomb. He is able to help her survive her memories so that she can face the future.

In Italy, the 1950s were distinguished by earthy comedies starring such glamorous stars as Gina Lollobrigida and Sophia Loren. Neorealism was not entirely forgotten, however. In *General Della Rovere* (1959), Roberto Rossellini returned to the form to tell the true story of a small-time swindler (Vittorio De Sica) who is forced by the Germans to impersonate an important partisan general. The real general is dead, but a group of imprisoned partisans don't know it, and the Germans want the pathetic con man to help them identify the partisans' leaders. When he is put in the prison, the prisoners be-

lieve he is General Della Rovere, their hero and savior. The prisoners worship him and confide in him. He is profoundly affected by their love and respect for him, and he eventually becomes the man he is impersonating. Rather than betray his comrades to the Germans, he faces a firing squad.

In *The Great War* (1959), directed by Mario Monicelli, two goldbricking soldiers (Vittorio Gassman and Alberto Sordi) do their very best to avoid fighting but end up in the roles of heroes and martyrs. The film is not about World War II, of course: it is about the Italians fighting the Austrians during World War I.

World War I was also the setting for the best American war movie of the decade, *Paths of*

Above: *The two children (Brigitte Fossey and Georges Poujouly) in* Forbidden Games *(1952).*

145

Glory (1957), directed by Stanley Kubrick. The novel, by Humphrey Cobb, on which the film was based had been published in 1935, but its subject—based on an actual incident—was not an appealing one, and Kubrick had difficulty finding financial backing for the film. The story is set in the trenches of the western front in 1916, "after two grisly years of trench warfare." The French General Staff, responding to pressures from newspapers and politicians, decides that an attack must be made. The prime objective is a German strongpoint known as the Anthill. When the plan is broached to the general (George Macready) whose men are to take the Anthill, he wavers, but his mind is made up when the commander (Adolphe Menjou) informs him that the action will probably lead to a promotion.

The generals, with their gray hair and goa-

tees, are corrupt politicians. For them, the war is an opportunity for self-aggrandizement, and they don't concern themselves with the welfare of their soldiers; Macready estimates that 60 percent of the men in the attacking force will be killed, but that is all right. To him, the soldiers are members of a "lower order," good only because "they absorb bullets and shrapnel."

The officer who is to lead the attack (Kirk Douglas) thinks otherwise, but he performs his duty. The hour arrives, he blows his whistle, and the men clamber out of the trenches and run toward the German lines. None of them makes it. They are cut down by machine guns and blasted into the air by artillery (Winston Churchill is said to have admired the realism of the battle scenes).

The attack is an absolute failure; the French soldiers do not succeed even in getting beyond

146

their own line of wire. The failure cannot be blamed on the officers who devised the suicidal attack; the failure is blamed on the soldiers. They are accused of cowardice. "If those little sweethearts won't face German bullets, they'll face French ones," vows Macready. Three men are chosen, one from each company in the first wave of the attack, to be shot as examples to the other soldiers. A mock trial is held (no record is kept, no charges are delivered, no witnesses appear), and the three men are condemned. They are lined up (one, suffering a skull fracture, is tied to an upright litter to face his executioners) and killed by a firing squad. "The men died wonderfully," comments Menjou.

Paths of Glory would seem to be less anti-war than antimilitary. The villains of the film are the corrupt generals; the Germans, theoretically the enemy, are never seen, not even from a distance. And that is the point: in the trenches, there is the constant sound of snipers' bullets whirring by, and explosions send clods of mud down on the crouching, frightened soldiers. It is the Germans who are shooting at them, but they have more to fear from the gray-haired old men mouthing platitudes about heroism and honor.

Like *All Quiet on the Western Front, Paths of Glory* is not about American doughboys. It is about French soldiers and is not an indictment of the American military. The French government did not overlook this fact, and the film was banned in France until 1975. The American military wasn't fooled, however, and for a period after the film's release, it was banned on military bases in the United States.

World War I was remembered in a much different light—the warm glow of nostalgia—in *Lafayette Escadrille* (1958), directed by William Wellman. Wellman, whose *Wings* had first introduced audiences to the wonders of World War I's air war, had a personal story to tell, his own affectionate memoirs of his days serving as an American volunteer with the Lafayette Flying Corps. Cast in the role of William Wellman as a young man is William Wellman's son, Bill Wellman. Among the other fliers are Jody McCrea (son of Joel McCrea), Clint Eastwood, and Tab Hunter.

Lafayette Escadrille is the story of "Ameri-

Above: *Kirk Douglas after leading the disastrous attack in* Paths of Glory *(1957).*

Above: Paths of Glory *(1957)*.

cans who wore French uniforms, flew in French planes, and fell in love with French girls." The only American to fall in love with a French girl is Hunter. He meets and falls in love with Etchika Choureau (who had had her first fling with a Yank during World War II in Wellman's *Darby's Rangers*). The love story is traumatic; the scenes of the youths learning to fly are comedic.

World War III was the subject of several films during the 1950s, all of which are concerned not with the possible causes of such a war but with its aftermath. *Five* (1951), written and directed by Arch Oboler, is a low-budget production about five survivors of an atomic war. Part of the plot involves the clashes between a white man and a black man over the one girl in the group. There is a similar situation in *The World, the Flesh and the Devil* (1959), directed by Ranald MacDougall, which posits a world destroyed by isotopic poisoning. Harry Belafonte and Inger Stevens believe they are the only survivors; then Mel Ferrer shows up.

On the Beach (1959), directed by Stanley Kramer and based on a novel by Nevil Shute, was the first film to seriously question "the bomb" as a deterrent to war. It takes place after a devastating nuclear war; radioactive fallout is spreading across the world. The only place where there is still human life is Australia, and that situation is soon going to end: the Australians are told they have only five more months. Gregory Peck is the commander of an American submarine that arrives in Australia and then goes on a journey, searching for life, along the western coast of the United States. There is no one alive anywhere. A scientist (Fred Astaire) explains that there is no simple explanation for why the war happened. As he says, "The war started when people decided to defend themselves with bombs."

Samuel Fuller, whose *The Steel Helmet* had been the first film about the Korean War, made the first American film about another Asian war. *China Gate* (1957) begins with newsreel footage informing viewers of a faraway conflict being fought by the French against the Communists. The film stars Angie Dickinson as a tough lady named Lucky Legs who leads a group of French

Foreign Legionnaires (among whom are Gene Barry and Nat "King" Cole) in an attack on a Vietcong munitions dump.

The squabble in French Indochina was also the subject of *The Quiet American* (1958), directed by Joseph L. Mankiewicz. Based on a novel by Graham Greene, the story concerns an American who goes to Vietnam and becomes involved in that country's complicated politics. Reviewers complained about the casting of the lead role, but it is exquisitely fitting that the mild-mannered American, who arrives in Saigon with his trusty dog, Duke, and his own schemes for settling the conflict, is played by Audie Murphy. Having been to hell and back, he had yet one more stop to make.

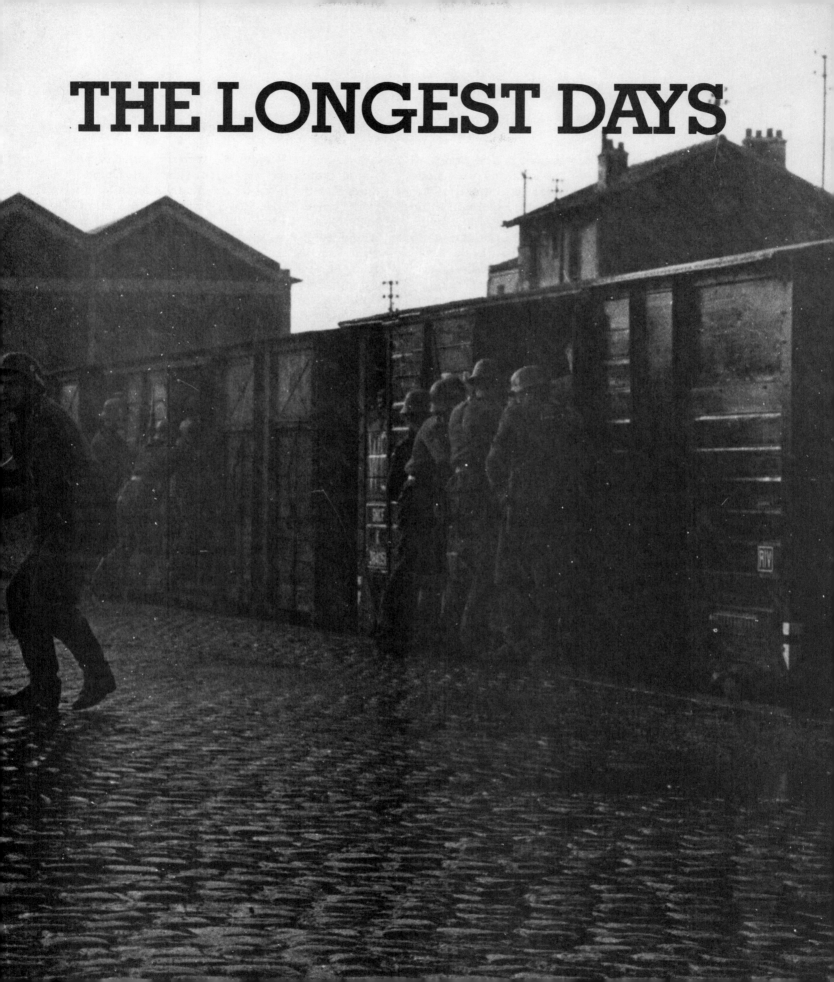

THE LONGEST DAYS

In one of the last scenes of *The Bridge at Remagen*, one of the last war movies of a decade woefully full of war movies, a German officer (Robert Vaughn) is executed by a German firing squad. Just before he is shot, the officer hears the rumble of aircraft passing overhead.

"Ours or theirs?" he asks a nearby soldier.

"Enemy planes," answers the soldier.

"But who," asks Vaughn, "is the enemy?"

It was a good question. Identifying the enemy during the 1960s was not always an easy task, and uniforms and national insignia offered little help. If a German officer (played by a popular American actor) was uncertain of the issues, so, too, was a new generation of filmgoers. There was a war going on during the 1960s, the war in Vietnam, but almost no films were made about it. Public opinion in the United States was fiercely divided, and American filmmakers, faced with financial difficulties, took no risks. They left the Vietnam War to their competition, television, and sought refuge in a safer war, World War II. That war reached new heights of popularity during the 1960s, but it did so by leaving behind any residual animosities.

The 1960s was a decade of large-scale war epics, most of them made in Europe. By the middle of the decade, 50 percent of all American films were being made in foreign countries. Sets and labor were less expensive overseas, and the studio system rapidly was being replaced by independent productions, many of which involved the efforts—and money—of more than one country: several of the war movies of the 1960s were coproductions of former enemies. It is not surprising that these reenactments of great events present their stories with scrupulous impartiality: they were made for a world market.

The makers of war movies had yet another reason for going to Europe: although it had become difficult to obtain vintage World War II war material in the United States, many European countries still had the tanks, planes, and weapons needed. Thus, a crowd of international stars changed uniforms from film to film as World War II was recreated year to year. War became theater, uniforms became costumes, and the identification of the enemy was sometimes a dramatic revelation.

Under Ten Flags (1960), a coproduction of the United States and Italy directed by Duilo Coletti, stars Van Heflin as an eminently humanitarian Nazi named Reger. Reger commands the *Atlantis*, a German pirate ship that wreaks havoc on Allied freighters. In order to get near the Allied ships, the *Atlantis* masquerades as a friendly ship. At a moment's notice, the wily crew of the *Atlantis* can repaint their vessel, change their uniforms, run up an appropriate flag, and cover the ship's guns. Once near the unsuspecting quarry, down go the gun covers and up goes the German flag. It works wonderfully, and Reger never mistreats the prisoners he takes—he even saves Jews from those of his countrymen who are less philanthropic. Stalking the *Atlantis* is an exasperated British admiral (Charles Laughton). The German is the hero.

The screenplay for *Under Ten Flags* was based on the diaries of Bernhard Rogge. Following his career sinking Allied ships during World War II, Rogge became an admiral in the West German Navy and an officer in NATO. Although based on fact, the film was rejected by Israeli censors. They knew it would not be well received in their country. Adolf Eichmann had just been located in Argentina and brought to Israel to stand trial.

The distinguishing characteristic of the war movies of the 1960s was size. Filmmakers were trying to lure audiences away from their television sets, and they believed that the best way to do that was to offer what television could not: lengthy, wide-screen spectaculars with all-star casts. The first of these epic-size war movies was *The Guns of Navarone* (1961), directed by J. Lee Thompson. The screenplay was written by Carl Foreman based on a novel by Alistair MacLean. The story concerns six commandos (including Gregory Peck, Anthony Quinn, and David Niven) sent to the island of Navarone to destroy two large German guns. Each of the men chosen for this perilous mission has some special skill (even if it is only killing) and a character to match it. These men are not to be confused with a squad of GIs—they are professionals. As one says, "If you want to win a war, you have to be just as nasty as the enemy." It is their leader (Peck) who, in responding to this statement, pro-

152

vides a clue to the war movies to come: "What worries me is that we're going to wake up one morning and find out we're even nastier than they are." (He was correct: in just six years, the good-guy Allies awoke to find themselves *The Dirty Dozen*.) They succeed in their mission, and the final explosion of the guns so pleased both audiences and the filmmakers (the film's special effects won an Academy Award) that explosions like it provided the exciting conclusions to a cycle of similar films.

The wide screen could be used to tell true stories, too, and there were lots of stories to tell. Bernhard Rogge and Adolf Eichmann were only two of the survivors of World War II still living: the world was full of men who had served on one side or the other during the war. When historian Cornelius Ryan began assembling material for a history of the D-day invasion, he located and interviewed hundreds of men who had participated in the battle. The resulting book, a reconstruction of D day from the personal reminiscences of the men who lived through it, is a masterpiece of popular history, and it led to the next of the monster war spectaculars of the 1960s, *The Longest Day* (1962).

Right: *Fabian* (center) *and Robert Wagner in* The Longest Day *(1962).*

The production of the film rivaled the logistics necessary for the original battle. Three directors were required—Ken Annakin (for the British sequences), Andrew Marton (for the American sequences), and Bernhard Wicki (for the German sequences)—and more than fifty actors were given parts (among them John Wayne, Richard Burton, Peter Lawford, Henry Fonda, Robert Mitchum, Robert Ryan, Rod Steiger, Robert Wagner, Paul Anka, Sal Mineo, Fabian, and Sean Connery). Some have important roles; some appear in brief cameos. Using recognizable actors helps viewers keep track of who is whom, but it also detracts from the film's authenticity: John Wayne is John Wayne no matter what name he is given. The Germans in the film speak German; the French speak French. Each character is identified when he or she first appears, and the story of the battle moves forward as a series of vignettes, cutting back and forth from the invaders to the defenders.

It is an impressive spectacle. The myriad, simultaneous events convey a sense of the battle's enormous breadth, and some of the scenes—the British sloshing ashore to the accompaniment of bagpipes or the Americans cheering as they rush across the sands of Utah Beach—almost touch the wonder of the moment. The incidents of heroism are matched by incidents of humor or irony, and the film tries to be fair to both sides. "I sometimes wonder which side God is on," mutters John Wayne in one scene, and the same statement is soon made (in German) by a German officer.

The Longest Day was made on location in France, and officers and enlisted men who had taken part in the battle, both Allies and Axis, acted as advisers and consultants. The battle scenes were reproduced with such care that stills from the film are reputedly indistinguishable from pictures taken during the battle. A great many soldiers were needed for these scenes, and the producers were loaned thousands of NATO troops. When, in August 1961, during the shooting of the film, the East Germans began constructing the Berlin Wall, the absence of these NATO soldiers was not appreciated by the American government, and when some of the soldiers complained that they had been forced to work on the film, the result was a congressional investigation that led to changes in the Pentagon's policies governing cooperation with filmmakers.

The difficulties involved in getting US government cooperation did nothing to curtail the production of war movies. The success of *The Guns of Navarone* and *The Longest Day* led to a cycle of large-scale war epics. David Lean followed the success of his *The Bridge on the River Kwai* with *Lawrence of Arabia* (1962), the story of T. E. Lawrence (Peter O'Toole) and his exploits as a leader in the Arab revolt against the Turks during World War I. Few films present a more appealing vision of war—it is exciting and personally fulfilling. With a score by Maurice Jarre that makes the desert seem like the sea, *Lawrence of Arabia* is an intimate sort of spectacle, the story of one man living out his personal fantasies.

Carl Foreman independently produced *The Victors* (1963); he also directed the film and wrote the screenplay. The film begins with newsreels of the kaiser, World War I, and the rise of Hitler.

Above: *George Peppard* (left) *and Vince Edwards in* The Victors *(1963).*

Below: The Victors *(1963)*.

The newsreels continue, showing England during the Blitz, Roosevelt declaring war, and, finally, a squad of American GIs firing at a sniper in a small Sicilian town. But this last newsreel comes to life: the GIs making their way cautiously through the streets include Eli Wallach, George Hamilton, and George Peppard. The film follows the story of this squad of Americans from the fighting in Sicily to the occupation of Berlin. The story mixes newsreels with episodes involving the various members of the squad, small incidents that reflect aspects of the war. Some of the incidents are so odd, so wonderfully ironic, that it seems they must be true, based on personal remembrances; some are so bitter that they seem contrived; all show the destructive effects of war on both the victors and the vanquished.

The absurdity and horror of the war are in the smallest details of the film as well as in its largest scenes. There is the terrible buzzing of flies as gas-masked men pile up the bodies of dead soldiers; the members of the squad are marched through snow to act as witnesses to the execution of a deserter while on the soundtrack Frank Sinatra sings Christmas carols. The wartorn Europe the soldiers walk and ride through is full of streets and squares whose names and monuments are all dedicated to peace. The victorious Americans include GIs who enjoy "coon hunting"—beating up black soldiers. Eli Wallach, the squad's sergeant, disappears from the stories without an explanation. In a later episode, George Peppard goes to visit him in a hospital, and Wallach no longer has a face—it has been blown away. The film ends in East Berlin, a dark city of gutted buildings and bomb craters. Making his way through the rubble, George Hamilton encounters a drunken Russian soldier. There is a plank laid across a crater; each soldier wants the other to cross first. Their politeness turns to anger, and they have a fight with knives; each kills the other in a grim first encounter of the Cold War.

155

The Great Escape (1963), directed by John Sturges, provides a more pleasant view of the war. The screenplay for the film, written by James Clavell and W. R. Burnett, was based on the book by Paul Brickhill that had helped inspire the cycle of 1950s POW films. Like those earlier films, *The Great Escape* is about courageous POWs who outwit their German captors and escape, but *The Great Escape* is a much larger and longer film, and to the traditional British inhabitants of the prison camp are added some very independent Americans. The prison camp, Stalag Luft Nord, is a special camp for prisoners who have made repeated escape attempts. As the not unlikable German commandant (Hans Mesemer) explains, "We have in effect put all our rotten eggs in one basket, and we intend to watch this basket carefully."

Putting all those men together is a foolish mistake, and they are soon busy digging three tunnels (named Tom, Dick, and Harry) and preparing for the mass exit of 250 men. The prisoners believe it is their duty to escape, for even if they don't make it to freedom, they will pull German troops away from other duties. The ingenuity and resourcefulness of the POWs are inspiring, and most of the film deals with their preparations for the escape. Air pumps and a miniature railway are constructed for the tunnels, and while some men dig, others make maps, compasses, clothes, identification papers, and various other items. The major actors are neatly divided by their special skills: Charles Bronson and John Leyton are the "tunnel kings"; Donald Pleasance is "the forger"; James Garner is "the scrounger"; David McCallum is in charge of "dispersal," getting rid of the dirt from

the tunnels; James Coburn is the "manufacturer"; Nigel Stock is "the surveyor"; Gordon Jackson is "intelligence"; and Richard Attenborough is "Big X," the mastermind of the entire affair. More important than any of these is Steve McQueen as Hilts, "the cooler king," who is rarely seen because he spends most of his time tossing a baseball against the walls of the cooler, where he is kept in solitary confinement.

Only seventy-six men escape, and of those only three make it to freedom. The others are recaptured. The film's most spectacular scenes are of McQueen trying to jump a motorcycle over a barricade on the Swiss border. Fifty of those who are captured are executed by the Gestapo. McQueen is not one of these—he is brought back to the camp and proudly walks off toward the cooler, a friend tossing him his baseball on the way.

A novel by James Clavell served as the basis for *King Rat* (1965), directed by Bryan Forbes. The setting for the film is the Changi jail in Singapore, a Japanese POW camp full of Allied prisoners. Here there are no daring escape attempts, no schoolboy high jinks. The prison is a squalid cage, and the prisoners are rats, struggling to survive. Corporal King (George Segal), an unscrupulous con artist, takes merciless advantage of his fellow prisoners and connives his way into

luxury and power. King's hold over the other prisoners ends only with the surrender of Japan. When the camp is liberated, he becomes just one more GI.

The Hill (1965), directed by Sidney Lumet, is about another kind of prison camp, a British military detention camp in North Africa. The inmates are British soldiers guilty of some wrongdoing—thieves, cowards, deserters, black marketeers—and the officials and guards are British soldiers. The "hill" is a man-made mound of sand constructed at a sixty-degree angle. The prisoners are made to march up and down this hill carrying full packs in temperatures of 115 degrees. They march until they collapse. One of the prisoners is Sean Connery; the cruel master sergeant in command of the camp is Harry Andrews.

Italiano Brava Gente (Attack and Retreat) (1964), directed by Giuseppe De Santis, was the first motion picture to be jointly sponsored by Italian, Russian, and American production companies. The film was made on location in the Soviet Union, with Russian, Italian, and American actors. Shot in black and white in a realistic, documentary style, the film centers on the Italian campaign in Russia, from 1941 to 1943, and though it is told from the point of view of the Italian invaders, it is the Russians who are the

real heroes. Sprawling and episodic, the film relates the personal stories of a series of Italian soldiers: each man tells his own tale, and each tale ends in the death of the speaker. Although the separate incidents are intensely personal, each has the sense of being monumental: a battle with a Russian tank in a playground, a soldier who dies in a field of blossoming sunflowers, Russian peasants singing the "Internationale." In one scene, a squad of Italians is ordered to shoot a group of saboteurs among whom is an innocent young girl (Shanna Prokhorenko). The Italians line up and shoot—and no one shoots the girl. Peter Falk, a raincoat thrown over his shoulders, appears as a wealthy man's son, a doctor whose ongoing monologue mixes humorous comments with quotations from Italian poet Eugenio Montale; Arthur Kennedy plays a Fascist major with a crippled left hand.

The Train (1964), a coproduction of the United States, France, and Italy directed by John Frankenheimer, includes the kind of international cast commom to movies of the sixties—Burt Lancaster, Paul Scofield, Jeanne Moreau, Albert Remy, and Wolfgang Preiss. The film asks a pertinent question: are objects of art as valuable as human lives? Set in 1944, the story concerns the efforts of the French Resistance to prevent the Germans from shipping French art treasures to

157

Germany. The Germans consider the paintings "decadent art," but they recognize their value and intend to use them to finance the war. Many of the partisans who risk their lives to save the art have never set foot in a gallery or museum, but the works represent "the heritage and glory of France." Lancaster is the leader of the hijackers; Scofield is the German colonel trying to get the art to Germany. The film develops into a spectacular chase, and the trains themselves establish their own dramatic presence.

Trains are also of central importance to *Von Ryan's Express* (1965), directed by Mark Robson. Frank Sinatra stars as Colonel Ryan, an American flier shot down over Italy and taken to an Italian POW camp. There he comes into conflict with the ranking British officer (Trevor Howard). Because the British have been undertaking their traditional escape attempts, they are being deprived of medicine and clothing. Ryan, who outranks the Briton, puts an end to the escape attempts, even shows the Italians where the British tunnels are. This traitorous act earns him the nickname "von." When Italy capitulates, the Italian guards flee, and Von Ryan, aided by a sympathetic Italian (Sergio Fantoni), leads the four hundred prisoners out of the camp. Before they can reach the Allies, however, they are recaptured by the Germans, who put them on a train bound for Germany. Von Ryan and his men commandeer the train and take off on a mad dash for the Swiss border. (Part of this daring escape involves the Allied officers dressing up in German uniforms.)

It sometimes seemed during the 1960s that the outcome of World War II had been determined not by armies but by small groups of men. *Operation Crossbow (The Great Spy Mission)* (1965), a coproduction of Great Britain and Italy directed by Michael Anderson, is about the destruction of the German rocket installations at Peenemünde. The story is based on actual incidents, but in the end it is George Peppard who saves the day by pulling the correct lever to open the doors and allow British bombers to destroy the installation—and he does this while wounded and firing a machine gun. It is the kind of role Errol Flynn had fun with during the war. The large cast includes Sophia Loren, in a very small part; the German rocket factory, full of flashing colored lights and an array of control panels, is a wonderland of German ingenuity.

The Heroes of Telemark (1966), directed by Anthony Mann, is about the heroic efforts of Norwegians to prevent the Nazis from developing the atomic bomb. This film is also based on actual incidents, but once again the heroics of the main characters detract from the story's plausibility. A Norwegian professor (Kirk Douglas) and a Norwegian partisan (Richard Harris) battle each other and the Germans in their efforts to destroy a shipment of "heavy water" before it can reach Germany.

The worst of the large-scale war epics to follow *The Longest Day* was *Battle of the Bulge* (1965), directed by Ken Annakin. Filmed in Spain in Cinerama, it covers the familiar story of the famous battle and its familiar elements, including the English-speaking German infiltrators; McAuliffe's "Nuts"; the massacre at Malmedy; the power of the German tanks; and the influence of the weather on the outcome of the battle (although it is pointed out many times that the poor weather is preventing American air support, many of the scenes take place under cloudless blue skies). The leader of the Germans is a humorless panzer commander (Robert Shaw). This veteran of many fronts is delighted with the new tanks he is offered—monster King Tigers—but unhappy with the large number of boys who are to serve as the crews. The boys prove their dedication by stamping their feet and singing a rousing chorus of "The Panzerlied." The Ameri-

Left: *Tom Courtenay* (left) *and George Peppard in* Operation Crossbow (1965).

can forces facing this fearsome attack include Telly Savalas, who uses his meek Sherman tank in his lucrative black-market business; James MacArthur (who survives the massacre at Malmedy); and Henry Fonda, as a former police inspector whose warnings of an imminent German attack go unheeded. In this version of the battle, the contest finally comes down to possession of one fuel dump. When Fonda and his crew deny the Germans access to the fuel (Shaw burns up in his tank to the tune of "The Panzerlied"), the King Tigers run out of gas and are left standing all across the treeless plains of Spain. As an American officer says of the Germans, "They've abandoned their tanks, and they're walking back to Germany."

In Harm's Way (1965), directed by Otto Preminger, stars John Wayne and Kirk Douglas as naval officers fighting the Japanese in the Pacific. The film begins with the attack on Pearl Harbor. "We got ourselves another war—another gut-bustin', mother-lovin', navy war!" announces Douglas, barely hiding his pleasure, but the two men have to fight their way through several personal problems (including nurses, an estranged son, and a case of rape) before they can get at the Japanese.

In *Cast a Giant Shadow* (1966), produced, directed, and written by Melville Shavelson, Kirk Douglas plays David "Mickey" Marcus, the American officer who became a general in the Israeli Army. When Marcus is asked to help train the ragtag Israelis, his friend General Randolph (John Wayne) cautions him not to go, but go he does, leaving behind his beautiful wife (Angie Dickinson). In Israel, he is so successful at training the army that he is made commander of all Israeli forces. He also meets and falls in love with a freedom fighter (Senta Berger). Before this romantic biography ends, Yul Brynner, Frank Sinatra, and Topol make appearances in cameo roles.

Kirk Douglas appears briefly in the role of General Patton in *Is Paris Burning?* (1966), directed by René Clement. Douglas is only one of a crowd of stars in this rambling account of the liberation of Paris in August 1944. The cast also includes Jean-Paul Belmondo, Charles Boyer, Leslie Caron, Glenn Ford, Anthony Perkins, Simone Signoret, Robert Stack, and Orson Welles. The screenplay was written by Gore Vidal and Francis Ford Coppola based on a novel by Larry Collins and Dominique Lapierre; the title comes from Hitler's supposed demand to General Die-

159

Top and above: *Battles in the streets of Paris between Germans and members of the Resistance in Is Paris Burning? (1966).*

trich von Choltitz, whom he had ordered to destroy the city if it could not be held. (Von Choltitz died a few days before the film's release.) As with so many of these epics, the film is composed of a series of vignettes, each of which has its star and its little story to tell. In this case, the small parts do not join to create a coherent whole.

An inevitable result of all these international coproductions with their efforts to tell the story of World War II from both sides was that the Allies sometimes became the villains. Such is the case in *The Saboteur, Code Name Morituri (Morituri)* (1965), directed by Bernhard Wicki. Like *The Sea Chase* and *Under Ten Flags*, this involves an anti-Nazi sea captain (Yul Brynner). Among his passengers is a German civilian (Marlon Brando) who is being blackmailed by British Intelligence agents into spying for them— he is Jewish, and his Allied tormentors threaten to inform the Nazis.

The Battle of El Alamein (1968), an Italian-French coproduction directed by Calvin Jackson Padget (Giorgio Ferroni), recreates the famous battle from the point of view of the Italians and their German allies—the British are the villainous enemy. Rommel (Robert Hossein) is heroic; Montgomery (Michael Rennie) is thoroughly un-

Above: *The ship carrying the heavy water sinks in* The Heroes of Telemark *(1966).*

Above: *Checking road signs that have been changed by German infiltrators in* Battle of the Bulge *(1965).*

Above: *The final explosion of the bridge in*
The Bridge on the River Kwai *(1957).*

Below: *Richard Burton* (right) *in* Raid on Rommel *(1971).*

sympathetic. The film was shot on location in North Africa.

The character of the German officer still displayed some of its "cultured swine" heritage. In *Counterpoint* (1968), directed by Ralph Nelson, a music-loving German general (Maximilian Schell) controls the fates of an American symphony conductor (Charlton Heston) and his entire orchestra. It is December 1944, and the haughty conductor and his musicians are in Belgium on a USO tour. They are interrupted during a rendition of Beethoven's Fifth by news of a German breakthrough: the Battle of the Bulge. Still wearing their tuxedos, they scramble aboard their bus and, following directions offered by some very amiable military police, they soon find themselves the prisoners of some very cold-hearted Germans (the helpful MPs were English-speaking German infiltrators, of course). They are taken to a nearby castle, headquarters of the cultured German officer, who sips Moselle and never travels without his clavichord. Although he has orders to kill all prisoners, the general wants the conductor, whose work he has long admired, to give one last performance. The conductor stalls, well aware that when the music ends so will his life and the lives of his seventy musicians.

Night of the Generals (1967), directed by Anatole Litvak, is about three German generals (Peter O'Toole, Donald Pleasance, and Charles Gray). All three are responsible for the deaths of many people, but one of them is a maniacal murderer of prostitutes, and a Wehrmacht Intelligence officer (Omar Shariff) is determined to bring the man to justice. The search ends twenty years after the war, when the guilty general kills again.

Anzio (1968), an Italian production directed by Edward Dmytryk, is about the stupidity of two American generals (Arthur Kennedy and Robert Ryan). One is overly cautious, the other is eager to make headlines, and their combined foolishness leads to disaster for the American landing force. Robert Mitchum plays a newspaper correspondent determined to find out the truth about the battle. He and a squad of GIs (among them Peter Falk) take a trip behind enemy lines. On their way back, in the film's best scenes, they are nearly all killed by German snipers.

One of the most ambitious of these epic recreations of historic events was *Battle of Britain* (1969), a British film directed by Guy Hamilton. The film boasts a giant cast (including Harry Andrews, Michael Caine, Trevor Howard, Curt Jurgens, Laurence Olivier, Christopher Plummer, Michael Redgrave, and Ralph Richardson) and some remarkable scenes of aerial combat. (The producers had difficulty locating the correct aircraft, but they found that the Spanish Air Force still flew the same Heinkel bombers used by the Luftwaffe during the war.) The story to be told—of how a tiny force of British fliers fought off overwhelming numbers of German fighters and bombers and ended Hitler's plans to invade Britain—is one of the most dramatic of the war. The film, however, is surprisingly undramatic. Its best scenes are those in which the wonderful Spitfires fly circles around the lumbering German bombers. The terrible truth of the battle is only glimpsed, as in scenes of the sky over London, a glowing red haze. Although the film tries to be fair to both sides, the Germans seem wooden-headed—led by a comical Goering—and the British have extremely stiff upper lips. The film ends with lists of the numbers of men killed on both sides during the battle.

The Battle of Neretva (1969), directed by Velijko Bulajic, was a mammoth coproduction of the United States, Yugoslavia, Italy, and West Germany. The film tells the compelling story of how a small army of Yugoslavian partisans fought against masses of German, Italian, and Chetnik forces to bring four thousand of their wounded safely across the Neretva River. It was a great victory for the Yugoslavian partisans, and Josip Broz Tito had long wanted to make it into a film. The stars of the film include Yul Brynner, Curt

161

Jurgens, Hardy Kruger, Franco Nero, and Orson Welles. Kruger plays the commander of the German invasion forces; Welles has a few scenes as a representative of the Chetnik government.

The Bridge at Remagen (1969), directed by John Guillermin, relates yet another exciting story of World War II—the capture of the last bridge left standing over the Rhine. The production of the film proved that using European locations for the recreation of battles can be perilous. The producers of the film found the kind of bridge they needed in Czechoslovakia; they leased vintage tanks, half-tracks, and armored cars from the Austrian Army. The vehicles, film crew, and actors were all assembled on location in Czechoslovakia. Filming began in the late summer of 1968, during the last days of the "Prague Spring," the brief period of democratization brought about under the leadership of Alexander Dubček. The filming came to an abrupt end in August, when the modern tanks of the Soviet Union and its Warsaw Pact allies rolled across the Czech borders to crush Dubček's liberal government. The local newspapers charged that the "American" tanks were there in support of Dubček; the East Germans called the film a CIA cover-up. The actors and crew fled the country in a fleet of taxis, a new bridge was constructed at Castel Gandolfo, Italy, and the filming resumed.

The completed film tells the story of the capture of the bridge at Remagen, and, in the tradition of *The Longest Day*, both sides of the engagement are presented. Robert Vaughn, wearing sunglasses instead of the once-customary monocle, is the commander of the Germans defending the bridge. He has orders to destroy the bridge, but he hesitates because to do so would cut off the retreat of a German army. The Americans, led by E. G. Marshall, are surprised to find the bridge still standing, and they rush to secure it. Among the GIs are George Segal and

162

Left: *An RAF airfield under attack in* Battle of Britain *(1969).*

Ben Gazzara. The latter claims that he is "going to get out of this war rich," and he habitually robs the dead. The Germans fail to destroy the bridge, and when the gallant Vaughn returns to headquarters for reinforcements, he is put under arrest and executed. He has just enough time to deliver his terse query about the identity of the enemy.

It was not the purpose of *The Bridge at Remagen* to identify the enemy. The purpose of the film was to make a historic event into an exciting, entertaining spectacle. The characters of the participants are incidental to the well-staged battle scenes. That one of the GIs is robbing the dead made the film seem more "realistic" to an increasingly cynical audience. The Vietnam War was responsible for some of this cynicism: the antiheroic stance of many of these films reflects a growing disillusionment with the military.

This cynicism expressed itself most clearly

in the offspring of *The Guns of Navarone*. By 1967, these films had grown older and meaner, and mixed with their cynical view of the war was increasingly graphic violence. American films in general, responding to a youthful audience's thirst for thrills, were becoming more violent: 1967 was the year of *Bonnie and Clyde*. Violence in films increased in measured increments in the same way and during the same period that nudity in films increased. Buttocks in one film prepared the way for breasts in another; after seeing dripping blood in one film, viewers were inured to the sight of gushing blood in the next.

Tobruk (1967), directed by Arthur Hiller, is about Allied commandos sent to Tobruk to destroy its fuel dump and seize its fortifications as preparations for an invasion. The unit is composed of British commandos (led by Nigel Green), an American (Rock Hudson), and members of something called the Special Identification Group—German Jews who are fighting for the Allies (led by George Peppard). The plan calls for the Jews to dress up in German uniforms and get the British commandos through the Axis checkpoints as prisoners. "It's suicide!" complains Hudson. "It's orders!" states Green. Once inside the city, the commandos go to work on the German and Italian defenders. The Allies, the heroes of the film, make extensive and,

163

at times, almost gleeful use of flamethrowers and manage to blow up one of the massive guns (this *Navarone*-like scene was reused in 1971's *Raid on Rommel*). The scenes involving flamethrowers are particularly gruesome.

Robert Aldrich had presented a preview of this mixture of violence and cynicism in *Attack!* Loyalty to the military establishment was replaced by loyalty to a peer group; fighting for a cause was replaced by fighting for personal rewards. In *The Dirty Dozen* (1967), a coproduction of the United States and Great Britain, Aldrich stretched these notions to their nastiest limits and presented war as a mindless exercise in brutality.

The plot of the film is simple: twelve men, psychopaths and sadists, murderers and rapists, in prison and condemned to death, are told that their crimes may be forgiven if they will take part in a suicidal mission behind enemy lines. Since they face certain death if they stay where they are, they agree to go. These twelve (among them John Cassavetes, Charles Bronson, Jim Brown, Telly Savalas, Clint Walker, Donald Sutherland, and Trini Lopez) are led by an iconoclastic major (Lee Marvin) and a tough sergeant (Richard Jaeckel). The major puts the hoodlums through rigorous training. He knows the twelve have become a team when they, as a group, refuse to shave in cold water. He counters their refusal by forbidding them to wash at all, and they thus become "the dirty dozen." With their killing skills honed to perfection, these men are parachuted into Brittany: their mission is to invade a French château used by high-ranking

German officers for recreation and kill as many of the Germans as they can. The method they use is both simple and alarmingly sadistic: they trap the Germans and their female companions in the château's bomb shelter and then, pouring in gasoline and grenades, they incinerate them.

The members of "the dirty dozen" are not fighting to bring an end to Hitler and Nazism—they are fighting for themselves. And although they wear American uniforms, their methods resemble those of the SS. They are the quintessential war movie commandos.

Commandos were popular throughout the 1960s. Commandos do not experience the misgivings or fits of fear that plague GI Joes; commandos are professionals, and they usually enjoy their work. Cynical and antiheroic, they have no respect for officers (who usually send them on suicidal missions) and are not profoundly concerned with the reasons for the war they are fighting. They are detached from the vagaries of ideology, and their nationality is of no importance. Indeed, the most destructive groups of commandos are frequently composed of a mixed bag of nationalities, the best killers and explosives experts from several nations, men who share something more than a language or a fondness for the same cuisine: killing. Commandos are the ultimate symbol of war detached from moral or historical concerns: in a world of specialists, war is something that commandos do. This notion, engendered by movies, led to the belief prevalent during the 1970s that all men who fight in a war must be ruthless killers.

Among the most popular commandos are the

164

Opposite: *Vietcong attack in* A Yank in Viet-Nam *(1964).*

French Foreign Legionnaires. They seem willing to fight and die for anything. Since they operate for France, their enemies are often unfamiliar and appealingly foreign. The enemies of the Legionnaires in *Commando* (1964), an Italian film directed by Frank Wisbar, are Algerians. Stewart Granger stars as the leader of a group of twelve commandos sent to rescue an Algerian rebel leader. Most of the commandos are killed during the suicidal mission, and at the end, with the rebel delivered, it is learned that it was all for naught: a ceasefire has been signed.

Some other former enemies of the French, already encountered in Samuel Fuller's *China Gate*, are fought by Americans in *A Yank in Viet-Nam (Year of the Tiger)* (1964), directed by Marshall Thompson (who is also the film's star). This low-budget production was one of the few American films about Vietnam made during the 1960s. Filmed on location in South Vietnam, it is about an American marine major (Thompson) who is rescued by South Vietnamese guerrillas when his helicopter is shot down by the Vietcong. He joins the guerrilla band and takes part in a raid against the Vietcong. He also falls in love with one of the guerrillas. *A Yank in Viet-Nam* went relatively unnoticed in the United States; Swed-ish critics felt it was a particularly repugnant film.

In *The Devil's Brigade* (1968), directed by Andrew V. McLaglen, other misfits volunteer their way out of jail and become fearsome soldiers. Unlike *The Dirty Dozen*, this film was based on a true story, and it was made with the assistance of the Pentagon. The story concerns Colonel Robert T. Frederick (William Holden), who takes "the scum of the stockade" (among whom is Richard Jaeckel with his head shaved) and turns them into a crack fighting unit, the First Special Force. The Americans comprise only half of this unit; the other half is made up of quite normal Canadian soldiers. This group achieves great victories in daring commando raids, particularly in the capture of Monte La Difensa, an important obstacle in the battle for Cassino. Their actions brought them great praise from Winston Churchill, but they were even more pleased when the Germans nicknamed them "the Devil's Brigade."

In *Attack on the Iron Coast* (1968), a British film directed by Paul Wendkos, Canadian commandos led by Lloyd Bridges take part in Operation Mad Dog, an attack on a German naval base in France. In *Commandos* (1968), a joint production of Italy and West Germany, a group of

tough Americans (including Lee Van Cleef) leads Italian commandos in an attack on an oasis in North Africa. Aldo Ray and four British commandos parachute into Germany on the eve of the Normandy invasion and destroy an airfield in *Suicide Commando* (1969), an Italian film directed by Camillo Bazzoni. In another Italian film, *Battle of the Commandos* (1969), directed by Umberto Lenzi, Jack Palance leads six "jailbirds" (incarcerated misfits who volunteer their way out of jail) on a pre-Normandy raid to destroy two German observation posts and a railway gun. A German fuel dump in the North African desert is the target for a group of British commandos in *Play Dirty* (1969), a British film directed by Andre de Toth. With the exception of the captain (Michael Caine) who leads them, all of the commandos are ex-cons.

One of 1968's films about commandos was not popular with all audiences. Based on a novel by Robin Moore, *The Green Berets* (1968) was produced and directed by John Wayne (Ray Kellogg helped with the direction). Made with the full cooperation of the State and Defense departments (army officials were later criticized for the vast amounts of men and material they loaned out), the film recounts the exploits of a team of

US Special Forces—Green Berets—led by Colonel Michael Kirby (John Wayne) in Vietnam. In the first part of the film, the Green Berets defend a "strike" camp against hordes of Vietcong; in the second, they kidnap an enemy general. The character of the enemy is made clear: the Vietcong rape and torture, pillage and destroy; they are led by generals who swill champagne, eat caviar, and ride in limousines. The cause of the Green Berets is therefore just, and even a skeptical journalist (David Janssen) who accompanies Colonel Kirby to Vietnam eventually picks up a rifle and joins in the fray: like the members of the audience, he has learned the truth about the war and is eager to fight the barbaric Vietcong. The film ends with Colonel Kirby walking off into the sunset with an adoring South Vietnamese orphan.

The Green Berets was the only major American film about the Vietnam War made during the war, and it was not well received. Most critics were appalled by its simpleminded politics and its praise of violence; antiwar groups picketed it. American soldiers had been fighting and dying in Vietnam for more than seven years when *The Green Berets* was released, but they were there without the customary support of Hollywood. It

166

was more than proper that it was John Wayne who made the film. Having led marines in heroic charges off beaches and through jungles to face other Oriental enemies, he would have been the right man to follow. He had been there, at Bataan and Iwo Jima, had been in enough American war movies that he had no trouble identifying America's enemies, and he knew what an American victory was like. When many soldiers in Vietnam tried to imagine themselves heroes, they imagined themselves John Wayne. But they couldn't be John Wayne heroes, there was to be no great victory, and their frustration became a national frustration. *The Green Berets* made money, but it didn't change the attitudes of the American public. Ironically, the film's theme song, "The Ballad of the Green Berets," gave a hint of the opinion

of the war eventually shared by many Americans: "Fearless men who jump and die," runs one line of the song—it sounds suspiciously like suicide.

Yet another group of commandos is assembled for yet another daring mission in *Where Eagles Dare* (1969), directed by Brian G. Hutton. But in this movie, which was based on a novel by Alistair MacLean, the limits of this type of story are reached and gleefully passed. Richard Burton and Clint Eastwood are the leaders of a special unit parachuted into Bavaria to rescue an American general from an inaccessible and impregnable German fortress, Schloss Adler ("Castle of the Eagles"). Dressed in German uniforms, the two superheroes massacre regiments of Germans when not rescuing each other from situa-

Opposite: Attack on the Iron Coast *(1968).*

167

tions of dire peril. There are many twists to the exciting story, and all the killing is done in a spirit of good, clean fun.

World War II was the most popular topic of the 1960s on screens of various dimensions. Programs about the war replaced westerns as the staple of television. Some of the television series about the war were based on characters or themes created by movies, and some were pure invention. "McHale's Navy," "The Gallant Men," "Garrison's Gorillas," "Hogan's Heroes," and "Mister Roberts" were among the World War II programs offered during the decade. The best, however, was "Combat," which ran from 1962 to 1967, starring Vic Morrow, Rick Jason, Jack Hogan, and Pierre Jalbert.

The popularity of the war on television did nothing to abate the production of war movies, and the war epics were accompanied by a flood of other World War II films. The early years of the 1960s saw a number of biographies of war heroes. Like *To Hell and Back*, *Hell to Eternity* (1960), directed by Phil Karlson, relates the story of a war hero from his childhood to his military service. At the age of eleven, Guy Gabaldon (played at this stage by Richard Eyer), an orphan of Spanish descent, is adopted by a Japanese-American family. By the time of Pearl Harbor, he (played now by Jeffrey Hunter) speaks fluent Japanese, and although he is barely over five feet tall, he is accepted by the Marine Corps. During the fighting on Saipan, he puts his knowledge of Japanese to good use, coaxing thousands of die-hard enemy soldiers into surrendering.

The Gallant Hours (1960), directed by Robert Montgomery, is a documentarylike account of the career of Admiral "Bull" Halsey (James Cagney). *The Outsider* (1961), directed by Delbert Mann, tells the story of Ira H. Hayes (Tony Curtis), a Pima Indian and one of the marines who took part in the famous flag raising on Iwo Jima. Samuel Fuller presented another of his straightforward and grim accounts of infantrymen in combat in *Merrill's Marauders* (1962), the story of General Frank D. Merrill (Jeff Chandler, in his last film role). The film has no subplots and no flashbacks to wives or sweethearts. Rather, it is a series of hard-fought battles as the gray-haired

168

Merrill and his scruffy, sweaty volunteers grapple with the Japanese in Burma. The men, who suffer from typhus and malaria, are pushed by Merrill to the limits of their endurance. In one scene, they don't know what day it is and can't even agree on whether it is morning or evening: they exist only to fight the enemy. Of the original three thousand, only one hundred remain in action, and the film ends with the statement that their tradition is being carried on by the Special Forces.

The most celebrated war biography of the 1960s was *PT 109* (1963), directed by Leslie Martinson, a unique film if only because its leading character was at that time president of the United States. Kennedy made three requests of the filmmakers: that the film be accurate, that any royalties due him be given to the survivors of his crew or to their families, and that he have final approval of the actor who would impersonate him. The actor chosen was Cliff Robertson; Kennedy approved.

Several films during the 1960s made antiwar statements by focusing on the dehumanizing effects of war on soldiers. *War Hunt* (1962), directed by Denis Sanders, is set in Korea during the last weeks before the final truce that ended the war. The loudspeakers are there, of course—the North Koreans use them to broadcast propaganda and, just before attacks, loud music. Among the Americans facing the North Koreans is Private Endore (John Saxon). For Endore, killing the enemy is an impersonal act: he kills without conscience. Every night, dressed in black and armed only with a stiletto, Endore goes out alone to kill. He returns from his nocturnal forays with

information about the enemy positions, making him a valuable soldier, much appreciated by his officers. What they don't know is that Endore has become a compulsive killer; he performs an animallike dance over every soldier he kills. He has no friends except for a young Korean orphan named Charlie, and he resents anyone else even speaking to the boy. "I used to wonder about that guy," says one soldier of Endore. "I'm sure glad he's on our side." Private Loomis (Robert Redford, in his screen debut) is less certain. Loomis worries about Endore's influence on Charlie. When a ceasefire is declared, everyone worries about Endore: if he goes out and kills during the ceasefire, the hopes for a truce will be ended. Endore goes out, and the other Americans hunt him down. They have to kill him.

The theme of *War Hunt* goes back to *They Gave Him a Gun* and prefigures the rash of films made during the 1970s and 1980s about Vietnam War veterans who—because they have been soldiers, trained to kill—cannot adjust to peace. An ad for the film stated, "It happened on a raging battlefield, but he could have been a murderer stalking a city's streets!" The war hero was on his way to becoming a social misfit.

The War Lover (1962), directed by Philip Leacock and based on a novel by John Hersey, stars Steve McQueen as an Army Air Corps captain who considers the war "work"—and he loves his

job. Indeed, the war is his life. He has no home to go back to, is cynical about personal relationships, and lives only to fly in his B-29, called *The Body*. As one of his fellow airmen points out, he could be on either side. He and his copilot (Robert Wagner) become involved in a love triangle (with Shirley Ann Field). It is McQueen who dies, heroically trying to save *The Body*.

Hell Is for Heroes (1962), directed by Donald Siegel, presents a brutal story of World War II in which terrifying violence is made more acute by an atmosphere of loneliness. Steve McQueen stars as an embittered combat veteran for whom the war is a very personal affair. A courageous soldier, he is a cynical loner who believes that human relationships are ruled by expediency. "People do the same all over the world—go with the time," he says. He and the other nine men in his squad are sent to defend an area along the Siegfried Line that would normally be defended by a company. Until reinforcements can arrive, they have to make the Germans believe that they are a much larger force. The battle scenes, including one in which James Coburn tries to destroy a pillbox with a flamethrower, are vivid; the film's tension is destroyed somewhat by unneeded comedy supplied by Bob Newhart (in his first movie) as a clerk carrying on an extended phone monologue for the benefit of German eavesdroppers. The reinforcements finally arrive, and there is an all-out attack on the pillbox. Mc-

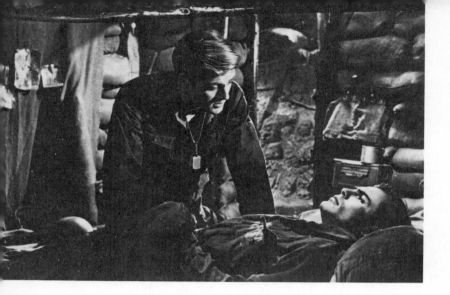

Queen dies heaving a satchel charge into the opening of the pillbox. He disappears into the opening, swallowed by flames. The last scene is of GIs running toward the pillbox, men falling dead on every side, the opening of the pillbox engulfed in fire. It is in the middle of this battle that the film ends; the words "The End" appear written over the flames.

War Is Hell (1963), a movie about the Korean War that was produced, written, and directed by Burt Topper, begins with an introduction by Audie Murphy in which the most decorated soldier of World War II discusses the impact of war on soldiers. One of the things war does to soldiers is make them hungry for medals and glory. Such is the case with one particular GI named Keefer (Tony Russell). He and three other GIs are sent to destroy a North Korean pillbox; the other three men die in the action, and Keefer claims sole credit for destroying the pillbox. When a lieutenant (Topper) expresses doubts, Keefer kills him and assumes command, leading the men in merciless attacks against the North Koreans, even after a ceasefire has been declared.

Captain Newman, M.D. (1962), directed by David Miller, provides a more compelling depiction of what war does to soldiers. The film relates the story of an air force psychiatrist (Gregory Peck) and his patients. Among them are a former squadron commander (Eddie Albert) who has gone insane and recites over and over the names of the men he sent to death, and a flier (Bobby Darin) suffering ulcers and insomnia because of a truly horrific experience.

Two of the best war movies of the 1960s are about the effects of war on noncombatants. *Two Women* (1961), a French-Italian coproduction directed by Vittorio De Sica, tells the deeply moving story of a mother and daughter trying to

survive in Italy during the Allied invasion. The film follows a widow (Sophia Loren) and her thirteen-year-old daughter (Eleanora Brown) as they travel from war-ravaged Rome to the safety of a village in the south. The two women are raped by Moroccan soldiers, mistreated by Fascists, and strafed by planes. The screenplay for the film, written by Cesare Zavattini, was based on a novel by Alberto Moravia.

Closely Watched Trains (1966), a Czech film directed by Jiri Menzel, is the humorous and compassionate story of a seventeen-year-old trainee (Vaclav Neckar) at an unimportant railway station in Czechoslovakia during World War II. The boy, whose one desire is to "stand on a platform and avoid hard work while others slave," has his first sexual encounter with an attractive conductress, but he fails miserably. He does much better with a female Resistance fighter. His involvement in a plan to blow up a German train leads to his death.

At a distance, enemy soldiers are targets; close up, they are men, and killing them is not so very easy. This truism of war, used to great effect in the antiwar films of World War I, appears in films about other wars. *The Long and the Short and the Tall (Jungle Fighters)* (1961), a British film directed by Leslie Norman, is about a platoon of British soldiers in Malaya in 1942 who are cut off and surrounded by the enemy. When they capture a Japanese scout (Kenji Tagaki), there are arguments about what to do with him. The bumbling sergeant (Richard Todd) insists that they get their prisoner safely back to their lines; a very individualistic private (Laurence Harvey) agrees; the other men want to shoot the Japanese. There is a similar situation in *The Hook* (1963), directed by George Seaton, but the setting is the Korean War. Three Americans (Kirk Douglas, Nick Adams, and Robert Walker) are returning to their headquarters aboard a neutral freighter with a North Korean prisoner (Nehemiah Persoff). They learn by radio that the North Koreans have destroyed a village, and a vindictive South Korean officer orders them to kill their prisoner. The sergeant (Douglas) orders the privates to carry out the order; they refuse. The screenplay for the film was based on a novel by

Vahe Katcha, *L'Hameçon*, the setting of which was yet another war, the Algerian war.

Taxi for Tobruk (1965), a French film directed by Denys De La Patelliere, is about four Free French soldiers in North Africa who capture a German Afrika Korps captain (Hardy Kruger) and a German truck. The Frenchmen take their prisoner, who speaks French, and drive the truck toward their lines. En route, they find that they have much in common with the enemy soldier, and they come to depend on and even like him. One of the Frenchmen (Charles Aznavour) is Jewish, but he, too, eventually accepts the German. This small peace comes to a sudden end when the German truck they are in is spotted by an Allied tank.

None But the Brave (1965), directed by Frank Sinatra (this was his first film as director), is about another separate peace established between enemies. The scene of the film is a small island—so small it doesn't appear on maps—in the Pacific during World War II. The only inhabitants of the island are a platoon of Japanese soldiers who are virtually marooned there. They have no radio and no contact with the outside world until a plane carrying a platoon of American marines crash-lands on the island. The Americans' radio is damaged in the crash, so they, too, are marooned. The two opposing forces are equal. Indeed, the film takes great pains to show that they are identical: the commander of the Japanese (Tatsuya Mihashi) is very similar in his beliefs to the commander of the Americans (Clint Walker)—they are both "brothers in the loneliness of command"—and the soldiers of both groups are given matching personalities; each group has one hothead eager for combat. The two platoons snipe at each other for a while, but then the Japanese officer asks the American pharmacist's mate (Sinatra) to inspect the leg of one of his wounded men. Sinatra saves the man's life, and there is a truce. For a short period, the two groups coexist happily on their isolated island. The peace ends when the American radio operator succeeds in fixing his radio and sends for help. When the rescue ship arrives, the two groups return to their warlike attitudes, and there is a bloody battle in which all the Japanese and most of the Americans are killed. The film ends with the title "Nobody Ever Wins."

171

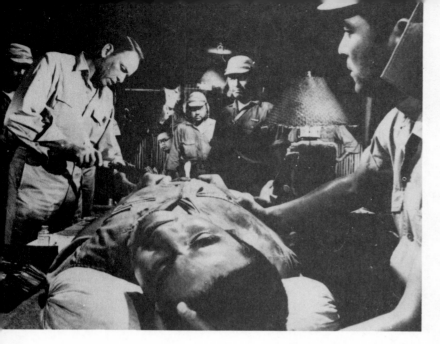

near a wounded Japanese soldier. The two boys make feeble efforts to help each other. Their moment of peace is short-lived. Just as the Japanese lifts his arm to pass the American a match, other marines appear and shoot him. From a distance, he was an enemy soldier; to the wounded marine, he was just another scared boy.

The most cynical view of heroism and the nobility of war was couched in a comedy, *The Americanization of Emily* (1964), directed by Arthur Hiller. The screenplay, by Paddy Chayefsky, was based on a novel by William Bradford Huie, and the theme of the film—that live cowards are better than dead heroes and that glorifying war dead only creates the mood for more wars—did not please everyone. It is James Garner, an admiral's aide stationed in London, who espouses this philosophy. He is a "dog robber": his duties are to supply an admiral (Melvyn Douglas) with hotel accommodations, bourbon, delicacies, bridge partners, and female companionship. He is absolutely without scruples in this scrounging and in his determination to avoid combat. He believes that the men who get themselves killed are not heroes but gullible fools and that the women who venerate the dead are just paving the way for more wars.

His ideas shock the patriotic Englishwoman (Julie Andrews) with whom he falls in love. She has lost her husband, father, and brother to the war, and she believes Garner's selfish attitudes are the result of his American materialism. Then the overpressured admiral, in the throes of a breakdown, decides that the first man to die on Omaha Beach during the coming D-day invasion should be a sailor—the navy needs the publicity. The man chosen is Garner, who survives the ordeal to become a "dead" hero.

How I Won the War (1967), a British film directed by Richard Lester, is not just an antiwar film—it is an anti-war-film film. The man who "won the war" is Lieutenant Goodbody (Michael Crawford). With ponderous stupidity, Goodbody leads a platoon of soldiers through battles in North Africa and Europe, never learning from his experiences and forever endangering everyone near him. Goodbody survives the war, but none of his men does. They all die grisly deaths, in-

Hell in the Pacific (1968), directed by John Boorman, tells the same story with a much smaller cast: one Japanese (Toshiro Mifune) and one American (Lee Marvin). Mifune, a Japanese naval officer stranded on a remote island, discovers that he is no longer alone when he spots a raft. The new arrival to the island is an American flier (Marvin), and he, too, soon realizes that he is not the only one on the small island. The two stalk each other for a while, then Mifune captures Marvin, tortures him, and nearly starves him to death. Marvin gets free and does the same to Mifune. They finally stop fighting and, although neither speaks the other's language, they become friends and collaborate on the construction of a raft. After several days at sea, they reach another island, where they are reminded of the war. Their peace is quite literally blown apart.

Beach Red (1967), directed by Cornel Wilde (who also stars in the film), tells the story of a marine landing on a Japanese-held island. Like the many films made during the 1950s about such events, the film uses flashbacks to establish the characters of the marines, but unlike those earlier films, there are also flashbacks for the Japanese defenders. *Beach Red* also differs from other beachhead films in that it is full of horrific violence: when a wounded marine, lying in the water near the beach, stands up, his severed arm stays behind, floating in the bloody foam. Each step of the battle is an agony of brutally graphic deaths. The fear of the young marines (among them Burr De Benning and Patrick Wolfe) becomes palpable, and there is no letup in the tension until one of them, wounded, falls

cluding Private Gripweed (John Lennon), who, shot in the stomach, looks out at the audience and says, "I knew this would happen. You knew this would happen, didn't you?" Each of the battles is introduced by a colored bubble-gum card, and the men who are killed remain with the platoon as ghosts tinted to match the color of the battle in which they died.

The film was attacked by critics for making fun of a serious subject, and British critics were particularly upset by its derisive characterizations of Churchill and Montgomery. American audiences had too much trouble understanding the dialogue to be offended.

The connection between the Beatles and World War II was made firmer in 1976's *All This and World War II*, directed by Susan Winslow. This is a compilation of World War II newsreels set to the music of the Beatles as performed by several groups and performers, including Elton John, the Four Seasons, the Bee Gees, Frankie Laine, the London Symphony Orchestra, Helen Reddy, Leo Sayer, and Tina Turner.

Most of the comedies about World War II are

less cynical, and most are set in Italy, tacitly acknowledged as the most enjoyable of World War II's theaters of operations. *What Did You Do in the War, Daddy?* (1966), directed by Blake Edwards, is about a company of American infantrymen sent to capture a Sicilian town. When they enter the small town, they find it is occupied by Italian troops. The commander of the Italians (Sergio Fantoni) asks the Americans if they wish to surrender. "Hell, no!" responds the American captain (Dick Shawn). "Do you surrender?" "Of course," replies the Italian. There is one small hitch: the Italians demand a day's delay to celebrate a traditional wine festival. The captain is persuaded by his lieutenant (James Coburn) to allow the festival to go on, and even the arrival of some belligerent Germans does nothing to end the merrymaking.

In *The Secret War of Harry Frigg* (1968), directed by Jack Smight, five Allied generals, captured while enjoying a Turkish bath in North Africa, are imprisoned in a villa in northern Italy. The villa is a very pleasant place—it is run by a former manager of the Ritz Hotel—and the generals are making no attempts to escape. Private Harry Frigg (Paul Newman), an incorrigible rule-breaker who is adept at breaking out of prisons, is made a temporary general and sent to free the generals.

The Secret of Santa Vittoria (1969), directed by Stanley Kramer, is about a small Italian town and the heroic efforts of its denizens to keep the Germans from confiscating their one million bottles of wine.

Castle Keep (1969), directed by Sydney Pollack, is a surrealistic fairy tale about "eight walking-wounded misfits"—a group of GIs led by a one-eyed major named Falconer (Burt Lancaster)—who stumble upon a castle in Belgium. They set up residence in the castle, which is full of priceless art treasures. One of the GIs (Patrick O'Neal), an art historian, becomes dedicated to preserving the castle and its art. One (Scott Wilson) falls in love with a Volkswagen. He loves the car because it is indestructible. "Someday," he vows, "the world is going to be populated by nothing but Volkswagens." One of the GIs (Peter Falk), a Brooklyn baker, finds a bakery and a baker's wife in the nearby town and happily re-

173

Left: *Patrick Wolfe as a young marine about to face the Japanese in* Beach Red *(1967).*

sumes his trade. With the blessings of the impotent count of the castle (Jean-Pierre Aumont), the major undertakes to impregnate the countess. The group's would-be writer (Al Freeman, Jr.) provides occasional narration, but it is a dreamy, talk-filled film, and it moves easily from scenes of humorous philosophizing to stylized battles. The castle happens to be on the road to Bastogne, and with the snow of that famous Christmas of 1944 falling in the castle's rose garden, the GIs try to defend the castle from hordes of Germans.

King and Country (1964), a British film directed by Joseph Losey, begins with a view of a World War I memorial amid busy London traffic. The Great War was not forgotten during the 1960s: the trenches of the western front remained the most popular symbol of war's futility and the best setting for an antiwar film. *King and Country* is about a British Army private named Hamp (Tom Courtenay) who decides one day to go for a walk. Leaving the rain and mud of Passchendaele, he sets off for home. A volunteer from the first year of the war, he has been in the trenches too long and is suffering from shell shock. He makes it as far as the embarkation point of Calais, where he is arrested by military police and brought back to stand trial for desertion. The captain who defends him (Dirk Bogarde) realizes that he is innocent, but there is nothing he can do to save him. Were Hamp's wound physical, he would be considered a heroic war veteran; since it is mental, he is condemned to death.

King of Hearts (1967), a coproduction of France and Great Britain directed by Philippe De Broca, is a sweet, eccentric comedy about a Scot-

174

tish private (Alan Bates) who is sent into a French town to disarm a time bomb left there by retreating Germans. The townspeople have all fled, leaving open the gate to the local insane asylum. The inmates wander out of the asylum, dress themselves up, and take over the town. When the private arrives, the lunatics make him their king. Ultimately, following a truly insane battle in which the Germans and the British slaughter one another, the private is no longer certain of who is sane and who isn't.

World War I's ever-exciting air war is presented from the German point of view in *The Blue Max* (1966), directed by John Guillermin. The title refers to Germany's highest award to its World War I aces, a blue cross nicknamed "the Blue Max" for Max Immelmann, one of its most celebrated recipients. Among the aristocratic airmen eagerly shooting down Allied aircraft to earn this coveted medallion is one son of the working class (George Peppard). The count (James Mason) in charge of this particular squadron wants to make the unscrupulous social climber a hero. It is 1918, Germany is losing the war, and the working class is growing increasingly discontented. They need a hero. The countess (Ursula Andress) and the proletarian ace have some steamy love scenes, but the film is most exciting when it's in the air.

Fräulein Doktor (1969), an Italian-Yugoslavian film directed by Alberto Lattuada, is another story of World War I told from the German viewpoint. The fräulein of the title (Suzy Kendall) is a German espionage agent whose missions include involvement in the death of British Field Marshal Kitchener and the theft of the secret of poison gas. The gas is put to fearsome use, and the scenes of skin peeling off the arms and hands of Allied soldiers gassed by the Germans are grisly. The crack female spy is pursued by the director of British Intelligence (Kenneth More).

Richard Attenborough, who had his first acting role in Noel Coward's *In Which We Serve*, made his debut as a director with *Oh! What a Lovely War* (1969). The film begins with a "happy family called Smith" attracted to a special show on Brighton's seaside pier. "World War One," announces an illuminated sign over the entrance;

"Songs, battles, and a few jokes," promises a poster. The family buys tickets to the war and enters. The film switches from the cheerful seaside amusement park, where famous battles can be viewed through peep-show machines and a giant Casualty Scoreboard keeps count of the dead, to scenes of men dying in muddy shell holes. It is the songs of the period that provide the framework for the film. All those jaunty little patriotic ditties are revealed as being more than just pleasant music-hall numbers. There is a bitterness and a tragic irony behind them, and the film tries to make the viewer understand the truth of the war, a truth sometimes lost in nostalgia. The final scene of *Oh! What a Lovely War* is unforgettable—rows and rows of white crosses stretching out as far as the eye can see.

In *Panic in Year Zero* (1962), directed by Ray Milland, a husband (Milland), wife (Jean Hagen), and their children (Frankie Avalon and Mary Mitchel) go for a little drive out of the city. They have not gone very far when the sky behind them is suddenly lit up by a bright flash of light. They soon learn that there has been a nuclear attack and that Los Angeles and four other American cities have been destroyed. The family manages to survive the ensuing period of mayhem—looting, rioting, murder—by taking refuge in a cave.

It was a topical film. Until 1962, most Amer-

icans had preferred to ignore the threat of nuclear attack, but the Cuban missile crisis made the possibilities of World War III terrifyingly apparent. Nuclear war became a constant worry for a great many people.

Dr. Strangelove or: How I Learned to Stop Worrying and Love the Bomb (1964), directed by Stanley Kubrick, did absolutely nothing to allay anyone's fears. It is General Jack D. Ripper (Sterling Hayden) who, convinced that the Communists are out to destroy his "precious bodily fluids," sends his B-52s to obliterate the USSR. While RAF Group Captain Lionel Mandrake (Peter Sellers) tries to break the recall code to stop the bombers, US President Merkin Muffley (Sellers) confers with Soviet Ambassador de Sadesky (Peter Bull) and General "Buck" Turgidson (George C. Scott). Mandrake breaks the code, and all the bombers are stopped—all but one (its radio has been broken), the one piloted by the "rootin', tootin', shootin', and salutin'" Major T. J. "King" Kong (Slim Pickens). Kong accepts the situation with heroic aplomb. "Well, boys," he tells his crew, "I reckon this is it: nuclear combat, toe to toe with the Ruskies." He assures his men that regardless of "race, color, or creed," they'll all be in line for promotions when the war is over. Meanwhile, President Muffley has located Soviet Premier Dimitri Kissof, and he apologizes to Dimitri for the "silly thing" that has happened. The premier has some startling news for the president: the Russians have deployed a Doomsday Machine, a device to destroy all life on the earth that is set to go off if any nuclear bomb explodes on Soviet territory. The president seeks the advice of Dr. Strangelove (Sellers), director of weapons research and development. The former Nazi scientist, mumbling about radioactive half-

175

lives while trying to keep his right (bionic) arm from giving a Nazi salute, gleefully reports that such a machine is indeed feasible. When the bomb-bay doors of Kong's B-52 refuse to open, there is a last bit of hope for continued life on earth, but Kong heroically climbs aboard his bomb and, whooping and hollering, takes a ride. The film ends with a series of blossoming mushroom clouds.

Dr. Strangelove is a comedy, a very black comedy about one way in which the world might end. Experts rushed to claim that its scenario was impossible, but not everyone was convinced. *Fail Safe* (1964), directed by Sidney Lumet, is not a comedy. In *Fail Safe*, it is not a deranged general that sends bombers toward Russia, it is a mechanical malfunction. When the failure of the "fail-safe" device leads to the bombing of Moscow, the US president (Henry Fonda) offers the Soviet premier a way of avoiding total war: the bombing by US planes of New York City.

The Bedford Incident (1965), directed by James Harris, presents yet another scenario for World War III. In this case, the war is started by the fanatical commander of an American destroyer, the *Bedford*. The mission of the *Bedford* is to track the movements of Soviet submarines in the North Atlantic. When a Soviet sub is detected within the territorial waters of Greenland, the commander of the *Bedford* (Richard Widmark) relentlessly tracks the sub in an effort to force it to surface and thus embarrass the Soviet Union. The commander has as adviser a former German U-boat commander (Eric Portman), who cautions him that what he is doing is dangerous, but the commander, who styles himself an "old-fashioned patriot," refuses to let up. He drives his crew so hard that one of them accidentally launches a missile. The film ends with swirling mushroom clouds. (Widmark claimed that he modeled his character in the film on the mannerisms and speeches of Senator Barry Goldwater during the 1964 presidential campaign.)

York City.

World War III is only narrowly averted in *Ice Station Zebra* (1968), directed by John Sturges. A Soviet satellite falls to earth near the North Pole. Inside the satellite are photographs of all the missile emplacements in both the United States and the Soviet Union. Both sides want the film, and both are willing to go to war for it. There are spies involved, and the final encounter in the polar snow is diverting. (This was one of Howard Hughes's favorite films: he watched it more than 150 times.)

The only film to depict the actual effects of a nuclear war was *The War Game* (1965), a British film written and directed by Peter Watkins. Made for BBC-TV, the film combines simulated newsreels and street interviews in a straightforward, documentarylike account of a nuclear war.

It shows the effects of a nuclear attack on Great Britain in horrifying detail. In fact, the film is so disturbing that the television producers who commissioned it refused to show it, and it was banned from television in Great Britain.

Another British film, *The Bed Sitting Room* (1969), directed by Richard Lester, provides a more palatable version of the effects of a nuclear war. Based on a play by Spike Milligan and John Antrobus, *The Bed Sitting Room* is a comedy set three years after the world's shortest war (it lasted all of two minutes and twenty-eight seconds). The twenty-odd survivors of blasted London find themselves changing into things: one woman turns into a cupboard; her husband becomes a parrot. Without warning, Ralph Richardson becomes a one-room apartment.

THE SEVENTIES AND ANOTHER WAR

The viewers of 1953's *Battle Circus*, a film about combat surgeons saving the lives of wounded GIs in Korea, were given a clear, topical message: donate blood. There was a war going on, and the men fighting it needed support from the home front. The viewers of 1970's *M*A*S*H*, another film about combat surgeons in Korea, were also given a clear, topical message: war is insane. There was a war going on in 1970, too, but there were no appeals to the home front from American filmmakers. The war in Vietnam caused a great rift in American society, and American filmmakers, lacking a clear consensus of opinion to follow, chose to bide their time. The only film about the Vietnam War to appear in 1970 was a low-budget production called *The Losers (Nam's Angels)*, directed by Jack Starrett, an implausible tale of members of the Hell's Angels taking part in a suicide mission somewhere in Cambodia.

To many Americans, the war in Vietnam was itself a suicide mission. An apparently endless conflict that could not be won, the Vietnam War destroyed one of the most cherished beliefs of many Americans, the belief in the infallibility of their armed forces. It was a belief engendered in large part by films: Americans were used to seeing hordes of Oriental enemies mown down with ease; now they were faced with television newscasters reporting daily casualty figures for a war without victories. The despair and frustration brought on by Vietnam led Americans to question their faith in the military establishment, and although there were no major films about the Vietnam War during the early 1970s, it had effects on films about other wars. The 1970s began with two antiwar comedies, one biography of a general, and one mammoth reenactment of a battle. None is about Vietnam, but all are examinations of the American military.

The setting for *M*A*S*H* (1970) is the 4077th Mobile Army Surgical Hospital, a collection of tents located three miles from the front and seven thousand miles from home. The fighting is never seen, only its aftermath: an endless stream of mangled bodies. The bodies are torn and bleeding, ripped open and squirting blood. There is no letup in the nauseating spectacle. The situation never gets better and only gets worse, until the viewer wants to look away, afraid of what might come next. This is the antiwar statement of *M*A*S*H*. None of the actors ever says a word about this terror, no one cries out or faints or vomits. But the bodies are everywhere: they are what war is.

The members of the audience can look away; the surgeons and nurses operating on the ground-up boys cannot. They have other ways to maintain their sanity, and their responses to the carnage of war are what the film is about, for, in this most unlikely of places, *M*A*S*H* is a comedy, an irreverent satire of war and the people and institutions that accept and perpetuate it. From a mock recreation of *The Last Supper* (a good-bye party for a dentist who, fearing he is a victim of latent homosexuality, is committing suicide) to a madcap football game in which the doctors drug their opponents' best player, the film is merciless in its ridicule. Those people who hold on to rules and rituals—whether military, religious, or social—are exposed as fools and frauds. Their clumsy salutes and mumbled prayers mean nothing against that blood-red background.

M*A*S*H was director Robert Altman's first important feature film, and in it he used the techniques for which he has since become famous, techniques that create a texture of compelling realism. There is no one story to follow in *M*A*S*H*—the "story" of the film is the environment of the hospital, a real world peopled by real people. The viewer is never formally introduced to anyone and must labor to understand what is happening. The characters of the leading players—Hawkeye Pierce (Donald Sutherland); Trapper John McIntyre (Elliott Gould); Major Frank Burns (Robert Duvall); Major Margaret O'Hoolihan (Sally Kellerman); Duke Forrest (Tom Skerritt); Colonel Henry Blake (Roger Bowen); Corporal "Radar" O'Reilly (Gary Burghoff); Father Mulcahy (Rene Auberjonois)—must be pieced together, assembled from a mixture of overlapping conversations and relationships. Like Hawkeye and Trapper John, the viewers have been drafted for a certain period of time, and the end of the film is not the end of the war or the end of a story—it is just the end of their tours of duty.

Preceding pages: Just Another War (Uomini Contro) *(1970)*.

The irreverence of the comedy—religion is the favored subject for ridicule, but army regulations, sex, and sports are among the other targets—shocked many people, and the film's cynical portrayal of army life led to its being banned on all American military bases for a short time after its release. But the world created by Altman and scriptwriter Ring Lardner, Jr., was enormously popular. The film was a hit and led to a long-running television series.

Less popular was *Catch-22* (1970), directed by Mike Nichols. Based on a best-selling novel by Joseph Heller, *Catch-22* adheres so closely to its source that those viewers who hadn't read the book had trouble following the film. Like *M*A*S*H*, *Catch-22* is an antiwar comedy about efforts to survive the insanity of war. And like *M*A*S*H*, *Catch-22* has at its heart a nightmare of death. But in *Catch-22*, there is only one body being ripped open, and one of the characters has a great deal to say about the horror around him. Yossarian (Alan Arkin) knows exactly what is going on: people are trying to kill him. He is a very sane man in a very insane situation, a situation in which what is logical and what is eth-ical have no significance, for there is always a catch—Catch-22.

Catch-22 is a comedy, but beneath the humor is a powerful mixture of horror and helplessness. The setting for the film is an American Army Air Force bomber base located on an island in the Mediterranean during World War II. In command of the base are colonels Cathcart (Martin Balsam) and Korn (Buck Henry), who continually increase the number of missions required before a flier can be rotated out of combat. There is also a major named Major (Bob Newhart), an officer who can be consulted in his office anytime he isn't in his office. The ostensible commander of these men is General Dreedle (Orson Welles), but the man really in charge is Milo Minderbinder (Jon Voight), creator of M&M Enterprises. It is Minderbinder's global capitalism that is running the war, and his thoroughly nonpartisan methods make perfect sense to the bureaucratic, self-serving officers. As Minderbinder says, "There are tremendous profits to be made." Minderbinder trades the fliers' silk parachutes for cotton from Alexandria. In place of each parachute, he leaves one share in M&M Enterprises. When he

Above: *Mixing golf with surgery, Elliott Gould (left) and Donald Sutherland being driven by Bobby Troup in M*A*S*H (1970).*
Right: *Sutherland and Gould in M*A*S*H.*

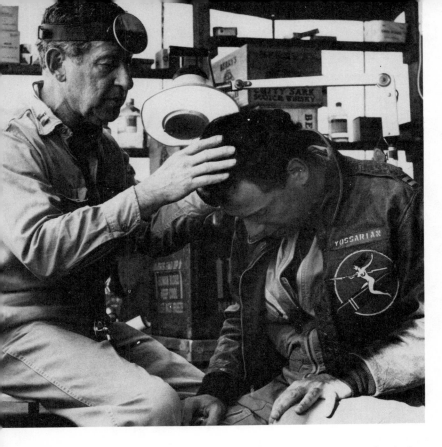

Left: *Jack Gilford* (left) *examines the very sane Yossarian (Alan Arkin) in* Catch-22 *(1970).*
Opposite: *George C. Scott in* Patton *(1970).*

fails to find a profitable way to get rid of the cotton (including turning it into candy), he accepts payment from the Germans in return for which he has American bombers bomb the American base. As he says, "What's good for M&M Enterprises is good for the country."

Yossarian knows that all these people are insane, and he knows that it is crazy to continue flying combat missions. In fact, since he keeps flying the missions, he, too, must be crazy and should therefore be grounded. But when he reports to the flight surgeon to get himself grounded for being crazy, he is informed of Catch-22: his wish to stop flying proves conclusively that he is sane and must keep flying combat missions. The viciously circular logic of Catch-22 is encountered throughout the film: it is a symbol of the mindless military bureaucracy.

Patton (Patton: Lust for Glory) (1970), directed by Franklin Schaffner, is an examination of one particular military mind, that of General George S. Patton. The most flamboyant and controversial American general of World War II, Patton alternately delighted and enraged the American public; the film honestly depicts the many aspects of his complex character, exposing his ruthlessness and egotistical delusions of grandeur while also portraying his audaciously bold leadership, his courage, and his dedication to his country. The film is most famous for its open-

ing scene, in which Patton (George C. Scott), standing before an enormous American flag, delivers a speech to his soldiers: "Men, all this stuff you've heard about America not wanting to fight, wanting to stay out of the war, is a lot of horse dung. Americans traditionally love to fight. All real Americans love the sting of battle. . . . Americans play to win all the time. That's why Americans have never lost and will never lose a war, because the very thought of losing is hateful to Americans. . . . I want you to remember that no bastard ever won a war by dying for his country—he won it by making the other poor dumb bastard die for his country."

The film follows the career of Patton from the battles in North Africa to Sicily and finally to Europe. It is in Sicily that he slaps a shell-shocked soldier, accusing him of cowardice; it is in Europe that he kisses an officer who has just come through a savage battle and, surveying the bodies and wreckage, cries, "I love it. God help me, I do love it so—more than my life!" To Patton, war is a glorious adventure, a rare and wonderful opportunity to make history. The great leaders of the past—Caesar, Hannibal, Napoleon—are forever with him. His war—World War II—is his chance to outdo the heroics of the past. The battle scenes in *Patton* are remarkable and include a reenactment of the Battle of the Bulge in which the deciding factor is not the weather but the arrival of Patton's troops. The film ends with Patton getting himself into trouble for his unfriendly attitude toward the Soviet Union.

Patton is neither an antiwar film nor a prowar film: it is a compelling biography of a singular man. To some viewers, Patton seemed like a madman, the kind of war lover that gets other people killed; to others, he was an inspiring hero. The film won eight Academy Awards, including best picture, best director, and best screenplay. The screenplay, based on a book by Ladislas Farago, was written by Francis Ford Coppola and Edmund H. North. Coppola's success with *Patton* helped his career, and in 1972, he directed *The Godfather*, one of the most successful films ever made. He was becoming an important leader among American filmmakers.

The image of *Patton* was tarnished somewhat when it was learned that President Nixon

had watched it and liked it so much that he had seen it again, just five days before ordering American forces to invade Cambodia.

Another book by Ladislas Farago—*The Broken Seal,* about the cryptographic war that preceded Pearl Harbor—together with a book by Gordon W. Prange served as the basis for *Tora! Tora! Tora!* (1970), a chronicle of the events leading to the Japanese attack on Pearl Harbor that ends in a spectacular recreation of that battle photographed on location in Hawaii. The title of the film is the code word sent by the commander of the Japanese planes to the carriers to confirm that complete surprise had been achieved and that the raid could go forward as planned (*tora* is Japanese for "tiger"). The film was a coproduction of the United States and Japan, the two former enemies working together to create another blockbuster film in the tradition of *The Longest Day.* Like that film, *Tora! Tora! Tora!* required several directors: the American portions were directed by Richard Fleischer; the Japanese were directed by Toshio Masuda and Kinji Fukasaku. And like *The Longest Day, Tora! Tora! Tora!* cuts back and forth between the opposing sides and is scrupulously impartial—both sides make blunders as they move toward confrontation. The story stresses American incompetence and unpreparedness. It was an expensive film—$25 million—and its producer, Darryl F. Zanuck, placed an advertisement in *The New York Times* explaining the reasons for the film: "The basic reason for producing this film . . . was to arouse the American public to the necessity for preparedness in this acute missile age when a sneak attack could occur at any moment."

The production of war movies declined dramatically following the release of *M*A*S*H, Catch-22, Patton,* and *Tora! Tora! Tora!* There were no more large-scale war movies until 1976, when *Midway* reintroduced the war epic. Disillusionment with the war in Vietnam was making itself felt. Although that war had only rarely appeared in American movie theaters, its end, in 1973, was followed by the customary brief respite from war movies.

Many of the war movies made during the six years before *Midway* are about personal wars involving antiheroic—if not psychopathic—individuals who fight for their own reasons. *Murphy's War* (1970), a British film directed by Peter Yates, is a psychological study of one man and his very private war. Murphy (Peter O'Toole), an Irish seaman, is the only survivor of a ship torpedoed by a German submarine in South American waters during the final days of World War II. The crew of the ship is massacred by the Germans; Murphy is saved by a Quaker missionary (Sian Phillips), and with the help of a French oil engineer (Philippe Noiret), he sets out to avenge himself on the German submarine. The official end of the war does nothing to diminish Murphy's determination. Stirling Silliphant wrote the screenplay for the film based on a novel by Max Catto, and the film was shot on a remote part of Venezuela's Orinoco River.

The Last Grenade (1970), a British film directed by Gordon Flemyng, is about another private search for revenge. Based on *The Ordeal of Major Grigsby*, a novel by John Sherlock, the film begins in an unnamed African country where British mercenary Grigsby (Stanley Baker) is ruthlessly double-crossed by his American associate (Alex Cord). The remainder of the film follows Grigsby's relentless efforts to destroy his archenemy. Along the way, he falls in love with the wife (Honor Blackman) of a general (Richard Attenborough) and is deserted by all of his cohorts. He takes on his final mission alone.

Michael Caine and Cliff Robertson star as two very reluctant heroes in *Too Late the Hero*

(Suicide Run) (1970), directed by Robert Aldrich. The setting is an island in the Pacific during World War II. There is a British garrison on the southern tip of the island; the remainder of the island is controlled by the Japanese. Caine and Robertson are part of a patrol sent through the Japanese-held portion to destroy a radio transmitter. The mission is suicidal, of course, but the patrol manages to blow up the radio and locate an enemy airstrip. With this very valuable information, they try to get back to the garrison. One by one, the members of the patrol are killed; two (Lance Percival and Martin Horsey) are taken prisoner. The last men left, Caine and Robertson, have to make their way through a jungle in which the Japanese have placed loudspeakers. The Japanese commander (Ken Takakura) broadcasts favorable surrender terms and forces the two prisoners to plead with their comrades to surrender. Caine and Robertson do not surrender, and the film ends with an exciting run across an open field.

Like Aldrich's two previous war movies, *Attack!* and *The Dirty Dozen*, *Too Late the Hero* is violent and cynical. Advertisements for the film showed a dead soldier lying across the word *war*

with the legend, "It's a dying business." The advertisement is notable because the soldier's weapon, resting on his chest, is an M-16, the weapon of Vietnam, not World War II.

Brian G. Hutton directed *Kelly's Heroes* (1970), a comedy variation of *The Dirty Dozen*. When Kelly (Clint Eastwood) learns that there is $16 million in gold in a bank thirty miles behind the German lines, he organizes a small force to steal it. Among his antiheroic companions are Don Rickles, Telly Savalas, and Donald Sutherland. The last is an anachronistic hippie whose very personalized tank includes a stereo system and a loudspeaker. He changes the tunes to suit what he is doing; while blasting away at German railroad workers, he plays "I've Been Working on the Railroad." With the help of a German Tiger tank, the heroes get the gold.

The most popular POW-escape film of the 1970s was *The McKenzie Break* (1970), directed by Lamont Johnson. In this film, the daring prisoners who dig their way out of a POW camp are Germans. The prison camp is located in Scotland; among the German POWs are twenty-eight submariners, led by a cunning officer (Helmut Griem). The German prisoners make life for their British captors so hard that a specialist, an Irish Intelligence officer (Brian Keith), is brought in to calm things down. He and the German officer engage in an exciting battle of wits.

Raid on Rommel (1971), directed by Henry Hathaway, recounts a story very similar to that of 1967's *Tobruk*: a group of commandos makes its way through the German lines to Tobruk to destroy the big guns there as preparation for a landing. The story is similar; many of the action sequences are truly identical, taken directly from the earlier film. The film dispenses with *Tobruk*'s German Jews dressed in German uniforms: they are replaced by Richard Burton, who wears a German uniform to infiltrate a German POW convoy. In addition to Burton, the film offers an intriguing scene in which Rommel (Wolfgang Preiss) and a British medic (Clinton Greyn) get into a gentlemanly argument about a stamp, the 1906 two-pfennig brown issue. Prior to this film, Rommel was known as a warm family man and a courageous officer (usually when portrayed by James Mason); that he was also a phi-

latelist comes almost as no surprise.

The war movies made for television during the early 1970s display a fun-loving, good-natured view of the war. *The Birdmen (Escape of the Birdmen)* (1971), directed by Philip Leacock, is about Allied prisoners in a German castle who build a glider and fly to freedom in Switzerland. Doug McClure leads the escapees; Richard Basehart plays the gentlemanly Nazi commandant of the castle. McClure also shows up in *Death Race* (1973), directed by David Lowell Rich. He is one of the pilots of a crippled P-40 fighter that becomes involved in a duel with a German tank—the German tank commander is Lloyd Bridges. Battle footage from *Patton* shows up in *Fireball Forward* (1972), directed by Martin Chomsky. This stars Ben Gazzara as a general who takes over command of a division of American GIs suffering bad luck and worse morale. The only truly serious television war movie of the early 1970s was *The Execution of Private Slovik* (1974), directed by Lamont Johnson, which stars Martin Sheen as Eddie Slovik, the only American soldier since the Civil War to be executed for desertion (in 1945). The screenplay was adapted from a book by William Bradford Huie.

Having tried on German uniforms in *Where*

Eagles Dare and *Raid on Rommel*, Richard Burton finally plays a German in *Massacre in Rome* (1973), an Italian film directed by George Pan Cosmatos. The story of the film is based on an actual incident—the execution of 330 Italian civilians in reprisal for an attack on German soldiers. The film follows the events, day by day, that led to the massacre, presenting the actions of both the Resistance fighters and the German officers. Burton is an idealistic German colonel; Marcello Mastroianni is a priest who restores art. When a group of SS soldiers is attacked in a street and thirty-three men die, the colonel is ordered to execute ten Italians for every German soldier killed; the priest tries to reason with him. The executions are performed in the Ardeatine caves, limestone tunnels near Rome. The film ends with a list of the names of those killed and gives the subsequent fates of the German officers involved.

The Pedestrian (1974), a German film produced, written, and directed by Maximilian Schell, is about the postwar fate of one German officer. Gustav Rudolf Sellner stars as a West German industrialist, a member of parliament, a proud grandfather, and a well-respected man. He is the "pedestrian"—he has lost his driver's license because of an accident in which his oldest son (Schell) died. The accident was the result of a violent argument between the father and son, and it leads the editor (Peter Hall) of a sensationalist German newspaper to investigate the wartime record of the industrialist. He discovers that Sellner was one of two German officers responsible for the slaughter of a Greek village. The film examines the relevance of individual war guilt in a society that condones, even dismisses, war. In one remarkable scene, four elderly ladies (Peggy Ashcroft, Elisabeth Bergner, Francoise Rosay, and Lil Dagover) discuss—in German, French, and English—the wars they have lived through and only vaguely remember.

The memory of World War I was kept alive in several films during the 1970s. Dalton Trumbo made his debut as a director with *Johnny Got His Gun* (1971). A World War I infantryman (Timothy Bottoms) survives a bomb blast with his mind and the trunk of his body intact; his arms, legs, and face are gone, and he lies in a hospital bed, blind, deaf, dumb, and paralyzed. His dreams—which include encounters with Christ (Donald Sutherland)—and his memories are in color; the rest of the film is in black and white. He is left alone, kept alive but neglected, until a nurse (Diane Varsi) writes "Merry Christmas" on his chest. Using telegraphy—bouncing his head on a pillow—he is able to make known his thoughts. And what he wants is to be taken out and shown to the world so that people will see the truth about war.

Trumbo based the film on his 1938 novel. The novel had done nothing, of course, to prevent World War II, and it had taken a long time for him to realize his dream of making the book into a film. The antiwar sentiments of the 1970s, brought on by another war, made its theme pertinent once again.

Just Another War (Uomini Contro) (1970), an Italian-Yugoslavian coproduction directed by Francesco Rosi, is about Italian soldiers condemned to suicidal attacks on an Austrian stronghold by a glory-seeking general. The hero is a young lieutenant (Mark Flechette) who begins to believe that it is wrong to obey insane orders; he is supported by a very political-minded lieutenant (Gian Maria Volonté). Like *Paths of Glory*, the film makes clear the class distinctions between the generals and the soldiers. Most of the soldiers are Sardinians. They know neither why they are there nor for what they are fighting; their generals view them as worthless expendables.

There is similar exploitation in *Black and White in Color* (1976), a coproduction of the Ivory Coast and France directed by Jean-Jacques Annaud. The film is set in West Central Africa in 1915. Although there is a war raging in Europe,

186

the inhabitants of adjoining French and German colonial outposts are blissfully unaware of it. Their peaceful coexistence comes to an end when a package, lined with old newspapers containing news of the war, arrives at the French outpost. The French are surprised to find that their enemy is Germany, not Britain, but they go about recruiting a company of blacks to attack the Germans. The Germans also hear of the war, and they, too, assemble an army of blacks and train them to be good Prussian soldiers. The two forces fight their way to a standstill, with the opposing armies facing each other from muddy trenches ("As good as any in the newspapers," proudly states one Frenchman). This little war is ended by the arrival of an Indian officer leading a platoon of kilted black soldiers who take over

the German colony in the name of the British Empire.

Zeppelin (1971), a British film directed by Etienne Perier, is also set in 1915. The Germans are busy perfecting a new weapon, the zeppelin, and the British, understandably concerned, send an agent to spy on the monstrous airship. The man chosen is a young Scottish lieutenant of Anglo-German parentage (Michael York). When he "defects" to the Germans, his friends and family in Britain think he's a traitor, and many of the Germans are suspicious of his motives. The wife (Elke Sommer) of the designer of the airship (Marius Goring) is particularly doubtful of his sudden change of heart, but she's more concerned with preparations for the zeppelin's final trial run. The plan is to raid a Scottish castle and steal some British national treasures, "including," remarks one German, "the Magna Carta. That will upset British morale." The man chosen to act as navigator is the Scottish mole.

Von Richthofen and Brown (The Red Baron) (1971), directed by Roger Corman, is a philosophical sort of film about the death of Germany's legendary World War I ace. The film follows the careers of Baron von Richthofen (John Phillip Law) and Roy Brown (Don Stroud), the man who eventually shot down the baron. The baron is an old-fashioned Prussian aristocrat; Brown is a Canadian farmer, a thoroughly modern man who does not share the baron's antiquated view of war. To Brown, war is a dirty, mechanical job. As he says, "I change things. Put a man and a plane in front of me, and I change them into a wreck and a corpse."

The screenplay for *Aces High* (1976), a British film by Jack Gold, was based in part on *Journey's End*, the 1929 play by R. C. Sherriff that was made into a movie in 1930. The setting for *Journey's End* is a dugout on the western front; *Aces High* relocates the story to an airfield in France, but the characters and the plot are essentially the same. The squadron leader is a Stanhope-like character (Malcolm McDowell) who cannot get into his plane unless he is drunk; among his fliers is the brother of his sweetheart (Peter Firth). The film recounts seven days in October 1917, beginning with the arrival of a rookie pilot (Firth) and ending with his death. There are cameo appearances by John Gielgud, Ray Milland, Trevor Howard, and Richard Johnson. Sherriff did not live to see this adaptation of his play. He died in 1975.

In 1976, the United States celebrated the two-hundredth anniversary of the Declaration of Independence. One of the films conceived as a tribute to the bicentennial was *Midway* (1976), directed by Jack Smight. Although a film about the Battle of Trenton or the Battle of Saratoga might have been more appropriate, the American Revolution has never been a popular subject with American filmmakers, and its battles are therefore not familiar to all Americans. The Battle of Midway, one of the most critical battles of World War II—it was the turning point of the war

in the Pacific—is better known. And even if viewers of *Midway* were not familiar with the history of the battle, they were acquainted with many of the scenes in the film, for *Midway* is composed in large part of wartime battle footage, newsreels, and borrowings from *Thirty Seconds Over Tokyo* and *Tora! Tora! Tora!* A celebration of a great American victory, *Midway* is also a celebration of American war movies.

The story of the film is the story of the battle, which took place early in June 1942. Although it was a sea battle, fought by American and Japanese carriers and battleships, the enemy ships never came in sight of one another: the fighting was done by planes. Like most epic reenactments of battles, *Midway* presents both sides of the story, shifting from meetings aboard American battleships to meetings aboard Japanese battleships. The Japanese ships are commanded by Admiral Yamamoto (Toshiro Mifune); the American ships are commanded by admirals Nimitz (Henry Fonda), Halsey (Robert Mitchum), and Spruance (Glenn Ford). In addition to these stars, there are James Coburn, Hal Holbrook, Cliff Robertson, and Robert Wagner. The central character, however, is Charlton Heston, and mixed into the story of the battle is a contrived love story: Heston's son (Edward Albert) is in love with a Japanese-American girl.

Midway is a war movie, but it may also be included among the "disaster" movies that were popular during the 1970s. The film was originally released in Sensurround, the special-effects system that adds low-frequency air vibrations to the sound track. Exploding bombs, roaring plane engines, the impacts of planes crashing onto the decks of carriers were all made tangibly real, giving audiences the exciting sensation of being right in the middle of the famous battle. Sensurround was first used for another film starring Heston, *Earthquake* (1974).

Midway was only one of several large-scale war movies released during the late 1970s, the best of which was *A Bridge Too Far* (1977), a British film directed by Richard Attenborough. Like *The Longest Day*, *A Bridge Too Far* is based on a book by Cornelius Ryan (William Goldman wrote the screenplay), and, like its predecessor, *A Bridge Too Far* has an enormous cast of famous

Opposite: *Robert Redford* (center) *as an airborne officer leading a makeshift attack on one of the crucial bridges in* A Bridge Too Far *(1977).*

Below: *Larry Csonka (left), Charlton Heston, Henry Fonda, and Robert Webber in Midway (1976).*

189

actors. There are more than one hundred speaking roles in the film, and the cast includes Dirk Bogarde, James Caan, Michael Caine, Sean Connery, Edward Fox, Elliott Gould, Gene Hackman, Anthony Hopkins, Hardy Kruger, Laurence Olivier, Ryan O'Neal, Robert Redford, Maximilian Schell, and Liv Ullmann. The theory is that using well-known actors helps the viewer follow a narrative composed of many separate stories, but all the famous faces detract somewhat from the film's realism. Even so, *A Bridge Too Far* is one of the best war movies ever made. It presents such an accurate depiction of war that it makes a powerful antiwar statement. Part of its poignance is the result of its subject, a disastrous Allied defeat, but few films convey a more compelling sense of the cost of war. *A Bridge Too Far* is ultimately a depressing film, and for that reason it was not very popular.

Operation Market Garden, the subject of *A Bridge Too Far*, was a bold plan, conceived by Field Marshal Montgomery, to drop thirty-five thousand British and American paratroopers behind the German lines into Holland. The airborne soldiers were to seize and hold six strategic bridges across rivers and canals, providing a corridor through which ground troops could drive into the Ruhr. It was a plan "to end the fighting by Christmas and bring the boys back home." Had it been successful, Operation Market Garden might have ended the war in 1944. It wasn't successful, and the Allies suffered more casualties in Market Garden than in the Normandy invasion.

The film covers each step of the operation, the efforts to capture each of the bridges and the

efforts of the ground forces to move forward. There are problems and delays at each step. Instead of meeting resistance from only "Hitler Youth and old men on bicycles," as they had expected, the British and American airborne troops find themselves fighting panzer regiments; the ground forces are constantly attacked as they try to make their way down the one, narrow highway, and each delay has an effect on all the soldiers involved. It is the bridge over the Rhine at Arnhem, the last bridge, that is the "bridge too far." The plan had called for the British paratroopers at Arnhem to hold on for two days; instead, they have to hold on for nine days before they are withdrawn. The ground troops make it to within one mile of the Arnhem bridge, but they can go no farther.

The battle scenes in *A Bridge Too Far*, particularly the street fighting by the British "Red Devils" at Arnhem, are among the most spectacular ever filmed, but the power of the film is in the way it makes clear that nothing was so dramatic as the heroism of the men involved. The fact that the film is composed of true stories contributes to its impact. Only a film based on a factual account could include such unlikely characters as a paratrooper who jumps holding a chicken, a British officer who carries an umbrella into battle, and another British officer who blows a small horn to urge his men on.

A Bridge Too Far was not the only film made in an effort to capitalize on the success of a previous film. *Force 10 from Navarone* (1978), a British film directed by Guy Hamilton, is supposedly about the subsequent adventures of two of the commandos who destroyed the big guns in the popular 1961 film. Based on another novel by Alistair MacLean with another screenplay by Carl Foreman, *Force 10 from Navarone* stars Robert Shaw (this was his last film) and Edward Fox in the roles played by Gregory Peck and David Niven in *The Guns of Navarone*. These two and a group of international pros (including Harrison Ford) are parachuted behind the German lines into Yugoslavia to blow up a strategic bridge.

MacArthur (1977), directed by Joseph Sargeant, was produced by the same man who produced *Patton*. Like *Patton*, *MacArthur* is the biography of a controversial American general.

The film begins with MacArthur (Gregory Peck) delivering a speech to West Point cadets. "Duty, honor, country," he tells them. "Those words dictate what you ought to be." Whether or not they dictated what MacArthur was is the subject of the film. He is revealed to have been a vain man, heedless of the opinions of others and frequently blind to the truth; he is also shown to have been courageous and a source of inspiration to those who served under him. The film follows the important points of his career: Corregidor, the invasion of New Guinea, his triumphant return to the Philippines, his acceptance of the Japanese surrender and his direction of the Allied occupation of Japan, the Korean War, and his dismissal by Truman.

The most remarkable war movies of the 1970s were those in which the heroes are Germans. The first of these was *The Eagle Has Landed* (1976), a British film directed by John Sturges. Michael Caine stars as Colonel Kurt Steiner, commander of a unit of German paratroopers. Steiner's heroic character is established early in the film when, returning with his men from the Russian front, he attempts to save a young Jewish girl from some brutal German guards. He and his paratroopers are chosen to take part in a daring plan to kidnap Winston Churchill. It is Robert Duvall, as a German staff officer, who plans the operation. Among the

191

other Germans are Anthony Quayle as Admiral Wilhelm Canaris and Donald Pleasance as Heinrich Himmler. Steiner and his men dress up as Polish soldiers and are transported to a Norfolk village where Churchill is reportedly planning to spend a few days. There is a German agent in the village (Jenny Agutter) as well as an IRA soldier (Donald Sutherland) eager to help the Germans. Pretending to be friendly Polish soldiers on maneuvers, the Germans have no trouble getting into the village, and the operation goes according to plan until a young girl falls into the village's water mill and one of Steiner's men, kindhearted to a fault, leaps in to save her. His tunic is torn in the process, revealing his German uniform (which he is somehow wearing beneath his Polish uniform). The Germans, now exposed, herd the villagers into the local church, there is a confrontation with American soldiers, and even a surprise ending.

Another German soldier named Steiner is the hero of *Cross of Iron* (1977), a British-West German production directed by Sam Peckinpah. Peckinpah has directed many films about battles between groups of armed men; this was his first in which both sides wear uniforms. The action of the film takes place in Russia in 1943 during the disastrous German retreat. Things are not going well for the Wehrmacht, and Corporal Steiner (James Coburn) and his dirty, bearded veterans must fight just to survive. Steiner is an exemplary man, tough, independent, and re-

sourceful. He is something of a myth, both to his own men and to the entire regiment. He has an Iron Cross, but he doesn't value it, and he doesn't care when he is promoted to sergeant. "A man is generally what he feels himself to be," he says. He hates all officers, and he hates his uniform; his only loyalty is to his platoon. Steiner's commanding officers include Colonel Brandt (James Mason), the philosophical Captain Kiesel (David Warner), and Captain Stransky (Maximilian Schell). Stransky, an arrogant, aristocratic Prussian, desperately wants an Iron Cross. He claims that he cannot go home and face his family without one. He tries to take credit for leading an attack and wants Steiner to serve as witness to his heroism. Steiner refuses; Stransky tries to get him killed.

And all the while the Russians attack and the Germans counterattack. There is no order or sense to the battle scenes, no way of discerning who is winning or losing, who is in a safe place or who is in danger. It is all one savage horror. The bodies of the dead are everywhere, and the bodies of the still living squirt blood when pierced by bullets or are blasted apart and thrown into the air by artillery shells. Much of this gore takes place in slow motion. Director Peckinpah is famous for his "ballets of death," and *Cross of Iron* is full of them. (The film was severely cut before its American release in order to avoid an X rating.) Even when a battle is not taking place, there is the ever-present threat of death. There are constant artillery bombard-

192

Above: *Michael Caine as Colonel Steiner in* The Eagle Has Landed *(1976).*

Above: *George C. Scott in* Patton *(1970).*
(The Bettmann Archives)

Above: *Clint Eastwood (left) and Don Rickles
in Kelly's Heroes (1970). (Courtesy MGM/UA)*

Above: *The members of The Dirty Dozen (1967). (Courtesy MGM/UA)*

Right: *Clint Eastwood (left) and Richard Burton in Where Eagles Dare (1969). (Courtesy MGM/UA)*

Above: *Nick Nolte in* Under Fire *(1983).*
(Courtesy Orion Pictures)

ments. A truck carrying Steiner and his men back to the front rolls over the decomposing corpse of a German soldier.

The Germans in *Cross of Iron* are aware of their tarnished reputations. "You think they'll ever forgive us for what we've done? or forget us?" asks Steiner. The fact that the Germans are losing is essential to the film. Their grim acceptance of their fate is what they have in place of the innocence of the German boys in *All Quiet on the Western Front*. Like Paul and his comrades, Steiner and his men become detached from their uniforms. They could be wearing any uniforms, and they could be fighting in any war. The end of the film is not the end of a story or even the end of a battle. Indeed, the film ends in the middle of a battle. The closing titles appear along with a series of photographs of war victims, victims of World War II and victims of other wars, including Vietnam.

Cross of Iron was very successful, especially in West Germany, and it led to a sequel, *Breakthrough (Sergeant Steiner)* (1978). This film was financed for the most part by West Germans, but it was directed by an American who, like Peckinpah, is known for westerns, Andrew V. McLaglen. As a concession to American audiences, the setting for *Breakthrough* is the western front; Richard Burton plays Sergeant Steiner this time, and he becomes involved in a conspiracy to assassinate Hitler and saves the life of an American officer (Robert Mitchum).

The issues and the distinctions between the heroes and the villians are far more traditional in *Soldier of Orange* (1979), a Dutch film directed by Paul Verhoeven. Based on a novel by Erik Hazelhoff, it tells the story of six Dutch university students who face the terrors and hardships of the German occupation. Each of the six meets a different fate: one, a Jew, is tortured and killed; one becomes a traitor and collaborates with the Germans. The hero of the film (Rutger Hauer) becomes involved in the Dutch underground and takes part in a dangerous mission to get a group of Resistance leaders to England.

The period of World War II was fondly remembered in a series of films about wartime romances. In *Summer of '42* (1971), directed by Robert Mulligan, a teenager (Gary Grimes) and

a young war bride (Jennifer O'Neill) have a brief love affair by the ocean. *Summer of My German Soldier* (1978), a television movie directed by Michael Tuchner, is about "first love" between a Jewish teenager (Kristy McNichol) and an escaped German POW (Bruce Davison) in the South. *Yanks* (1979), directed by John Schlesinger, recreates the period between the winter of 1943 and June 1944, when thousands of American soldiers were stationed in England. The film deals with the romantic relationships of three Americans (Richard Gere, William Devane, and Chick Vennera) and three Englishwomen (Lisa Eichhorn, Vanessa Redgrave, and Wendy Morgan). All are sweet films about a better time, a time of innocence when it was acceptable to be patriotic and when the men who wore American uniforms were heroes.

The longest war in American history ended in 1973. One of the last films made about the Vietnam War while it was still being fought was *Limbo* (1972), directed by Mark Robson. *Limbo* presents the emotional crises experienced by three women (Kathleen Nolan, Kate Jackson, and Katherine Justice) whose husbands are either prisoners of the North Vietnamese or are listed as "missing in action." The women live near an air force base in Florida, and while waiting for their husbands to return—or for confirmation that they are dead—they struggle with loneliness and their marital responsibilities. Although they are different in their political and religious views, the three women become close friends. They go together to Paris in the hope of getting information about their husbands from the North Vietnamese delegation to the peace talks. The North Vietnamese have no kind words for them; instead, they show the women photographs of atrocities supposedly committed by American fliers in Vietnam. Most of the film is told in flashbacks while the three women ride to an airport to which one man, the husband of one of the three, is returning. The film was made without the assistance of the air force because the plot includes unfaithful wives, and air force officials believed it would be bad for the morale of the fliers in Vietnam.

One of the first attempts by American filmmakers to deal with the effects of the Vietnam War on Americans, *Limbo* was ahead of its time. Its title is an apt description of the place the Viet-

194

nam War occupied in film history during the early years of the 1970s, for there were no major films about the Vietnam War until the last years of the decade. There were plenty of screenplays about Vietnam making the rounds of Hollywood studios, but no one dared touch the subject. Not until 1975, when Francis Ford Coppola announced his plans to make *Apocalypse Now,* did American filmmakers show any interest in films about Vietnam. Coppola showed the way, and the industry followed: four major films about Vietnam appeared in 1978.

Although there were no major films about the Vietnam War, scenes from that war began showing up in films, usually as nightmarish flashbacks, early in the decade. A new character appeared in American movies during the early 1970s: the Vietnam veteran. Since he had never been made into a hero by Hollywood, and since he had participated in an unpopular war—of which the most famous name was My Lai—the Vietnam veteran found himself portrayed as a killer. The popular image of the Vietnam veteran, a man trained in all the deadly arts, fit right into the morose self-image of America during the early 1970s. The theme of most movies about returning Vietnam veterans is the same: searching for peace, they find only violence, for America is a violent place.

Some of the early films about returning Viet-

nam veterans were compared to *Easy Rider.* Outcasts from society, the veterans roam the country, trying to find a place to fit in. Like the heroes of *Easy Rider,* they are not encumbered by racial prejudices, and they follow their own code. *The Hard Ride* (1971), written and directed by Burt Topper, is about a Vietnam veteran (Robert Fuller) who escorts home the body of a dead black buddy (Alfonso Williams), inherits the dead man's motorcycle and white girl friend (Sherry Bain), and takes off on a long ride across California, looking for the Indian leader of a motorcycle gang to attend the funeral. The veteran is killed in a gang war.

In *Welcome Home, Soldier Boys* (1972), directed by Richard Compton, four former Green Berets travel across the country in a Cadillac. The four pals (Joe Don Baker, Paul Koslo, Alan Vint, and Elliott Street) plan to use their combined savings of $9,000 to operate a ranch in California. They never make it. With only $69 left, they arrive in a small town in New Mexico called Hope. Tired of waiting for the owner of a gas station to come sell them gas, they try to break the lock on a pump, and the owner shoots at them. The four open the trunk of their car and take out an arsenal of weapons. They put on their Green Beret uniforms, slaughter most of the town's inhabitants, and die in a battle with National Guardsmen.

Tracks (1976), written and directed by Henry Jaglom, is about another white Vietnam veteran escorting home for burial the body of a black buddy killed in Vietnam. Most of the film takes place on a train, the body in a flag-draped coffin in a baggage car, the veteran (Dennis Hopper) going through hallucinations that mix dreams about his fellow passengers with memories of the war. The film ends with the funeral. When no one shows up to honor his dead friend, the veteran jumps into the grave and opens the coffin—it is full of weapons. Yelling that he is going to show people what the war was like, the veteran charges from the grave as though it were a foxhole, weapons ready.

Black Vietnam veterans appear as the heroes in several of the so-called blaxploitation films (films made by blacks for a primarily black audience) of the early 1970s. *Slaughter* (1972), di-   195

rected by Jack Starrett, stars Jim Brown as
Slaughter, a former Green Beret captain who returns home to find his parents have been killed
in an automobile explosion set by the Mafia;
Slaughter goes to war on the syndicate. In *Gordon's War* (1973), directed by Ossie Davis, another former Green Beret (Paul Winfield) comes
home to Harlem to find his wife has been killed
by the Mafia. He organizes a small urban army
with his former Green Beret buddies and drives
the drug dealers, pimps, and Mafia chieftains
out of Harlem. *Mean Johnny Barrows* (1976), directed by Fred Williamson, is about a veteran
(Williamson), discharged for striking an officer,
whose homecoming is only the beginning of another war. Once again, the enemy is the Mafia.

In films throughout the seventies, Vietnam

veterans are forced to use their military training
against the violence and corruption of modern
America. *Clay Pigeon* (1971), directed by Tom
Stern and Lane Slate, is about a Vietnam War
hero (Stern)—he threw himself on a grenade to
save his comrades, and it didn't go off—who
agrees to help a narcotics cop (Telly Savalas)
break an underworld drug operation. *Trained to
Kill (The No Mercy Man)* (1973), directed by Daniel J. Vance, stars Stephen Sandor as a Vietnam
veteran forced to do battle with a sadistic gang
in his hometown. In *The Stone Killer* (1973), directed by Michael Winner, a crime boss named
Vescari (Martin Balsam) plans a massacre to
avenge the gangland slayings of his cronies.
The men he chooses for this malicious chore are
all Vietnam veterans.

196

Probably the most famous Vietnam veteran of the 1970s was Travis Bickle (Robert De Niro), the ex-marine who gets a job driving a taxi at night because he can't sleep. *Taxi Driver* (1976), directed by Martin Scorsese and based on a screenplay by Paul Schrader, is about alienation and vigilantism. Bickle kills. He kills to cleanse society, and he kills for catharsis. He becomes an urban guerrilla and makes plans to kill a presidential candidate. *Taxi Driver* gained unwanted fame when it was disclosed that John W. Hinckley, Jr., wrote letters to both Schrader and Jodie Foster (who plays a teenage prostitute in the film) before attempting to assassinate President Reagan.

Paul Schrader also wrote the screenplay for *Rolling Thunder* (1977), another film about a Vietnam veteran who becomes a vigilante. Directed by John Flynn, *Rolling Thunder* stars William Devane as Major Charles Rane, a pilot shot down over Vietnam and held prisoner for eight years. He returns to a hero's welcome: the people of his hometown, San Antonio, give him a Cadillac and one silver dollar for every day he was in "Hanoi's hellhole." Before he has a chance to reacquaint himself with his family—his son does not remember him, and his wife has been unfaithful—a gang of hoodlums arrives to steal the silver dollars. They kill Rane's wife and son and stick one of his hands in a garbage disposal before shooting him. He survives and becomes adept in the use of the steel claw he has in place of the hand. Putting a shotgun in his Cadillac, he takes off for bloody revenge.

Not all films about returning Vietnam veterans were so harsh. Robert De Niro plays a Vietnam War veteran having a good time trying to make pornographic movies in *Hi, Mom!* (1970), directed by Brian De Palma. Timothy Bottoms plays an ex-marine establishing his own sanity in a crazy world in *The Crazy World of Julius Vrooder* (1974), directed by Arthur Hiller. In *Heroes* (1977), directed by Jeremy Paul Kagan, Henry Winkler plays a Vietnam veteran who escapes from a veterans' hospital in New York and goes on a cross-country bus trip to visit his old army buddies. He plans to get all his friends together and start a worm farm in Eureka, California. He carries a box of worms under his arm

wherever he goes.

Most of the films about returning Vietnam veterans connect the violence of the war to the violence in American society. One film, however, blames the violence of the war on the American government. *Twilight's Last Gleaming* (1977), a coproduction of the United States and West Germany directed by Robert Aldrich, combines a World War III thriller with a message about Vietnam. A former air force major (Burt Lancaster), who was framed on a murder charge because of his opposition to the war, and three other inmates on death row break out of prison and take over an underground missile site in Montana. The major threatens to launch nine missiles if his demands are not met. He wants $10 million and safe conduct for himself and his cohorts to a foreign country; he also wants the president (Charles Durning) to make public a secret document containing the minutes of a cabinet meeting that took place during the early years of the Vietnam War. The document reveals that the president and his advisers were fully aware that the war could never be won and that they decided to continue the war to prove to the Soviet Union that the United States was capable of irrational and inhuman acts. All the years of slaughter were nothing but an act put on as a warning to America's Cold War enemies.

Few reviewers felt there was anything remarkable about such a "revelation," and, anyway, no secret government document could explain the Vietnam War to the American people. For their part, the American people awaited

documents of another sort: films, films that would provide them with a way to understand the war and its effects on America.

The long-awaited films came, all at once, one right after another, and if they failed to explain the war, they finally gave Americans the opportunity to experience it the way they had experienced other wars. The eager anticipation that preceded the release of these films—*Coming Home, The Deer Hunter, Apocalypse Now*—demonstrates the important function war movies play in modern society. These films were regarded as statements—they were going to tell Americans how to feel about an event that had been central to their lives for more than a decade. Americans had had no films to make them angry at the North Vietnamese, and with the exception of *The Green Berets*, they had had no feature films praising the valor of their sol-

diers. After so many years of silence, and after the war was over, the songs of the sixties and the baleful sound of spinning helicopter blades filled movie theaters. Like the "happy family called Smith" in *Oh! What a Lovely War*, Americans paid their way into a war.

Ironically, *Apocalypse Now*, the film that inspired the cycle of Vietnam War films, was the last to appear. Among the first was another film about a Vietnam veteran, *Who'll Stop the Rain* (1978), directed by Karel Reisz. An ex-marine (Nick Nolte) becomes involved in a scheme to smuggle heroin from Saigon to California. Along with the wife (Tuesday Weld) of a war correspondent (Michael Moriarty), he goes on a wild journey through California and the Southwest that ends in a shoot-out in the mountains of New Mexico. The screenplay for the film was based on *Dog Soldiers*, a novel by Robert Stone; the title

198

of the film is from a song by the Creedence Clearwater Revival.

The Best Years of Our Lives was remade as a television movie, *Returning Home*, in 1975. Like the 1946 original, the film is about the veterans of World War II readjusting to civilian life. In some ways, *Coming Home* (1978), directed by Hal Ashby, is a sequel to *The Best Years of Our Lives*, updated for the veterans of the Vietnam War. But the years in *Coming Home* are not years to be celebrated—the film is set in 1968, during the worst years, the years of divisiveness and turmoil—and the war-wounded veterans in *Coming Home* are not worried about getting jobs and fitting back into civilian life: they are ostracized, cut off from society by their injuries and by their participation in an unpopular war. The action of the film takes place to a constant stream of music from the sixties: the Beatles, the Rolling Stones, Simon and Garfunkel, Jimi Hendrix. The music is there, and so is the growing self-awareness of women: it is all a little awkward. In one scene of the film, Jane Fonda, flipping through a high school yearbook, says, "It's so funny looking at the way we used to look." *Coming Home* gave American audiences a chance to look back ten years, and, like the pictures in a yearbook, the film is both embarrassing and saddening.

The story of the film is a love affair between the wife of a patriotic marine officer and a paraplegic veteran. The officer (Bruce Dern) goes off to Vietnam, eager to fight for his country; his wife (Jane Fonda) goes to work as a volunteer in a veterans' hospital, and it is there that she meets the veteran (Jon Voight), who is vehemently opposed to the war. The two bicker at first, then grow steadily closer until they become lovers. The experience changes the woman: she lets down her hair, both figuratively and literally, and experiences her own independence and sexuality in her first fully satisfying ways. The experience also changes the bitter veteran: he finds the way to use his anger constructively. When her husband comes home from Vietnam, emotionally destroyed by the disillusionments of war, he is informed of his wife's affair. There is nothing either his wife or the veteran can do to help him, and he commits suicide.

There are no scenes of battle in *Coming Home*. The war is described in other ways. The paraplegics are there, representatives of what war does to young men, and various characters in the film try to explain the war. The gung-ho husband has difficulty understanding the experience. "Television shows what it's like, but it sure as hell don't show what it is," he says. The soldiers in his command had chopped the heads off dead Vietcong—it was not the war he had expected. The paraplegic veteran has the opportunity to do what the maimed doughboy in *Johnny Got His Gun* wanted to do, talk to the public. Speaking from his wheelchair, he tells a group of high school boys, "It ain't like it is in the movies. . . . I have killed for my country, and I don't feel good about it." He also says, "If we want to commit suicide, we can find plenty of ways to do it right here." Of all the films about Vietnam released during the late 1970s, *Coming Home* makes the clearest antiwar statement. It was delivered, of course, woefully late.

The combat films of the Vietnam War resemble the films made during the 1920s about World War I: they are about innocent Americans thrust into a war they do not understand, a war in which their sense of morality serves only to get them killed. *Go Tell the Spartans* (1978), directed by Ted Post, is about American military advisers in Vietnam in 1964. Some are inexperienced and enthusiastic, eager to "kick ass"; some, including their major (Burt Lancaster), are weary, burnt-out professionals. They spend most of their time performing mindless bureaucratic chores, like counting mosquitoes, and reassuring one another that they won't repeat the mistakes of the French. "We won't lose," says one, "we're Americans."

The conflict they are involved in eludes their comprehension. There is no way to distinguish the enemy; even children cannot be trusted. Their morals and their military code of honor have no meaning. Six of them are sent to help South Vietnamese forces reoccupy a former French outpost at a place called Muc Wa. They are told that the French abandoned Muc Wa in 1953 and lost control of the road it guards, leading to Dienbienphu. There is a cemetery at Muc Wa for the French soldiers who died defending it. A sign over the entry reads, "Stranger, when you find us lying here, go tell the Spartans that we obeyed their orders," a reference to the Spartans who died defending the pass at Thermopylae. The Americans rebuild the base and successfully fight off Vietcong attacks. They are then ordered to pull out and leave behind the South Vietnamese. One of the Americans (Craig Wasson) refuses, saying it would be wrong to leave them behind: the Americans got them there, the Americans should help get them out. Although he knows it is foolish, the major stays behind, too. The rest of the Americans leave in a helicopter. The South Vietnamese and the two Americans are ambushed by the Vietcong. Lancaster, the veteran of other American wars, does not survive. Shot, he slumps into a ditch, his last words a mumbled, "Oh, shit." The only survivor of the massacre (Wasson) wanders alone. Confronted by a Vietcong sniper, he vows, "I'm going home, Charlie." Rather than "The End," the film concludes with "1964."

The Boys in Company C (1978), directed by Sidney J. Furie, picks up the story three years later, in 1967, with a group of boys arriving at a Marine Corps induction center. One (Craig Wasson again), a draft dodger, is delivered in handcuffs by FBI agents. Among the other inductees are Stan Shaw, Andrew Stevens, Michael Lembeck, and James Canning. Canning, a would-be writer, keeps a journal, and his entries provide the running narrative for the film, from the group's arrival at the induction center in August 1967 to January 1968.

The five boys go through basic training together. The training is brutal and dehumanizing, designed to make them think and act in unison. They are then sent, by ship, to Vietnam. As the ship docks, the shelling begins. Vietnam is a bewildering chaos composed of bureaucratic incompetence, callous officers interested only in monthly "body counts," and the constant threat of death. Their first firefight—there are no "battles," only sudden explosions or ambushes—occurs while they are part of a convoy bringing supplies to an army outpost. The "vital" supplies turn out to be crates of cigarettes and liquor and furniture being sent to a general for his birthday; two men die in the fighting.

The officers in the film are not heroes—most are idiots who endanger the lives of their men through blind adherence to rules or timetables; the soldiers are nervous and open fire on anyone and anything at the slightest provocation. The Vietcong are rarely seen, but the film suggests that they are not the only enemy. "You," says one of the American soldiers (Shaw) to an American officer, "you are the enemy." It is the answer to the question formulated during the sixties; it is what *M*A*S*H* and *Catch-22* are about: the enemy is he who sees a reason for war.

The Boys in Company C ends with a soccer game, the Americans against a team of South Vietnamese. The Americans are ordered by their officer to lose the game to bolster the morale of their ally. They are told that if they lose, they will see no more combat; if they win, they will be sent to Khe Sanh. They win, but the game ends in a Vietcong attack, at the end of which Canning, the writer, heroically throws himself on a grenade to save the lives of some children. The last entry in his journal ends the film: "We'll just keep on walking into one bloody mess after another until somebody figures out that living has got to be more important than winning."

In the opinion of some American filmmakers, Vietnam was suicide, an entire nation committing physical and moral suicide. *The Deer Hunter* (1978), directed by Michael Cimino, supplies an appropriate metaphor for the war: Russian roulette. The first part of the film is an elaborate ritual of life, a Russian Orthodox wedding ceremony in a Pennsylvania steel town. The wedding celebration establishes the rich sense of life and community among the people in the town. It is followed by another ritual: three friends, Michael (Robert De Niro), Nick (Christopher Walken), and Steven (John Savage), go deer hunting. While they are in a bar after the hunt, the film jumps to Vietnam. It is a startling jump: the sounds of the bar become the sounds of a helicopter, and the three friends are there, wearing Ranger uniforms, fighting the Vietcong. They are captured by the Vietcong and forced to play Russian roulette while their captors bet on who will survive. It is a nightmare, a ritual of death that more clearly than any battle scene conveys the hopeless terror of the Vietnam

200

Opposite: *Craig Wasson stumbles through the French cemetery in* Go Tell the Spartans *(1978).*

War, a war in which courage and moral codes seemed meaningless.

Michael helps his two friends maintain their sanity and engineers their escape. They are almost rescued by helicopter, and Steven's legs are injured: Michael carries him out of the jungle on his back, while Nick is taken out by helicopter. The friends are then separated. Michael returns home to find Steven, his legs amputated, in a hospital. Nick is still in Vietnam, and Michael goes back for him, back to the chaos of Saigon, a city on the brink of collapse. And he finds him there, the "star" of a secret civilian version of the Russian roulette game. The two friends reenact the ordeal they suffered as prisoners. Nick dies, and Michael returns home. The film ends with him and his remaining friends singing "God Bless America."

The Deer Hunter and *Coming Home* shared the Academy Awards for 1978. *The Deer Hunter* won five, including best picture and best director; *Coming Home* won three—best actor (Jon Voight), best actress (Jane Fonda), and best screenplay. The Vietnam War was finally an important subject for American filmmakers, but it was not yet a subject on which all Americans could agree: *The Deer Hunter* was attacked by many people for its portrayal of the Vietcong as cruel killers.

The Vietnam War was also the subject of a television movie, *Friendly Fire* (1979), directed by David Greene. Based on a book by C. D. B. Bryan, *Friendly Fire* is about an Iowa farm family whose patriotism turns to antiwar activism.

When a father (Ned Beatty) and mother (Carol Burnett) learn that their son has died in Vietnam from "friendly fire"—accidental shelling by American artillery—they try to find out more about his death. The mother, in particular, wants to know the truth, and her search involves her in governmental indifference and dissembling.

Francis Ford Coppola's long-awaited epic about Vietnam, *Apocalypse Now*, was finally released in 1979. Much was expected of the film. Coppola, who produced and directed it, said it was a "philosophic inquiry into the mythology of war and the human condition." He and John Milius wrote the screenplay, and they based it on Joseph Conrad's 1902 novella, *Heart of Darkness*. Like *Heart of Darkness*, *Apocalypse Now* is the story of a journey along a river into darkness and horror: in Conrad's book, it is a journey along the Congo to an outpost run by a Belgian trader named Kurtz; in *Apocalypse Now*, it is a journey along a river into Cambodia to the headquarters of a renegade American officer named Kurtz. In both works, the long journey is a search for the nature of evil, but in the film, it is also a search for the explanation of America's involvement in the Vietnam War. At the end of the journey, at the heart of darkness, is Kurtz, and he is dreaming the answer.

"I watched a snail crawling along the edge of a straight razor . . . and surviving. That is my dream." From deep in Cambodia, Walter E. Kurtz is broadcasting his dreams. The errant Green Beret colonel has assembled an army of Montagnard tribesmen and is waging his own war against the Vietcong. According to army officials, Kurtz's ideas and methods have become "unsound," and a certain Captain Willard (Martin Sheen) is sent to "terminate his command." "Terminate?" asks Willard. "Terminate with extreme prejudice," he is told. As one general (G. D. Spradlin) explains to Willard, "There's a conflict in every human heart . . . and good does not always triumph. . . . Every man has got a breaking point, and Kurtz has reached his."

Willard's thoughts provide the running narration of the film (this narration was written by Michael Herr, author of *Dispatches*). As the boat he is on travels upriver and the crewmen water-ski or sun themselves, Willard reads dossiers detailing Kurtz's history. It is an impressive story, and Willard begins to admire the man he is going to kill.

At one stage of the journey, the boat has to be airlifted to a river delta, and Willard and the

202

The Deer Hunter (1978).

crewmen are given the opportunity to participate in a dawn helicopter attack on a Vietcong village. In command is Colonel Kilgore (Robert Duvall), a surfing fan who has his helicopter's loudspeakers blare music from Wagner's *Die Walküre* during the attack because, "It scares hell out of the slopes." This attack is one of the most impressive ever filmed, the helicopters firing rockets, cannon, and machine guns as they make their passes over the Vietcong positions, the pilots chatting to one another on their radios, Kilgore complimenting them on each good strike. It is a thrilling display of organized mayhem. Before the battle is over, Kilgore is ready to sample the waves, but he calls in an air strike to quiet some enemy mortars. The planes drop napalm on the jungle. "I love the smell of napalm in the morning," says Colonel Kilgore. "It smells like victory."

From the river delta, the boat continues its trip upriver. There is another stop, at a USO facility, and then a stop at a bridge, the last army outpost on the river. "You're in the asshole of the world," says a soldier to Willard. It is an ongoing night battle, with the lights and music of a carnival. "Beautiful, it's just beautiful," comments one of the crew members in an LSD daze. They continue along a shoreline of lush jungle littered with the war's refuse: crashed jets, burning helicopters stuck in trees. They travel through fog and thick green mists. It becomes night more often, and as they near Kurtz's encampment they pass piles of skulls, crucified men, and bodies hanging from trees. Kurtz is waiting for them at the end of the river.

There are severed heads and dead bodies everywhere. A crazed photojournalist (Dennis Hopper) greets Willard and explains to him that Kurtz is an outstanding man—he even reads poetry out loud. Indeed, with his ponderous body hidden in murky shadows, his bald head and round face only rarely shining through the darkness, Kurtz (Marlon Brando) recites T. S. Eliot's "The Hollow Men" (an apt choice, since it begins

with a line from Conrad's novella). Kurtz's small library includes such books as Frazer's *The Golden Bough*: if anyone has come to an understanding of the Vietnam War, it must be Walter E. Kurtz, but all he has to offer are cryptic adumbrations. "Horror has a face," he tells Willard, "and you must make a friend of horror. We must make friends with moral terror." Leaning out of his shadows, he says, "It is judgment that defeats us." Willard carries out his orders, slaying Kurtz with a large knife. True to Conrad's *Heart of Darkness*, Kurtz's last words are, "The horror! The horror!"

With the exception of Kurtz's awkward cerebrations, *Apocalypse Now* is a masterful movie, but it provided no statement about Vietnam. The film seems to be less about Vietnam than about some other world, an exciting realm far beyond the moral or political considerations of that war. The assessment of the battle by the drugged soldier is accurate—it is beautiful, a very pleasant hallucination. From the first scenes of the film, in which a helicopter drops napalm on a jungle to the music of The Doors, *Apocalypse Now* is a thrilling vision of war, a vivid and, perhaps, pleasing dream of death.

Erich Maria Remarque, whose *All Quiet on the Western Front* established the trenches of World War I as an enduring symbol of the futility of war, died in 1970. The decade that began with his death ended with a remake of that masterpiece as a television movie, directed by Delbert Mann. Since it is in color, the 1979 *All Quiet on the Western Front* lacks some of the bleakness of the first version, but the story is still powerful and moving. Like the 1930 original, the film uses some very American actors in the roles of Germans: Richard Thomas plays Paul, and Ernest Borgnine plays the veteran Sergeant Katczinsky. But by 1979, Americans were used to seeing Americans dressed in German uniforms and were ready to accept Americans in the roles of demoralized soldiers fighting a losing war.

THE ONLY GLORY

Because the first films were in black and white, black and white have become the shades of the past, the colors of the modern world's flashbacks. It was in that black-and-white world that World War I took place, so, like a dream, it is in black and white that it is remembered. *The Big Red One* (1980) begins in black and white on a World War I battlefield, a lone American soldier cautiously making his way past the bodies of the dead. In a scene from a nightmare, he is attacked by a terrified, shell-shocked horse; then, near a wooden figure of Christ crucified, he is approached by a German soldier, who calls to him, *"Der Krieg ist vorbei."* He kills the man, only to learn that what the German was saying is true: "The war is over." From that day in November 1918 the film jumps to November 1942, to a war in full color. The same American infantryman (Lee Marvin) is now a sergeant leading a platoon onto a North African beachhead. He and the soldiers with him wear the armpatch of the First Infantry Division, a big red numeral one.

The Big Red One was written and directed by Samuel Fuller. He had been planning to make the film ever since the end of the war, for it is his own story, based on his own experiences as a GI in the First Infantry Division. Although it is in some ways similar to Fuller's other films about American dogfaces, *The Big Red One* has none of their contrived violence or strident propaganda: it is composed of love, a healthy, forthright love for the American soldiers of World War II. The first American war movie of the post-Vietnam era to look back sympathetically at Americans in war, *The Big Red One* is a very personal film, poetic and moving.

The film follows one squad of GIs from the landing in North Africa to fighting in France, Belgium, Germany, and, finally, to the liberation of a concentration camp in Czechoslovakia during the last days of the war. The squad is led by the World War I-veteran sergeant (Marvin), whose rank is all he has for a name. The other four GIs are Mark Hamill, Kelly Ward, Bobby Di Cicco, and Robert Carradine (playing a character, named Zab, patterned after Fuller). The replacements who join the squad are killed or wounded before their faces become familiar; only the original five members survive. There is no plot, only a series of episodes that make vividly clear the infantryman's war: a succession of dangerous situations. Those who survive each brush with death do not celebrate, for all they have to look forward to is the next encounter with the enemy. There are no mock heroics. Nor is there any real hatred for the enemy: they are soldiers very much like the GIs. "We don't murder, we kill," explains the American sergeant to one of his men, and a few scenes later, a German sergeant tells one of his men, "We don't murder the enemy, we kill them."

Although confined to the experiences of one squad, the story has great depth, and, perhaps because it is autobiographical, it has a dramatic sense of realism. There are moments of warm humanness, such as a scene in which the sergeant leaves a Sicilian town with flowers stuck in his helmet, and there are moments of fear, such as a scene in which the sergeant calls out the names of his men through the fog of a cold German forest. The film ends with an encounter that repeats the World War I incident. Sitting in the woods near the concentration camp, the sergeant is approached by a German, who calls to him, *"Der Krieg ist vorbei."* Again the sergeant stabs the German, but this time he finds out that the war is indeed over in time to save the man's life. As one of his men says, delivering the last line of the film, "Survival is the only glory in war."

Another film based on an autobiographical story of World War II reaches a similar conclusion. Lothar-Guenther Buchheim joined the crew of a German submarine as a photojournalist during the war and later put together his experiences in an autobiographical novel. The novel was enormously popular in Germany and served as the basis for *Das Boot (The Boat)* (1981). The production of the film cost $12 million, making *Das Boot* the most expensive German film since World War II and possibly the most expensive film in the history of the German cinema. It was the first large-scale German film about World War II since the war, the first German film in more than thirty-five years to present a sympathetic picture of Germans in war. It was also the most successful film of all time in Germany.

Das Boot was directed by Wolfgang Peter-

Preceding pages: *Lee Marvin* (third from left) *leads his squad ashore in* The Big Red One *(1980).*

Below: *Lee Marvin in* The Big Red One *(1980).*

sen, who also wrote the screenplay; its leading actor is Jurgen Prochnow, who plays the captain of the submarine. Both Petersen and Prochnow were born in 1941: the story of the film takes place in the autumn of 1941, during the battle for control of the Atlantic. After all the many films about Allied convoys fighting German submarines—films like *Action in the North Atlantic* and *The Cruel Sea*—*Das Boot* presents the German side of the battle, the story of one mission by one submarine, U-96. It begins with the statement that of the forty thousand German sailors who served aboard U-boats during the war, only ten thousand survived. It was not a matter of glory, and the film is about not Nazis but German sail-

ors, men desperately trying to survive.

The story begins with the departure of U-96 from La Rochelle in occupied France and ends with the submarine's return to port several months later. Almost all of the action takes place within the narrow interior of the submarine, in which are crammed forty-three men and the supplies they will need for their journey. There is no free space. To move, the men must climb over one another and around the salamis that hang from the ceiling. There is only one toilet for the entire crew, bathing is impossible, and the living quarters are so cramped that the men must sleep in shifts. It is in this claustrophobic's nightmare that the sailors must spend months at

sea, and most of the time the submarine is underwater. There is no escape; the sailors are locked in their metal coffin. There are no flashbacks, and there is no love triangle. The story does not follow the character developments of any of the men. There is, however, the spirit of the sailors. Although Germans, they cheer themselves up by singing, "It's a Long Way to Tipperary." It is hard to imagine them as the ruthless submariners who sent so many Allied ships to the bottom of the sea.

But that is who they are, and they do indeed attack Allied convoys. When they surface to sink the flaming hulk of one of the ships they have torpedoed, they are upset to see that there are still men aboard it, men who, afire, jump into the water. The film's most terrifying scenes, however, are those in which the submarine dives to great depths to avoid destroyers. The water pressure forces rivets out of the submarine's hull: they shoot out like bullets. The explosions of depth charges are followed by gushing water, water that threatens to fill the sub. The captain—and with him the viewer—cannot believe the efforts of his men to survive. But they do make it through and return to port, where another fate awaits them.

Perhaps inevitably, *Das Boot* was compared to *All Quiet on the Western Front*; *The Big Red One* was not. Even so, *Das Boot* and *The Big Red One* are very much alike; *The Big Red One* has a happier ending because it is about the victors, the ones who survived the war.

"Even true stories can end well." *The Night of the Shooting Stars* (1983), an Italian film directed by Paolo and Vittorio Taviani, recounts another story of World War II. It is a story told by a mother to her child at bedtime, a true story that has a happy ending: survival. The setting of the tale is a small town in Tuscany named San Martino. It is late in the summer of 1944: the Americans are coming, the Germans are pulling out, and the townspeople divide into two groups. The well-to-do follow German orders and remain in the town; the others set out to meet the Americans. "The end of the world is near," says the leader of this latter group (Omero Antonutti), "and it is our duty to survive." The story follows the fate of this group, which includes a spell-

binding battle they fight against Fascists in a wheat field. It is a dreamlike film, composed of vivid anecdotes that mix everyday occurrences with unreality: it is a sweet bedtime story about a long-ago war.

There is far less reality in *Victory* (1981), directed by John Huston. Ostensibly set during World War II, the story of the film concerns a group of Allied prisoners—British, Canadian, American, Australian, French, Dutch, and Belgian—in a German POW camp. A not unlikable German propaganda officer with the inevitable name of Von Steiner (Max von Sydow) hits upon the happy idea of having the Allied prisoners form a soccer team to play the German national team—all for the purpose of proving Teutonic superiority. The Allies agree, with the proviso that they be given players from Eastern European countries who are held in other German camps. Thus, the Allied team eventually comes to include eighteen of 1981's most celebrated soccer players, including Pelé of Brazil, Bobby Moore of England, Osvaldo Ardiles of Argentina, Paul Van Himst of Belgium, Kazimierz Deyna of Poland, and Hallvar Thorensen of Norway. The captain of the team is Michael Caine; its goalie is Sylvester Stallone. The Allies agree to play because they see the game as an opportunity to escape; contact is made with the French Resistance, and an elaborate plan is developed whereby the Allies will make their getaway during halftime. Halftime comes and the Allies are losing 4 to 1; the German officials have been overlooking the German players' flagrant infractions of the rules of the game (the Germans are beating up the Allies). But the Allies believe they can win, so rather than escape, they go back out to finish the game. The film has a suitably rousing score.

Lion of the Desert (1981), a coproduction of Great Britain and Libya directed by Moustapha Akkad, presents on a grand scale the story of Omar Mukhtar, the Bedouin leader who, from 1911 to 1931, fought a guerrilla war against the Italian invaders of Libya. For most of that time, Mukhtar's enemy was the Italian general Rodolfo Graziani, to whom goes the terrible honor of coining the term *concentration camp*: he "concentrated" all the various Bedouin Arabs in huge

Jurgen Prochnow in Das Boot *(1980).*

Ben Gazzara (left) *and Richard Roundtree
in* Inchon *(1982).*

camps. Graziani was also the first military commander to use tanks in the desert. In the film, Anthony Quinn plays Mukhtar; Oliver Reed plays Graziani. Rod Steiger makes an appearance as Mussolini, and John Gielgud appears as an Arab leader.

The film presents quite accurately the methods used by the Italians against the Libyans, the kind of barbaric methods usually associated with Nazis (the film was banned in Italy when first released). These methods include the Roman tactic of decimation: the Italians line up civilians and shoot every tenth man. They also pour cement into wells, build a wall of barbed wire across the desert, and mercilessly slaughter unarmed civilians. "Who," asks Mukhtar, "can fight such a war—not against armies, but against innocent people?" Mukhtar does a good job of fighting the Italians, but when he comes to

a peace conference he is treacherously captured, put in chains, and, in 1931 ("year nine of the Fascist era"), publicly hanged.

Like all epic war movies, *The Lion of the Desert* was expensive to produce. It cost more than $35 million and was financed in large part by Libya's Muammar Gaddafi.

The financing for another epic war movie came from an even more ironic source. *Inchon* (1982), a coproduction of the United States and South Korea directed by Terence Young, was partially financed by the Reverend Sun Myung Moon's Unification Church. The Reverend Moon also served as a special adviser for the film; the film's "spiritual adviser," however, was Jeane Dixon. This bizarre production recounts the US Marines' 1950 invasion of Inchon, which turned the tide of the Korean War. Laurence Olivier stars as General MacArthur, and among the other stars are Jacqueline Bisset, Toshiro Mifune, Richard Roundtree, David Janssen, Ben Gazzara, and, in the role of a newspaper columnist, Rex Reed. The film turned out to be one of the two or three most expensive ever made, costing a reported $46 million.

Philip Caputo's autobiographical book about his experiences during the Vietnam War, *A Rumor of War*, was made into a television movie in 1980, directed by Richard T. Heffron. Brad Davis stars as Caputo, and the film traces the changes wrought by the war on his character: he goes from idealism to bitter disillusionment. The war in Vietnam is not the war he—or his country—expected. It is a war with a "commuter schedule"; the marines are brought to it in helicopters. They do what they have been ordered to do and then get out as quickly as possible. All they want is to get out intact. There are no victories, only painful frustrations. Although the Americans are supposedly there to win the "hearts and minds" of the Vietnamese people, they remain detached. The enemy is rarely even glimpsed, but marines die. Caputo's friends die. And the anger and frustration have their effects on the American boys: "We relieved our own pain and fear by inflicting it on others," says Caputo. "We learned just how brutal a nineteen-year-old American boy can be." The officers are absurdly bureaucratic; they have no notion of the realities of the war they are waging, and the war becomes a brutal farce. In the middle of this nightmare of free-fire zones and body counts, Caputo finds himself charged with murder (following an informer's information, he and two of his men set up an ambush outside a village and killed the wrong people). The charges are dropped, and Caputo leaves the war. "I had survived," he says, "but that was my only victory."

Another true story of the Vietnam War was related in another 1980 television movie, *Fighting Back*, directed by Robert Lieberman. This recounts the inspiring story of Pittsburgh Steeler Rocky Bleier's (Robert Urich) miraculous comeback and subsequent football career after he was seriously wounded in Vietnam.

Americana (1981), directed by David Carradine, is about a Vietnam veteran (Carradine) who wanders the backroads of the Midwest. In a small town in Kansas, he comes upon a broken-down merry-go-round. He stops in the town long enough to refurbish the merry-go-round and then leaves. The film was adapted from a book by Henry Morton Robinson, *The Perfect Round*; Carradine coproduced, directed, and even wrote the film's score.

Most of the films about Vietnam veterans released during the early 1980s continued themes begun during the early 1970s: the veterans come home in search of peace but find only problems and violence. *Search and Destroy*, directed by William Fruet, was filmed in 1978 but not released until 1981. It begins in Vietnam in 1968 with a South Vietnamese official (Park Jong Soo) being escorted by a team of US Special Forces. The little group is ambushed by the Vietcong, and one of the Americans is wounded. The South Vietnamese refuses to aid the wounded American. This angers the remaining four Americans, who abandon the Vietnamese to face the Vietcong alone. Ten years later, the South Vietnamese official shows up in the United States, searching for revenge. He finds and kills two of the four; the other two (Perry King and Don Stroud) have a climactic battle with him at Niagara Falls.

Richard Pryor plays a Vietnam veteran with a somewhat comical postwar career in *Some Kind of Hero* (1982), directed by Michael Pressman. Captured by the Vietcong, Eddie Keller (Pryor) spends five years in a North Vietnamese prison camp. To get medical aid for a very sick compatriot, he agrees to sign a confession saying that the United States was engaged in an unjust and illegal war in Vietnam. When he comes home, a hero, Keller finds that his wife is in love with another man, that the two of them have ruined his bookstore business and spent all his savings, and that his mother has suffered a stroke and is about to be tossed out of the convalescent home she is in because of nonpayment of bills. Then he finds that because of the confession he signed the army will not give him his back pay. He needs money, of course, and he ultimately becomes involved with the Mafia. During the 1970s, he would have killed the underworld louts; but *Some Kind of Hero* was made during the get-rich-quick 1980s: Keller swindles the swindlers and rides away with a bundle of money.

Ten years after *Welcome Home, Soldier Boys*, in which four former Green Berets take on the National Guard in a New Mexican town called Hope, a lone former Green Beret arrives in an Oregon town called Hope and again battles the National Guard. *First Blood* (1982), directed by Ted Kotcheff, stars Sylvester Stallone as John Rambo, a Vietnam veteran and Medal of Honor recipient who wanders alone searching for the friends with whom he served in Vietnam. Near Hope, he finds the home of one of his friends, only to be told that his friend has died of cancer caused by Agent Orange. When he goes into Hope, looking for something to eat, Rambo runs into a mean policeman (Brian Dennehy) who doesn't like his looks and tells him to leave town. When Rambo doesn't, he is arrested and put in jail. Rambo's nightmare flashbacks to Vietnam (he was held prisoner by the Vietcong, who dumped excrement on him) mirror the treatment he receives at the hands of his fellow American citizens. He breaks out of jail and is pursued first by the local law-enforcement officials and then by five hundred National Guardsmen. Colonel Trautman (Richard Crenna), the Green Beret commander who recruited and trained Rambo and then sent him to Vietnam, shows up to rescue the police and the National Guardsmen from "his boy." When the policeman informs him that there are now more than five hundred men hunting for Rambo, Trautman says, "If you sent that many, don't forget one thing." "What?" asks the policeman. "A good supply of body bags," snaps the colonel.

Rambo is indeed more than a match for the men sent against him. His dark figure moves through the streets of Hope, the heartland of America haunted by a violent spirit it refuses to acknowledge. Trautman gets to Rambo and tries to reason with him, reminding him that he is now shooting at friendly civilians. "There are no friendly civilians," replies Rambo. Rambo cannot get the war out of his mind. "Nothing is over," he says. "You just don't turn it off." He goes on to deliver a moving speech about what he and his friends suffered in Vietnam, a speech made even more effective by the fact that it is Sylvester

Stallone, the hero of 1976's *Rocky*, speaking.

A similar speech, delivered by another sympathetic character, ends *Memorial Day* (1983), a television movie directed by Joseph Sargent. Mike Farrell plays a veteran of the Vietnam War who claims that he never thinks about the war. All he ever says about it is that it was a long time ago. He has become a successful lawyer, a husband and father, and most of his friends don't even know that he served in Vietnam. He is a master at hiding his feelings. But then one of the men he served with commits suicide, bringing on a crisis of conscience. The memories all return. "It just keeps coming up and coming up," he tells his wife. "It doesn't want to go away." His final breakdown occurs during a Memorial Day barbecue. Although they do not necessarily want to hear it, he tells his friends a story of Vietnam, a story about an ambush that he and his men set up in which five children, none of them older than seven, were killed. It is the memory of that night that is haunting him. "What do you want from us?" asks one of his friends. He tells them that everyone is responsible, and that "it's not over." "I lost part of me over there," he says, "and I'm never going to get it back."

The fate of the Americans left behind in Vietnam when the war ended—the POWs and MIAs—is the subject of *Uncommon Valor* (1983), another film directed by Ted Kotcheff. The film begins with a battle in Vietnam in 1972. The Vietcong are closing in on a group of Americans; helicopters arrive to rescue them, but some of the men are left behind, captured, and not heard from again. The film then jumps to 1973, to the United States, where the father (Gene Hackman) of one of the men captured decides to go rescue his son. (This was a very topical film; its appearance coincided with a similar, much-publicized plan to rescue American POWs from prisons in Southeast Asia.) A former marine colonel and veteran of the Korean War, the father visits Bangkok, where he is able to establish that his son is being held in a prison in Laos—he even gets photographs of the camp. He then visits each of the five members of his son's old squad and convinces them to help him raid the camp. They agree to go along, for none has been able to fully

adjust to civilian life, and they all share a fierce loyalty.

The father receives financial aid from an oil tycoon (Robert Stack), whose son is also a POW. In 1983, someplace north of Galveston, Texas, Hackman and the five veterans (plus another volunteer) build an exact replica of the Laotian camp and practice attacking it. Before he puts his commando unit through this special training, Hackman gives the men a little speech: "You're thought of as criminals because you lost; you cost too much and didn't turn a profit." But they're going back, he tells them, and no one can dispute the rightness of what they're doing. (What they're doing goes against the government, of course, and they are spied on by the CIA.) Their next stop is Bangkok; no date is given for this portion of the film, implying that it could be taking place in the present. In spite of

numerous setbacks (including the machinations of the CIA), they succeed in their mission.. The point of the film is very clear: there really are Americans still being held prisoner in Southeast Asia.

Purple Hearts (1984), directed by Sidney J. Furie, begins with a dedication to the Vietnam War's 347,309 Purple Heart recipients. The Vietnam War provides only the background to the film, which is a familiar war movie love story. Dr. Don Jardian (Ken Wahl), who works at a Mobile Army Surgical Hospital, falls in love with nurse Deborah Solomon (Cheryl Ladd), who works at a hospital in Da Nang. When not operating on wounded soldiers, Dr. Jardian finds excuses to visit Da Nang. ("I've felt dead inside ever since I got in country," he says. "That woman makes me feel alive.") His individualistic outlook irritates his superior officer, and he is sent to a base near the front ("Damn, I'm history," he laments). He survives the fighting there, and in exchange for a weekend in Manila with the nurse, he agrees to take part in a raid on a POW camp located twenty-one miles south of Hanoi. The American prisoners are no longer in the camp, and the Americans are attacked by the Vietcong. Dr. Jardian is reported killed. Very much alive, he returns to Da Nang in search of Nurse Solomon, only to be told that she has been killed in an attack on the hospital. She, too, is still alive, of course, and the two lovers are ultimately reunited. Such tear-jerking coincidences have been a staple of war movies since *The Birth of a Nation*. The happy ending of the film does not reflect the ending of the Vietnam War, and whatever tears viewers shed at the end are shed for the young lovers, not for the 347,309 men and women who received the Purple Heart.

The Odd Angry Shot (1979), written and directed by Tom Jeffrey, is an Australian film about Australians fighting in Vietnam. The story of a group of Australian professional soldiers serving a one-year tour of duty in South Vietnam, the film concentrates on the friendships among the men and mixes tough, biting comedy with remarkably realistic battle scenes. Like American soldiers in American films about Vietnam, the Australians want only to survive and return home safely. They aren't really certain that they belong in Vietnam; for them, it is somebody else's war.

Australia did indeed furnish troops to aid the US war effort in Vietnam, just as Australia furnished troops for the Korean War. Australian soldiers fought in South Africa during the Boer War, and Australian soldiers played important roles in both world wars. Even so, few Australian-made films about Australian soldiers were released worldwide until the early 1980s. *The Odd Angry Shot* was only one of several Australian war movies that were released during that period, each about a different war.

Breaker Morant (1979), directed by Bruce Beresford, relates the true story of three Australian soldiers court-martialed during the Boer War. The title of the film is the name of one of the three (Edward Woodward), who is a breaker of horses, a poet, and a soldier. The Australians are accused of having executed Boer prisoners and of killing a German missionary; they are tried by a British military court, and they ultimately become scapegoats of the British. The officer who serves as their defense counsel (Jack Thompson) pleads that the Australians were following unwritten but understood orders to take no prisoners, orders that came from the British. "The tragedy of war," he says, "is that horrors are committed by normal men in abnormal situations." Although the story of the film is set in 1901, many reviewers saw in it parallels to the Vietnam War.

There is also a true story behind *Gallipoli* (1981), directed by Peter Weir. As in 1930's *Tell England*, it is the story of the disastrous World War I Gallipoli campaign. *Tell England* relates the story of the battle from the experiences of two idealistic English schoolboys who enlist and go off to fight for England; *Gallipoli* is about two idealistic Australian boys who also eagerly enlist and are sent far from home to fight "an English war."

Gallipoli begins on a cattle farm in Western Australia in May 1915 and ends on a hill on the Gallipoli Peninsula in August of that year; it

Left: *Mel Gibson in* Gallipoli *(1981).*

begins and ends with one of the two Australian boys (Mark Lee) running. In the beginning of the film, he is running a trial race under the tutelage of his uncle. His uncle is training him to become a champion runner, and he takes him into a town to compete in a race. Among the other runners is Mel Gibson; he and Lee become friends and, like the other boys around them, they decide to enlist. They want to take part in the great adventure. The newspapers are full of reports of a battle being fought at a distant place called Gallipoli. Although most of the boys have little idea of where Gallipoli is and have trouble pronouncing the word, they are all impressed by the news. Some want to sign up because they have read of Turkish barbarities; one old woman expresses her anger at the Germans for "crucifying kittens on church doors." The boys do enlist (the underage Lee has to use a faked birth certificate), and they end up facing "Johnny Turk" in the trenches of Gallipoli. As one of the boys writes home in a letter, they believe they are "involved in an adventure that is somehow larger than life."

With the incessant danger and all the terrible deprivations, they remain cheerful and undaunted. They are proud and courageous, full of youthful energy. And they are uselessly, foolishly slaughtered. The Australians are ordered to attack the Turkish positions as a diversion while the English land at Suvla Bay. The Australian boys scramble out of their trenches only to be mown down by the Turkish machine gunners. Each group lines up in the trench and waits for its turn to die. It is finally the turn of Lee and his comrades to attack. "Remember who you are," their officer tells them. "The Tenth Light Horse, men from Western Australia." Lee climbs out of the trench and runs toward his death. The film ends with a freeze-frame shot of him speading his arms as though he were winning a race, the bullets cutting across his chest where the ribbon would have been (this image was compared to the famous photograph taken by Robert Capa during the Spanish Civil War of a soldier in the instant of being hit by a bullet).

Attack Force Z (1981), a coproduction of Australia and Taiwan directed by Tim Burstall, is about five commandos sent to a Japanese-held island during World War II to rescue the survi-

215

vors of a plane crash (one of whom is a Japanese diplomat involved in peace negotiations). The Japanese soldiers are cruel, the battles are brutal, and the film ends on a note of grim irony. Among the commandos are John Phillip Law and Mel Gibson.

Gibson plays the lead role in two futuristic war movies directed by George Miller, *Mad Max* (1980) and *The Road Warrior (Mad Max 2)* (1981). Both are about a very desolate, very violent post-World War III world in which the most valuable commodity is gasoline.

War itself has become a valuable commodity in the post-World War II world: it is news, exciting entertainment for those people fortunate enough to live far from it. Of the many ways in which the modern world might be divided is the division between those people who are photographed committing violent acts and those people who look at the photographs. This division coincides with the division between rich and poor, between those who live in safe places and those who don't. It is not surprising that photographers have become heroic figures to the well-to-do generations that have learned to believe what they see. Nor is it surprising that the "little wars" of the modern world have become the subjects for films, for regardless of their comparatively minor scale, these conflicts offer all the essentials for war movies: that heady mixture of violence and romance in a faroff land, that vicarious joy of seeing a hero's private destiny played out against a backdrop of grand events.

Circle of Deceit (1981), a coproduction of France and West Germany directed by Volker Schlondorff, is set during the 1976 civil war in

Lebanon (the film was shot in Beirut while the actual fighting was taking place). Bruno Ganz stars as a German reporter for an illustrated magazine who is in Lebanon with a photographer (played by Polish director Jerzy Skolimowski) to cover the situation. Although he is there to report on the violence outside, the German is caught in cruel introspection. Unhappy with his life, unhappy with his wife, he falls in love with a woman (Hanna Schygulla) and remains detached from the story taking place in the streets. He and the other foreign correspondents pass their time in a seaside hotel set in no-man's-land. There is a corrupt old Frenchman (Jean Carmet) who makes a living selling weapons to the Christian side in the conflict and then selling photographs of the resultant massacres to the international journalists. He sells packages of photographs to the highest bidder, reminding the newsmen, "It's what you need, isn't it? Dirty pictures for people who live in clean places." The German follows the story of his own life through the streets of the city, streets full of people running and trucks carrying guerrillas. The pleasant, sunny afternoons are broken by sudden bursts of machine-gun fire.

The Year of Living Dangerously (1982), an Australian film directed by Peter Weir, is set in Jakarta, capital of the Republic of Indonesia, in 1965, when Sukarno's rule was challenged by an attempted Communist coup. (The title of the film is from a statement made by Sukarno; it was his prophetic way of describing 1965.) Mel Gibson is there as an Australian newsman covering the story. He falls in love with a member of the British embassy staff (Sigourney Weaver) and befriends a cameraman named Billy Kwan (played by Oscar-winner Linda Hunt, a woman in the role of a man). He finds himself in trouble when he gets his hands on secret information.

Under Fire (1983), directed by Roger Spottiswoode, is about a prize-winning American photographer whose photographs help win a war. The film is set in Nicaragua in 1979; the Somoza regime is being toppled by the Sandinistas. When he arrives in Nicaragua, the photographer (Nick Nolte) is greeted by a familiar crowd of American journalists, people who make a living traveling from one "news event" to the next.

Gene Hackman confronted by military police in Under Fire *(1983).*

"You're gonna love this war," a radio news correspondent (Joanna Cassidy) tells the photographer. "Good guys, bad guys, and cheap shrimp." The "good guys" are the Sandinistas; the "bad guys" are the supporters of Somoza, among whom is the US government ("It's just another fascist regime that we're backing," comments a journalist). "I don't take sides, I take pictures," states the photographer, but his journalistic detachment does not endure long; his sympathies are drawn to the Sandinistas. He also becomes involved in a love triangle with the radio correspondent and her longtime lover, a senior correspondent (Gene Hackman), who soon leaves, having accepted a permanent job in New York City. When Rafael, the leader of the Sandinistas, is reported killed, Nolte is approached by the Sandinistas and asked to fake a photograph to make it look like the dead leader is still alive. The photographer takes the picture, the photograph helps revive the revolution, and Hackman returns to the scene, eager to get an interview with Rafael. Out in the street, the newsman is accosted by Somoza militiamen and, while the photographer watches and photographs, Hackman is shot dead. The photographer has film of the event, and although chased by a horde of Somoza soldiers, he and Cassidy get the film out of the country to be shown on American television. It causes a sensation. Comments one Nicaraguan, "Perhaps now Americans will be apprised of what is happening here. Perhaps we should have killed an American journalist fifty years ago." (It would have made little difference, of course: fifty years before Under Fire, American audiences were being thrilled by the heroics of Ralph Graves and Jack Holt battling Nicaraguan "outlaws" in Flight.)

Among the characters in Under Fire are a corrupt Frenchman (Jean-Louis Trintignant) who works for the CIA and an American mercenary (Ed Harris) who is only marginally aware of which side he is supposed to be fighting for. The action of the film takes place in terrain that has become woefully familiar: streets of blasted houses, walls covered with spray-painted acronyms and slogans, sandbags and anonymous dead bodies lying on rubble.

There are similar streets in Missing (1982), directed by Constantine Costa-Gavras. Although it is never stated, Missing is set in Chile following the bloody 1973 military coup that overthrew Allende; the film is based on the true story of an American who "disappeared" during the violence. The young American, Charles Horman (John Shea), is arrested after the coup; his wife (Sissy Spacek) reports him missing but receives no help in finding him from either the local authorities or the US diplomats stationed there. Then the man's father (Jack Lemmon), a well-to-do conservative businessman, arrives. To get at the truth, the father and his daughter-in-law must deal with the blatant dissembling of American diplomats; they are misled and lied to, but they eventually discover the truth: after he was arrested, Charles Horman was taken to the national soccer stadium and, along with hundreds of other people, killed.

The possibilities of a third world war, a nuclear war that would put rubble in the streets of all the world's cities, have not diminished since On the Beach. The first atomic bomb, the one dropped on Hiroshima in 1945, was the subject of a 1980 television movie, Enola Gay: The Men, the Mission, the Atomic Bomb, directed by David Lowell Rich. The film follows step-by-step the decision to drop the bomb, the training of the fliers, and, finally, the flight of the Enola Gay. Patrick Duffy plays the part of Paul Tibbets, commander of the plane.

World War III (1982), a television movie directed by David Greene, provides a plausible, step-by-step scenario for universal doomsday. The film begins in Alaska, sometime in the not-so-distant future. A special KGB unit parachutes down with orders to seize an important junction on the Alaska pipeline. The Russians have timed their attack to coincide with weather conditions that prevent the Americans from sending troops to stop them, but there just happen to be some National Guardsmen on maneuvers nearby, and they, led by a resourceful officer (David Soul), prepare to defend the junction. The Soviet plan is to destroy thirty miles of the pipleline if the United States does not withdraw a grain embargo. There is unrest in Russia, including violent food strikes. The Russians believe they have "military superiority" and that the United States would never go to war because of this cunning act of blackmail. While the battle goes on in Alaska, the Soviet premier (Brian Keith) and the American president (Rock Hudson) confer, but nothing is resolved, and the two sides begin to prepare for war. Each knows what the other is doing, and each matches the other's escalation. The escalation finally reaches a point at which neither side dares back down, and the film ends with scenes of people in countries all over the world looking up at the sky.

The Day After (1983), a television movie directed by Nicholas Meyer, presents one version of what life might be like the day after all those missiles struck the earth. The showing of the film was preceded and followed by a great deal of publicity and comment. The film was considered an important event, and before it was shown it provoked demonstrations both by groups in favor of disarmament and by groups opposed to disarmament; it was thus hailed as an antiwar statement while being assailed as "propaganda." The film attempts to depict what one commentator described as "that which no human being should ever see." Like *The War Game*, the pseudodocumentary by Peter Watkins that was commissioned by the BBC in 1965, *The Day After* is about the effects of a nuclear war. *The War Game* was so graphic in its depictions of a nuclear attack that it was banned from television; *The Day After* begins with a caution to parents warning them that some scenes in the film might be unusually upsetting to children.

The screenplay for *The Day After* was written by Edward Hume. The action takes place in Lawrence, Kansas, and the story follows the lives of the members of three families; the leading character is a doctor named Oakes (Jason Robards). The various people go about their daily lives paying little or no attention to radio and television reports of increasing tension between the United States and the Soviet Union. References are made to the Cuban missile crisis; it is announced that the Russians have evacuated Moscow. And then, quite suddenly, while some people are watching a football game and others are driving in their cars or just walking down a street, the war begins: the missiles lo-

cated in silos near Lawrence blast out of the ground and climb into the sky, and in a short time the Russian missiles arrive. Those viewers who kept their eyes open during the next scenes saw an earnest attempt to display human beings being destroyed by a nuclear blast. For some viewers, the effects shown were not horrible enough; for others, they were more than adequate.

The nuclear attack does not end the film: people—including the doctor and many of the other characters familiar to the viewer—survive, and the story continues. The day after the war is bleak. The president makes a radio speech declaring that "There has been no surrender, no retreat. We remain undaunted before all except God." The survivors lose their hair and go blind from burned retinas, flies buzz over charred corpses, and dark humanoid forms rob the dead. In the midst of the chaos are firing squads, evidently meting out punishment to the worst offenders. The local farmers gather in the shell of a building to discuss their plight—the topsoil has been completely destroyed. Although it is all very saddening, it is also somewhat misleading, for the film posits a future where there might very well be no future at all.

Testament (1983), directed by Lynne Littman, is also about the aftermath of a nuclear war. The film was originally planned as an hour-long television movie, but it grew into a feature film, even though its budget remained small ($750,000). The screenplay was based on a short story, "The Last Testament," by Carol Amen. The action takes place in a small town in northern California named Hamlin. There is no mention of international tension, and the film never concerns itself with which side started the war. It happens all at once: while Carol Wetherly (Jane Alexander) and her three children are watching "Sesame Street," their television set goes blank, and their living rooom is filled with a bright orange glow. There has been a nuclear attack, and Hamlin is isolated. Mr. Wetherly (William Devane), who has gone to San Francisco on a business trip, is never heard from. One by one, the inhabitants of the community die. Carol does her best to remain sane and sturdy for the sake of her children—who are painfully aware that they will never be adults.

Only one city is destroyed in *Special Bulletin* (1983), a television movie directed by Edward Zwick. The film uses the format of a television news program to cover, minute by minute, an exciting news event "taking place" in Charleston, South Carolina. There, a group of terrorists present the nation's leaders with nuclear blackmail: they threaten to detonate a nuclear device in the city's harbor if all of the detonators from the nuclear weapons in the area are not delivered to them. This is their form of instigating unilateral disarmament. The film covers the events just as they might be covered by a television news team (the simulated program looks so real that the network that broadcast the film inserted more than thirty disclaimers warning viewers that it wasn't). In the end, the device goes off. The scene of the city being destroyed is impressive: there is a big flash of bright light and a terrible blast of wind. It is the end of the city; there is nothing left but smoking rubble.

Modern technology has provided umpteen ways in which the world might end. *WarGames* (1983), directed by John Badham, is about a seventeen-year-old computer "whiz kid" (Matthew Broderick) who, using his home computer, accidentally breaks into the US government's missile-defense-system computer. The boy believes he has hooked into a computer-games manufacturer and is delighted when the friendly computer, whose name is Joshua, asks him, "Shall we play a game?" Among the games offered are Chess, Checkers, and Global Thermonuclear War. The enthusiastic teenager makes the obvious choice, and soon he and his girl friend (Ally Sheedy) are having a great time gulping soft drinks, eating potato chips, and trying—since they are playing the Russian side of the "game"—to blow up Seattle and Las Vegas. The fun ends the way so much of a young boy's fun ends—his father tells him to take out the garbage. He turns off the computer, ending—he thinks—the game. The computer, however, keeps right on playing. The planes, missiles, and submarines the computer is moving into preparedness for war are all very real, of course, and World War III is only narrowly averted. Having run through all the possible scenarios for this game called Global Thermonuclear War— all of which end in total worldwide devastation—Joshua reaches a sage conclusion: "A strange game. The only winning move is not to play."

Dean Williams

The Day After *(1983).*

219

Afterword

The 1941 comedy *Buck Privates* begins with Bud Abbott and Lou Costello selling neckties to passersby on a busy city street. Spotted and pursued by a policeman, the unlawful vendors try to hide by joining what they believe to be the line for a movie theater. It is actually the line for a draft board, and they end up enlisting in the army. For Abbott and Costello, the error is funny, just another of their characteristic blunders, but many people commit a similar, less humorous error: they, too, mistake the line for a draft board for the line to see a movie—they imagine that their experience of real war will be similar to the experience presented in war movies.

War is not a movie, but in our world those who line up to become soldiers are, in a sense, lining up to become actors. One of the reasons that modern wars are so well suited to the motion picture is that they are fought by armies of conscripted soldiers, armies made up of men and women who leave their homes and occupations—their "real" lives—to become actors in an enormous drama. Wearing identical costumes, with assigned ranks replacing the names their parents gave them, these citizen soldiers rehearse their parts in training camps and are then sent away to perform on distant stages, the farflung "theaters" of war. They lose their personalities before they risk losing their lives. Thanks to the motion picture, these conscripted soldiers don't go far when they leave home, for they immediately reappear as nearby as the local movie theater, where professional actors dressed in the same costumes revive those forfeited personalities. The stage fright suffered by the movie-lot buck privates helps them mimic the terror suffered by the taxicab drivers and would-be writers, the grocery clerks and soda jerks, the bankers and schoolboys on beachheads and in front-line bunkers. Each of the movie actors who, on cue, falls down and plays dead for the cameras is a stand-in for thousands of other "actors" who fall down never to rise up again.

War is an aberration, a period of unreality or, at least, of abnormality. The citizens who play the roles of soldiers, endangering themselves while trying to kill other citizens, are usually fighting so that they can return to their real lives, their normal selves. War is not the real world, and movies are not the real world. One of the most striking aspects of war movies is their obvious ambition to simulate the "reality" of war. Filmmakers take great care to reproduce accurately the destruction that would exist otherwise only as the result of tragedy. They hire military men and war veterans to serve as advisers and consultants; they borrow weapons from armed forces. And they aggressively assert that they are portraying the truth of war. Sometimes, the actors pretending to be soldiers are joined to the citizens pretending to be soldiers. Newsreels or actual combat footage are frequently spliced into war movies. Skillfully done, scenes of the "real" war can be seamlessly joined to the fake war, and the men whose fates are determined by a screenplay can seem to run alongside men whose fates are not so carefully foreordained. The

John Mills in Oh! What a Lovely War *(1969).*

realism of war movies makes them more entertaining: the viewer is given the thrill of "being there." Having actors speak foreign languages, the use of such devices as Sensurround, and the increasing amounts of red liquid that spurt from wounds all make the experience of war more dramatic.

The plot of all war movies is the same: the viewer survives. It is a notion that we carry with us when we line up for war. We may someday make the mistake of expecting World War III to have a similar outcome. Films about World War III are unique in that they deal with a war that has not yet taken place. Unlike the previous wars of this century, no special roles will have to be learned and rehearsed for World War III: the vast majority of its participants will play themselves. The passive act of watching movies, of calmly witnessing the reenacted deaths of others, has prepared us for our roles, making us the perfect victims of that most modern war.

The films about World War III suggest a new role for war movies: replacing their subject. All along, war and movies about war have struggled for the same audience. War and motion pictures offer the same appeals: escape from the annoying restrictions of ordinary life, transportation to a more exciting realm, a romantic place where stories reach gratifying conclusions and where power belongs to the virtuous. The offers of war are false; for their part, movies have provided generations with enthralling escape. If war must have a place in our world, then it belongs on film—and nowhere else.

Index of Movies